P9-AFI-648

THE
UNIVERSE BENDS
TOWARD JUSTICE

A
READER ON
CHRISTIAN NONVIOLENCE
IN THE U.S.

Edited by Angie O'Gorman
Foreword by Colman McCarthy

NEW SOCIETY PUBLISHERS
Philadelphia, PA   Santa Cruz, CA

Inquiries regarding requests to reprint all or part of *The Universe Bends Toward Justice* should be addressed to:

New Society Publishers
4527 Springfield Avenue
Philadelphia, PA 19143

ISBN 0-86571-177-1 Hardcover / ISBN 0-86571-178-X Paperback

Printed in the United States of America on partially recycled paper by R. R. Donnelley & Sons, Crawfordsville, IN

Cover and book design by Tina Birky and Barbara Hirshkowitz
Cover photo (Trefid Nebula in Constellation Sagittarius) by Glen Shapiro

To order directly from the publisher, add $1.75 to the price for the first copy, 50¢ each additional. Send check or money order to:

New Society Publishers
PO Box 582
Santa Cruz, CA 95061

New Society Publishers is a project of the New Society Educational Foundation, a nonprofit, tax-exempt, public foundation. Opinions expressed in this book do not necessarily represent positions of the New Society Educational Foundation.

All possible care has been taken to obtain permission from the copyright owners to reprint articles and selections protected by copyright. Materials not listed here are believed to be in the public domain. Any errors or omissions are unintentional and will be rectified in any future printings upon notification to the editors, who wish to express their gratitude for permission to reprint material from the following sources:

America Press, Inc., 106 West 56th Street, New York, NY 10019, and Beldon Lane for "Spirituality and Political Commitment: Notes on a Liberation Theology" by Beldon Lane, 1981, reprinted with permission. All rights reserved.

Associated Press for *The Lesson on the Mount II,* and the "Introduction" as reprinted from *The Substance of Faith and Other Cotton Patch Sermons,* Dallas Lee, Editor, 1972.

Daniel Berrigan for "The Sermon on the Mount, and the War that Will Not End Forever" and "Children in the Shelter."

The Catholic Worker for "The Catholic Worker Positions," by Thomas Merton. "Chant to Be Used in Processions around a Site with Furnaces," 1961, and *Nonviolent Napalm in Catonsville* by Thomas Cornell, 1968.

The Christian Century Foundation for *If America Enters the War What Shall I Do?* by Ernest Fremont Tittle, copyright 1941, reprinted from the February 5, 1941 issue of *The Christian Century*, and *Letter from Delano* by Cesar Chavez, copyright 1969, reprinted from the April 23, 1969 issue of *The Christian Century*.

Joan Daves for permission to reprint "Letter from a Birmingham Jail," copyright 1963, 1964, by Martin Luther King, Jr.

Dave Dellinger for *The Future of Nonviolence* by Dave Dellinger, as reprinted from *Studies on the Left*, 1965.

Fellowship of Reconciliation for *Pacifism and Class War* by A.J. Muste, as reprinted from *The World Tomorrow*, and *Blessed Are ₁ne Meek: The Christian Roots of Nonviolence* by Thomas Merton, as reprinted from *Fellowship Magazine*, May, 1967.

Renny Golden for *Theology of Sanctuary* as reprinted from *Sanctuary Nuts and Bolts*, 1983.

Graded Press for *The Idolatry of Deterrence*, as reprinted from *In Defense of Creation: The Nuclear Crisis and a Just Peace*, by the United Methodist Council of Bishops, copyright 1986. Used by permission of Graded Press, publisher.

The Herald Press, for "Communism and Anti-Communism" as excerpted from *War, Peace, and Nonresistance* by Guy Franklin Hershberger, by permission of Herald Press, Scottdale, PA 15683. All rights reserved. *God Against the Rich*, as excerpted from *Cotton Patch Parables of Liberation, 1976* by Clarence Jordan and Bill Lane Doulos, by permission of Herald Press, Scottdale, PA 15683. All rights reserved.

Philip P. Moulton for the excerpts from *The Journal of John Woolman* and *A Plea for the Poor*, as reprinted from *The Journal and Major Essays of John Woolman*, Philip P. Moulton, Editor.

New Society Publishers for *Fanny Lou Hamer: Baptism by Fire*, by Susan Kling, reprinted from *Reweaving the Web of Life: Feminism and Nonviolence*, and *Jesus' Third Way*, reprinted from *Violence and Nonviolence in South Africa*, by Walter Wink, 1987.

Peace Media Service for *The Power of Noncooperation* by Shelley Douglass as reprinted from the *IFOR Report*, April 1963.

Pendle Hill for the excerpt from *Of Holy Disobedience* by A.J. Muste, 1952.

The Village Voice for *Letter to the Weathermen*, 1970, reprinted by permission of *The Village Voice*, New York, New York.

TABLE OF CONTENTS

Colman McCarthy   Foreword .... **ix**

Angie O'Gorman   Introduction **1**

Margaret Bacon   Let Me Be the One: Mary Dyer:
Witness to Religious Liberty **9**

Robert Barclay   From: An Apology for the True
1678   Christian Divinity **15**

William Penn   First Letter
1681   to the Delaware Indians **19**

Germantown Friends   Germantown Friends' Protest
1688   Against Slavery **21**

John Woolman   Considerations on the Payment of a Tax
1755   Laid for Carrying on the War
Against the Indians **25**

John Woolman   A Plea for the Poor **31**
c.1763

Job Scott   War Inconsistent with the Doctrine and
c.1782   Example of Jesus Christ **35**

David Low Lodge   From: The Mediator's Kingdom
1809   Not of This World: But Spiritual **39**

Noah Worcester   From: A Solemn Review of
1814   the Customs of War **43**

Mary McGlone   The Orators in Petticoats:
Angelina and Sarah Grimke **49**

Angelina Emily Grimke   Appeal to the Christian Women
1836   of the South **55**

William Lloyd Garrison   Declaration of Sentiments **59**
1838

Charles K. Whipple   Evils of the Revolutionary War **65**
1839

William Ellery Channing   Has the Duty of Obeying Government
1841   No Bounds? **71**

Adin Ballou   From: Christian Non-Resistance
1846   in All Its Important Bearings **75**

Maggie Fisher   Harriet Tubman: Liberator **79**

Margaret Hope Bacon   I Ask No Favor for My Sex:
                            Lucretia Mott and Non-Resistance **85**

Lucretia Mott   From: Discourse on Woman **89**
1849

Sojourner Truth   "Ain't I a Woman?" **95**
1852

Charles K. Whipple   From: Non-Resistance Applied to the
1860   Internal Defense of a Community **97**

Walter Rauschenbusch   The Purpose of Jesus:
1907   The Kingdom of God **101**

Tom Cornell   A.J. Muste Remembered **105**

A.J. Muste   Pacifism and Class War **111**
1928

Kathleen De Sutter   An Active Glowing Force:
Jordan   The Nonviolence of Dorothy Day **117**
                            Catholic Worker Positions **123**

Ernest Fremont Tittle   If America Enters the War,
1941   What Shall I Do? **127**

Kirby Page   War in the Atomic Age **133**
1946

Dallas Lee   Clarence Jordan:
                            A Biographical Sketch **135**

Clarence Jordan   The Lesson on the Mount—II **141**
                            God Against the Rich **145**

A.J. Muste   From: "Of Holy Disobedience" **149**
1952

Susan Kling   Baptism by Fire
                            The Story of Fannie Lou Hamer **153**

Pat Coy	The Personalist Nonviolence of Thomas Merton	**159**
Thomas Merton 1961	Chant to Be Used in Processions Around a Site with Furnaces	**163**
Mennonite General Conference 1961	Communism and Anti-Communism ...	**167**
Martin Luther King, Jr. 1963	Letter from a Birmingham Jail	**171**
The Fellowship of Reconciliation	Ten "How To's" in Nonviolence	**185**
David Dellinger 1965	The Future of Nonviolence	**189**
Thomas Merton 1967	Blessed Are the Meek: The Roots of Christian Nonviolence ...	**195**
Tom Cornell 1968	Nonviolent Napalm in Catonsville	**203**
Cesar Chavez 1969	Letter from Delano	**209**
Daniel Berrigan 1970	Letter to the Weathermen	**213**
	Children in the Shelter	**219**
	The Sermon on the Mount, and the War that Will Not End Forever	**220**
Beldon C. Lane 1981	Spirituality and Political Commitment: Notes on a Liberation Theology of Nonviolence	**221**
Michael McConnell Renny Golden 1983	Theology of Sanctuary	**231**
Shelley Douglass 1983	The Power of Noncooperation	**235**
Angie O'Gorman 1983	Defense Through Disarmament: Nonviolence and Personal Assault	**241**
The United Methodist Council of Bishops 1986	The Idolatry of Deterrence	**249**
Walter Wink 1987	Jesus' Third Way	**253**
	Index	**267**

ACKNOWLEDGMENTS

A word of thanks is due to the people who helped create this book. Many authors acknowledge the person who typed their manuscript. I am fortunate to be able to thank not only Virginia Grumich for her help in this area, but also Jim and Mary Jo Brauner whose gift of a computer made it possible to produce a final manuscript with less anguish than usual. Elizabeth Kolmer, Chair of the American Studies Department at St. Louis University, gave invaluable help in locating documents from early U.S. history, and in advising me at a number of critical moments. Barbara Becnel was most helpful in allowing me generous access to her thesis research. The families in Sanctuary with whom I work at Casa Arco Iris patiently put up with my lack of time and energy at moments when their needs should have been my priority. My editor David Albert, who first suggested the idea for this book, guided me throughout the process of bringing it to reality. Jean Abbott, my dear friend and co-worker, generously took on much of my work in order to free me to concentrate on the book. Her belief in me as a person as well as in this project has much to do with the manuscript arriving at a publishable state at all. And lastly, a word of gratitude, strange though it may sound, to the individuals who provided me with hands-on learning through assault situations. They gave me the opportunity to experience the disarming power of nonviolence, within myself and within them. I am deeply indebted. As for my physical education instructor, she was mistaken.

Angie O'Gorman
St. Louis, Missouri, March 1989

FOREWORD

Colman McCarthy

In the belief that peace can always use a few more makers, I have been teaching courses in the history, theory and practice of nonviolence for the past seven years. I have had some 1,500 students from Georgetown University Law School, the University of Maryland, American University, George Mason University and several private and public high schools in Washington.

The first moments of the first class are a spot quiz. Identify the following:

1. Robert E. Lee
2. Sojourner Truth
3. Ulysses S. Grant
4. A.J. Muste
5. Napoleon
6. Adin Ballou
7. Caesar
8. John Woolman
9. Dwight Eisenhower
10. Dorothy Day

Most students, whether in law school, college or high school, know five: the generals. Who can't identify Lee, Grant, Napoleon, Caesar and Eisenhower? The other five are unknowns. Truth, Muste, Ballou, Woolman and Day were advocates of nonviolence. Each took personal risks by acting on the belief that the force of nonviolence is more effective, moral and enduring than the force of violence.

Although unsettling, it isn't surprising that students know warmakers but not peacemakers. They have been cheated in school. Curricula, sanctioned by school boards and promoted by learned faculty committees, guarantee it. Beginning in grade school, where children's minds are stuffed with prettified myths of Davy Crockett, Daniel Boone and other frontier gunmen, the cult of violence is taught as if fists, guns, armies and nukes were sacred liturgies of a peace creed.

As a pacifist, I am uneasy with the term "peace studies." It will do for now, but exactness will eventually be needed. What I have been teaching is peace through nonviolence. Students are hungry to learn it. A course on alternatives to violence isn't only about ending war or making life difficult for Caesar. It's about how to use what Gandhi called "soul force." It's to give one's mind and soul a chance to develop a philosophy of force. Every conflict or problem, whether among family or friends, between communities or governments, will be addressed either through violent force or nonviolent force. No third way exists. Those who choose nonviolent force—brave risk-takers like those pacifists in the quiz—opt for the force of justice, the force of love, the force of sharing wealth, the force of noncooperation, the force of ideas. Fighting with the strength of those forces is the essence of nonviolence. Pacifism is not passivity.

After the quiz, I ask my students to do an experiment: Leave the classroom and go to the nearest street corner; stand there and count as accurately as possible all the red cars and all the green cars that pass by.

Everybody got it? Red cars, green cars, 10 minutes. Come back in for two questions.

In every class, students have obeyed my command by dutifully counting the cars and coming back for the questions.

Question One: Didn't anyone think that standing there counting cars was stupid?

Question Two: If yes, why didn't you rebel and tell me to go waste my time counting the cars if I thought it was so important?

The experiment, as students quickly understand, is about questioning authority. Why do that? Because authority is not doing too well. Since 1900, more than 110 million people have been executed by governments. It's all been legal. In the United States, more than 7,000 people have been killed in death row executions. It's all been legal. The United States has had nine declared wars, and more than 140 undeclared wars—Grenadas, Libyas. They've all been legal. Some 40,000 children die daily from preventable diseases or hunger. There were more wars in 1987 than in any year in history. About 40,00 people are killed every month in more than 35 wars or conflicts. In the United States, some 9 to 12 million animals are slaughtered a day for food. Hunters slay 200 million animals a year. It's all legal.

The figures are numbing. But because authority—Supreme Courts, Supreme Soviets, parliaments, corporations, voter-installed legislators— decree that violence is necessary or that one more war or one more weapon system will bring peace or that animals are on earth to be killed for human pleasure, we go on counting red cars and green cars and rarely question the stupidity of it all.

Why do we dismiss nonviolence so quickly by saying that it's a wonderful theory but unreal and unworkable, while we are willing to endure—no, lavishly support—the fantasies of Congress that allow the Pentagon to spend $800 million a day on national insecurity? What Martin Luther King, Jr. said more than two decades ago remains true: "The greatest purveyor of violence in the world today (is) my own government."

It's not enough to keep remembering that. In 1983, I decided to move beyond mere caviling and go into schools as a volunteer to teach courses in alternatives to violence. I have trained teachers to teach peace courses. In the spring of 1989, I lectured at five colleges on the need to get courses on nonviolence into the curricula. At each school in the autumn of 1989, a new course in nonviolence was being offered. Students organized petitions demanding them. They understood the truth of Peter Kropotkin, the Russian anarchist and communitarian: "Think about the kind of world you want to live and work in. What do you need to build that world? Demand that your teachers teach you that." More than a few members of the faculty—from former Peace Corps volunteers to middle-aged professors who haven't lost their idealism—are eager to teach what is often the most relevant course on campus.

When students or teachers write to me, it is often to ask for literature on nonviolence. I suggest a number of titles, and happily the list will now include *The Universe Bends Toward Justice*. It is a powerful collection, as worthy as any peace anthology now available. I wish I had had a copy the other day when an administrator at one of our so-called prestigious universities told me that the reason his school didn't offer a degree in peace studies was that the subject was not academically rigorous. This, at a school with the nation's largest percentage of ROTC students. If academic rigor is wanted, start off with *The Universe Bends Toward Justice* and let the students absorb every page of its wisdom. They will have their minds shaken as never before.

This administrator was content to keep on processing students, not educating them. The rights and needs of students for a chance to create a peaceful society are ignored. Overlooked, also, are the rewards of teaching nonviolence. I recall what a student at Bethesda Chevy-Chase High School wrote last spring. She was in my course on nonviolence and wrote a column for her school newspaper: "In class, students argued, agreed, and offered their own solutions. Nothing was resolved but it didn't matter. The value of those and other discussions in peace studies does not lie in a tangible result, like a perfectly written five paragraph essay or an appropriate application of Boyle's Law. The discussions are important because they expose students to radical ideas, provoke thoughts on these ideas and diminish closemindedness."

Let the diminishing continue. With minds opened by books like *The Universe Bends Toward Justice,* the study of Woolman, Berrigan, Truth,

Day and the long list of others may lead to a moment of awareness and dissent, when no one will count the cars. Maybe, too, no one will carry out the crazed orders of violence-believing authority.

November 1989
Washington D.C.

PUBLISHER'S NOTE

New Society Publishers is proud to publish *The Universe Bends Toward Justice*. This volume is the first in a two-volume *Reader on Christian Nonviolence in the U.S.* and focuses on the theory and historical development of Christian nonviolence as it has been experienced since the first European Christian took up permanent residence on this continent.

Looking through this volume, it becomes apparent that the argument of Christian nonviolence as it has manifested itself in American history is in fact two arguments. The first centers on discovering a correct construction of the "Sermon on the Mount." The interpretation and reinterpretation of the Sermon on the Mount—the key foundation of the "love of enemies" tradition—takes on particular salience because of the belief that a proper understanding of the Gospels dictates the fitting course of an individual's behavior and, by extension, encompasses God's imperatives for the workings of all of human society. It is no wonder then that this argument has exercised Christians since the death penalty was administered by the ruling state to Jesus, with interpretations ranging from strict Christian pacifism and the refusal to participate in any institutions of power and violence, to the sophisms of Augustine who, later to be regarded as a pillar of Church authority, found it possible to argue that "loving one's enemies" does not rule out the possibility of killing them. One wonders to what degree Pontius Pilate might have approved of this construction.

The second argument running through the "love of enemies" tradition has more universal relevance and goes beyond the relatively less complex questions raised by Gospel-based pacifism. It argues that the "scrupulousness" of Jesus in obeying the dictates of conscience in the face of hostility from family, community, religion or state provides a moral standard to be universally followed. The Quaker iconoclast (and one is almost moved to say "prophet") John Woolman's appeal that we each "take heed to our own spirits" goes beyond the simply stated yet demanding moral dictum that one should refrain from killing or participating in violence under any circumstances to the perhaps more complicated but no less demanding principle that one weigh all individual moral choices with the gravity they deserve and in light of the moral example of Jesus, regardless of the personal consequences.

While this line of reasoning has existed to a lesser or greater extent within various cultures and societies, it has a peculiarly American cast in that the builders of the "New World" found it useful or even necessary to cast off previously respected forms of authority. Yet in the twentieth century, the obligation of individual conscience runs up against the strictures of an increasingly technocratic military-industrial state. The modern nation-state, whether or not it calls itself "democratic," ultimately rests on its power to extend the rights of citizenship only to those who commit themselves in advance to kill (or pay for the killing of) people they have never met, on the orders of those they may not have chosen or acknowledged, for purposes unnamed at the time they enter into the compact, for reasons with which they may or may not agree, in the cause of interests which they may or may not understand, let alone support.

I believe that generations from now people will look back upon this condition as a barbarity of the first order, for it denies the very human qualities of moral reasoning, judgment and responsibility, in short, that "conscientiousness" which should lie at the core of Christian ethics, or for that matter, any other ethics worthy of the name. From this vantage point, it is our belief that the voices represented in *The Universe Bends Toward Justice* will seem not so much lonely cries in the wilderness, but harbingers of a better world to come.

David H. Albert
for New Society Publishers
Santa Cruz, California
4 July 1989

In gratitude to the women whose struggle for life has touched my own:
Jean Abbott, Kathleen Kenny, Valentina Hernandez Augustine

and in memory of
Luz Leticia Hernandez Augustine
Disappeared
Guatemala City
November 1983

Forgive us for the violence

INTRODUCTION

IN A 1966 COLLEGE-LEVEL physical education class, I learned how to kill. It was a Catholic school and we were all would-be teachers. Clearly the instructor had the safety of our future students uppermost in her mind. She taught the technique, a simple strong shove in the right place, to help us defend them against intruders in the school or playground. I wondered at the time if there wasn't a better way. The image of myself as a teacher, rushing upon an intruder with my fists raised while school childen gazed on, brought to the surface my first questions about the place of violence in the Christian scheme of things. Defense seemed to require something different.

Later I encountered that difference in the Gospel of Matthew. There, Jesus seemed to rush upon the intruders in his life with his arms open rather than his fists raised. Even Matthew himself, a tax collector taking from his own people in order to support their Roman occupiers, was welcomed among Jesus' most intimate followers. Not only tax collectors, but a whole range of enemy-types were repeatedly invited to eat at the same table with Jesus, a recognized sign of personal bonding in his culture. Rather than distancing himself from his enemies, Jesus moved toward them.

The word nonviolence never appears in the Gospels, nor in Acts, nor in the Epistles, yet the dynamic of nonviolence is woven like the warp of a loom throughout the entire Christian Scripture. Hidden, it holds the other threads together. It forms the fabric. To miss it is to misunderstand the primary design in the Christian pattern: the power to apply love to hate. Too often, however, our cultural bias toward violent solutions to both personal and social threat, has interpreted nonviolence as powerlessness and equated pacifism with passivity.

The writings in this volume serve to counter that view. They reveal a variety of insights into the dynamic of Gospel-based nonviolence and how its power can be brought to bear on situations of sin and injustice. Even when the language is of a different era, what is said in these pages can be directly applied by today's Christian trying to understand the relevence of Gospel nonviolence in modern situations of personal and political injustice.

Historically, it was precisely this desire—to put faith into action—that gave birth to the nonviolent movement in the United States and has sustained it from

1

the personal witness of the first Quaker struggles for religious freedom in New England to the multi-issue movements of today.   Because different understandings of the Gospel's teaching have been emphasized in different historical contexts, the ethic has been expressed in a variety of ways depending on the level of experience, reflection, and Biblical criticism at a particular historical moment.   But always, it was the message of Gospel nonviolence which these men and women sought to weave into their response to a human community at war with itself.

The Gospel Base of Nonviolence

The Christian tradition of nonviolence is based on a group of teachings found in the Christian Testament, generally referred to as *The Love of Enemies* tradition.   While it is presented in several forms (Matthew 5:38-48, Luke 6: 27-36, Romans 12:14, 17-20, 1 Thessalonians 5:15, 1 Peter 3:9), the specific teaching to "love your enemies" as found in the Gospels of Matthew and Luke is perhaps the most well-known form of the tradition.

Jesus' teaching was undoubtedly rooted in the Hebrew Testament as well as affected by the works of religious sects in the region, Hellenistic Judaism and philosophical precedent. Each of these reference points, however, included a limit, some condition beyond which the love of one's enemy was not expected.   In the Israelite tradition, according to Leviticus 19:18, 34 *love of enemies* only extended to fellow believers or the sojourner who had become part of the Israelite community. In the writings of Hellenistic Judaism, separation from enemies or, like the Stoics, mastery of oneself through tranquility in the face of danger, were the key values. Jesus moved beyond these conditions and asked his followers to do likewise. His *Love of Enemies* teaching was new in that it was unconditional. It did not depend on the worth or status of the one receiving. It depended only on the reality of a God who loves like a parent and lets that love rain on the just and the unjust alike. (Matthew 5:45). "Love your enemies," was Jesus' response to a world he saw oriented by his God toward relational justice but at the same time stuck in destructive methods for confronting the reality of evil and thus blocked from moving on with the work of building the human community. *Love of Enemies* was the dynamic Jesus offered us for the disarming of evil.

This teaching is one of the few which has survived the long years of Biblical criticism as authentically spoken by Jesus. Scripture scholars agree that the command is crucial for understanding what this man Jesus wanted to accomplish. For all of that it is perhaps the teaching least understood and most disregarded by individual Christians as well as the churches to which they belong. Christians tend to acknowledge the generalized teaching of love of neighbors as at least desirable even if they feel unable to practice it in daily life. But love of "enemies?" It is generally assumed to be the musing of an idealist who miscalculated the arrival of the Kingdom he had hoped to usher in. While he may have intended it as a norm of the Kingdom come, he could not have meant it to be a part of the Kingdom coming. Clearly, so the thinking goes, Jesus did not understand the workings of evil in the human heart, nor the dilemmas of modern day political reality. As a result of this resistance to Jesus' insight, an insight profoundly attuned to the ways of evil in the world, Christians have often retarded the development of social justice as well as world peace.

Jesus did not so much lay down the rules for good behavior in his *love of enemies* teaching as he did the key ingredients of a dynamic and a process that tends to debilitate rather than to nurture evil; that tends to starve it out rather than cultivating the ground for its growth. One begins to learn this dynamic from the inside out, from engaging in inner disarmament and in the process learning what tends to promote disarming attitudes and what hinders them. The *love of enemies* tradition lies at the heart of Christian nonviolence, urging us to accept the process of disarming our own hatreds and violence so that we can learn to view others without projecting our own fears and sin on them. Then, perhaps we will be ready to enter into the role of peacemaker or liberationist. That is why Christian nonviolence can never be reduced to questions of strategy. Method, without spirit, is a trap, as easily vulnerable to the human weaknesses of greed and corruption as any other ideology.

Jesus invited those who chose to follow him to walk the extra mile before asking someone else to do so; to keep their own motives as free as possible from the desire for the kinds of power, control and the self-aggrandizement that motivate violent relationships. Thus nonviolence is not simply a response to war and death, it is a commitment to life. For those who would accept the struggle, the nonviolent way weaves a new pattern of perspectives for attaining personal as well as global well-being and security.

Forms of Gospel Nonviolence

It is astounding to realize that the same Christians who fled the Old World to found a society based on Christian principles also practiced exclusivity of belief and theological dogmatism, instituted slavery, took part in the burning of witches, and provided the same legal rights for their women as for their cattle. This was the environment in which the first attempts at Christian nonviolence were tentatively set out as Christians struggled against their own to create new criteria for faith and behavior in the New World.

The earliest efforts fall under the term "nonresistance" which seems to have been a strict application of the King James version of Matthew 5:39. In 1643 when the word "nonresistance" was coined in the English language, the King James translation was the only authorized version of the Bible. This translation of Matthew 5:39 reads, "But I say unto you, that ye resist not evil: but whosoever shall smite thee on the right cheek, turn to him the other also." Later Biblical criticism revealed important nuances in the meaning of the original text of "resist not evil." As will be seen from this collection, there is considerable difference between Barclay's *Apology* which attempts to apply the King James translation and one contemporary biblical scholar, Walter Wink, who argues that the words "resist not evil" were deliberately mistranslated in the English version of the Bible. Rather than counseling either violence or passivity, Wink argues, Jesus offered a systematic and strategic *Third Way* of nonviolent resistance.

In the early years, however, the teaching was practiced in the form of strict nonresistance to evil. The story of Mary Dyer as well as the early Quaker and Mennonite struggles emphasizing personal witness are good examples of the nonresistant approach. Later, the Abolitionists of the 1800's would update and apply nonresistance as a social change strategy to the issues of economic exploitation, slavery, and capital punishment. Whipple's *Non-Resistance Applied to the Internal Defense Of A Community* exemplifies the nonresistant approach to crime and penal reform.

Nonresistance was not a passive doctrine but rather emphasized witness in the face of social evil. Initially, nonresistance did not lend itself to organizing or strategizing for social change. It emphasized the personal living out of the Gospel witness regardless of the cost. Truth does carry power, and many believers in nonresistance held that the truth of the Christian ethic was powerful enough to overcome evil when good and evil came into sustained relationship. Witnessing to the truth, not strategic effectiveness, was the key. The suffering encountered in the meantime was endurable because the goal of realizing God's Kingdom on earth was in process. Thus, while many early Quakers might not have approved of the Boston Tea Party, they would have gladly refused to unload or drink the tea as a witness to the unacceptability of the tax.

There is a profound insight in the nonresistance approach when it is correctly understood. One twentieth century German theologian alluded to it when he said, "The only way to overcome evil is to let it run itself to a standstill because it does not find the resistance it is looking for. Resistance merely creates further evil and adds fuel to the flames. But when evil meets no opposition and encounters no obstacle but only patient endurance, its sting is drawn, and at last it meets an opponent which is more than its match."

Many modern day practitioners of nonviolent social change might find the nonresistance emphasis on personal witness inadequate to the magnitude of today's structural evil. But the kind of courage and commitment displayed by our forerunners in the tradition through their refusal to obey orders, to take oaths, or to cooperate with what they saw to be morally unacceptable, even to the point of death, has much to teach us in the context of current struggles.

Another form of nonviolence, "passive resistance," is, in fact, active, but still without harm to the opponent. It became the more emphasized understanding of Gospel-based nonviolence as organized resistance became the predominant mode. The organized non-payment of war taxes, the antislavery methods suggested by Angelina Grimke in *Appeal To The Christian Women Of The South,* and the later work slowdowns of the slaves and factory workers were all forms of passive resistance. This form emphasizes organized nonviolent action which works by withdrawal, refusal, and noncooperation and includes any number of methods such as the boycott, sit-down strikes, and going limp when arrested. Those who emphasize "passive resistance" embrace a strategy of social change through non-participation in the objectionable law, custom, or structure.

"Nonviolent direct intervention," a third general form, tends to be more assertive in trying to create the desired social change rather than solely protesting its absence. In this form, the traditional withdrawal or noncooperation may be involved, but the emphasis is on actions which in and of themselves change the unjust law or social structure. The Underground Railroad of the 1800's and the Sanctuary Movement of the 1980's are examples. People such as Harriet Tubman actually freed slaves. Providing housing, food, and transportation to Central American refugees fleeing the violence of their homelands gives precisely what the United States Government refuses to grant. The desired social change is being created in the action itself. Civil disobedience tends to play a role in these actions because the change is being put into effect to pressure for a change in an unjust law. The more radical tactics of the Catholic Left during the Vietnam War such as burning draft files, as well as the post-war Plowshares Actions in which military hardware is "disarmed," are also instances of nonviolent direct intervention. As will be seen from Tom Cornell's article, *Nonviolent Napalm in Catonsville,* these types of actions raised a new set of questions about the boundaries between nonviolent and violent approaches to social change.

Modern nonviolence is, in fact, a combination of these overlapping categories. In current campaigns they are so mixed as to become hardly distinguishable, each adding its own particular thread to the weaving of personal and social change. And of course that change has to do with more than war and peace. It has to do with life and its relationships; it is all of a piece. As is so well reflected in Woolman's *Plea to the Poor,* Christian nonviolence tends to affect one's lifestyle, employment, and choices about participating in social structures which are destructive of human liberation and community.

The Root Dynamic of Gospel Nonviolence

As rich as the tradition of Christian nonviolence has been in U.S. history, the term still conjures up for many the image of a bag of tricks. They look for words and actions which, if applied correctly, cause aggression and injustice to magically cease. Nonviolence is not magic. Nonviolence is a relational dynamic which, when brought to bear in situations of aggression, tends to be disarming. We must first understand the dynamic and how it engages with evil; only then can nonviolence be applied.

Nonviolence tends to counter dehumanizing elements inherent in conflict situations, not because of some magical power, but because of its ability to tap into the fundamental thrust of creation toward wholeness and its power to eventually reverse polarization and break the spiral of violent escalation. Dr. Martin Luther King, Jr. was referring to this dynamic when he told a convulsive Montgomery, Alabama, during the 1955 bus boycott, "The universe bends toward justice." The relational goals of nonviolence, rooted in the Gospel priorities of reconciliaton over revenge, mutuality over domination and mutual conversion over the destruction of opponents are quite different from the goals of the violent methodologies. Whereas proponents of violence stategize to increase fear in the opponent in the hopes that they will submit or at least limit their uses of power, as for example in nuclear deterrence, the nonviolent methodology calls for decreasing fear and defensiveness in order to increase the possibility of dialogue and mutual change. Whereas proponents of violence view the destruction of the enemy as a desired end or means to an end, proponents of nonviolence work to construct a new situation in which the causal dynamics in the enemy-relationship are resolved.

The "bag of tricks" mentality is inherent in the question, "But what would you do if someone was raping your grandmother?," a favorite query of draft board examiners and skeptics. Such questions beg for pat answers. But there are none. Those reading this collection may become frustrated if they are looking for a list of "how to's" guaranteed to provide security or social change. As with any method, some nonviolent actions which might work effectively in one situation of injustice or aggression might not work at all in another. This is because the key interactions happen within a specific context, with individual people or groups who have specific needs, fears and desires, and whose "will to power" must be reached in different ways by nonviolent practitioners who have different strengths and weaknesses. Not all rapists, for example, respond in the same way to verbal attempts to diffuse violence; nor to nonviolent physical attempts to de-escalate the assault; nor to a victim with a gun in her hand. The majority of rapists, however, will respond to violence with counter-violence, in the name of "self-defense" no less, just as nations have labeled the most plainly aggressive acts as national defense.

There is nothing magical about nonviolence. It requires courage and hard work, strategizing, self-discipline, strength, and a well-integrated spirituality. It requires a willingness to learn from our enemies, and at the same time the creativity not to limit our response by taking up their view of reality. It demands the ability on our part to desire their safety as well as our own; to love the enemy in them, even while we refuse to cooperate with it. These are the threads that weave security. These are the patterns that disarm. The message Jesus offered was simple. Our goals of security and peace are more readily attainable if we use methods which do not contradict them. We cannot reach security by creating insecurity. We cannot reach disarmament by arming. We cannot create a less violent world by using more violence.

Conclusion

This collection is not a history. It is a reader geared toward furthering interest in a deeper examination of the tradition of Christian nonviolence in the United States. The selections are arranged in chronological order to give the reader a sense of the tradition's development.

I suspect that few people will agree with everything contained in this volume. There are contradictions, questionable logic, and even disagreement among some of the most influential thinkers. Those working for justice in one area were sometimes unable to grasp the injustice in others. The use of exclusive language is an example. It is not until the 1980's that most Christian authors writing on issues of justice and nonviolence realized the violence inherent in the use of male pronouns to stand for all human beings. But all of this is important. It reminds us that even the people we may look to for guidance are in a process of coming to awareness. Much of our consciousness today was made possible by the journeys of these men and women. For this reason, and to retain the flavor of the period of each piece as authentically as possible, language has been left in its original form where available.

It is my belief that if Christians in the United States actually understood the nonviolence in their scriptures and were faithful to the priority given it by their founder, violence in U.S. domestic and foreign policy would be radically reduced. Too often the leaders of organized Christian churches, Catholic and Protestant alike, have refused to take the teaching seriously, either from fear, lack of understanding or political choice. This volume is a plea, specifically to Christians, to look into their religious tradition for the criteria by which to assess personal and political policies based on the violent suppression or elimination of people who threaten us by their aggression, ideologies, or simply because their needs conflict with ours. In a predominantly Christian nation where the extreme desire for profit and national security require the suppression of other peoples' access to basic life resources through militarism, economic and psychological warfare, racism, terrorism, torture, and death, Jesus has long been forgotten. This volume is an invitation to U.S. Christians to remember.

Angie O'Gorman
St. Louis, Missouri

LET ME BE THE ONE MARY DYER: WITNESS TO RELIGIOUS LIBERTY

Margaret Bacon

ON THE STATE HOUSE grounds opposite the Boston Commons stands the statue of Mary Dyer (~1617-1660), Quaker, with the inscription, "Witness for Religious Freedom, Hanged on Boston Common, 1660." The statue, created by Quaker sculptor Sylvia Shaw Judson, is of a serene woman of great inner strength.

Mary Dyer's struggle against the unjust laws of the Massachusetts Bay Colony, barring Quakers from exercising their freedom to worship, exemplifies the Quaker use of nonviolence in the middle of the seventeenth century. In England too Quakers were punished for their religious beliefs, and endured long prison terms rather than abandoning their witness to the truth. Their acceptance of suffering contributed to the development of religious toleration.

The persecution of Quakers in Puritan Boston was particularly acute. The right wing Puritans who had founded the colony intended to make it a theocracy, based on the Bible, and governed by male authority figures in both church and state, The ministers taught a harsh theology of predestination. Only those men and women who lived in strict accordance with Scripture, as interpreted by the ministers, could hope for a sign that they were among the elect, though despite their best efforts they might still be assigned to hell fire. Any deviation from the teachings of the ministers was considered heresy. Everyone was expected to spend long hours in cold meeting houses, listening to frightening doctrine. Public morals were enforced by the magistrates, and each home was to be strictly governed by the husband, with absolute authority over his wife, children and servants. The Quaker concept of a direct relationship between each person and the Divine Spirit, and the Quaker belief in the equality of women, represented a clear threat to this system.

9

Long before she became a Quaker, Mary Dyer rebelled against male authority in the Colony by supporting her friend, Anne Hutchinson. The Dyers had migrated from England to Boston in 1835 as newlyweds, and Mary Dyer, aged eighteen, had given birth to her first child, during the harsh winter. Hutchinson, who had medical skills, helped her during childbirth, and the two became friends.

Anne Hutchinson was already in trouble with the authorities for holding meetings for women in her home. Barred from asking questions in the church, women could discuss religious matters in these meetings, and Anne went so far as to criticize some of the ministers. In November of 1637, she was tried by the General Court for "maintaining a meeting in your house not comely in the sight of God, nor fitting to your Sex." She was banished to Roxbury, and the next spring brought back before the church to be excommunicated. As Anne Hutchinson walked slowly down the aisle to receive this punishment, Mary Dyer rose to walk with her.

Following Anne's banishment, Mary Dyer and her husband joined the Hutchinsons in founding a new colony, near Providence, Rhode Island, on land given them by Roger Williams, who believed each person should be free to worship God in his or her own fashion. Later, this colony split into two, the Dyers and their friends settling in what is now Newport. Here, the group declared itself a "democracie" and ordered that "none be accounted delinquent for doctrine."

In Rhode Island, the Dyers prospered as farmers and merchants, and Mary Dyer bore four more children. Her peace however was increasingly troubled by religious concerns. In 1643, after the death of her husband, Anne Hutchinson felt led to move to Long Island. Here she and most of her children were killed by hostile Indians. The Boston Puritans said it was a judgement upon her, and predicted that she would roast in hell. Mary Dyer found she simply could no longer accept the concept of predestination, or of a loving God who so punished his children.

In 1652 the Dyers took their five children back to England to visit Mary's mother. Here Mary Dyer encountered the Children of the Light, or Quakers, as they were then reproachfully nicknamed, who were just arising in the North of England. Their concepts of direct access to God, and de-emphasis on sin appealed to her. She became a convert, and was reluctant to leave when it was time to return to Rhode Island. Her husband and children eventually left without her and she traveled in the ministry up and down England, accompanied by another woman, as was the custom. Not until 1657 did she feel released to return to New England to preach the Truth in the new colonies.

In 1656, two Quaker women, Ann Austin and Mary Fisher, had arrived in Boston to preach, and were promptly searched for signs of witchcraft, thrown in jail, and then banished. To avoid further trouble, the Colony passed a new law ordering that if any more Quakers found their way into Boston they were to be arrested, whipped, placed in the house of correction, and prevented from speaking to anyone.

When Mary Dyer's ship at last arrived in Boston, she and her traveling companion were seized and thrown into jail, and the windows boarded up so no one could speak to them. Even the sea captain who had brought them into port, though ignorant of the new law, was fined one hundred pounds and ordered to take the other woman directly back to England.

Hearing of Mary's plight, Will Dyer came to Boston for her, and by posting a large bail, was permitted to take her to Rhode Island. Eager though she was to see her children, Mary left the Colony reluctantly, sure that it was her duty to preach the Truth to the Bostonians. While she bided her time, other Quakers dared to set their feet in Boston, and were met by harsher and harsher punishments. On October of 1857, a second law was passed, decreeing that any Quaker who returned to Boston after having been banished would have an ear cropped off. When three Quaker men endured this awful punishment, a third law was enacted that any Quaker returning to the Colony after being banished was to be hanged.

In September of 1659 two English Quakers, William Robinson and Marmaduke Stephenson, went to Boston taking with them an eleven year old girl, Patience Scott. The two men were thrown in jail, and the child closely confined in the home of the governor. Mary Dyer decided she must go and bring the girl home. She had a stormy interview with Governor Endicott, who formally banished her once and for all from the Colony. Stephenson and Robinson were also banished. They left, but in less than a month all three were back. On October 19 the General Court sentenced them to death by hanging.

The execution was set for October 27. The three Quakers were uplifted rather than depressed by their sentence, and spent their time in prayer and meditation. Each of them were furnished with writing materials so that they could write a final letter to their families. Mary Dyer decided to make an appeal to the governor, not for her own life, but to save him and his magistrates from the crime they were about to commit.

"In love and meekness I beseech you to repeal these cruel laws, to stay this wicked sentence. Though you have harmed us grievously, in the past, no life has been lost. But now, if you shed our innocent blood you will kill not only our bodies, but your infinitely more precious souls. For the wages of sin is death, and tis a heinous sin indeed to kill your fellowmen, children of God like you, who only seek to preach his Word. Relent, I beg you, repent I implore you, for if you persist you will surely feel God's heavy hand on Judgement Day....

"Therefore, let the light of Christ with its loving warmth soften your hearts and let the light bring your minds out of darkness to freedom and glory, for his is the way to everlasting life."

On the day of the execution the three walked to the gallows hand in hand. Mary Dyer told one of the magistrates that this was the hour of greatest joy she had ever experienced. "No ear can hear, nor tongue utter, and no heart understand the sweet incomings and refreshings of the Spirit of the Lord which I now feel."

Mary Dyer's joy was shortlived, however. She climbed the gallows with her companions and the hangman covered her eyes with a cloth, bound her legs and arms, and placed the rope around her neck. The other two went cheerfully to their deaths, but when it was her turn a court officer raced up with a last minute reprieve. The authorities feared the effect on public opinion of hanging a woman, and had planned this stratagem all along, hoping to frighten Mary Dyer into submission. Her eyes were unbound, her arms and legs freed, and the crowd cheered and urged her to step down from the gallows. She argued that she did not want to live unless the bloody laws were repealed, but it was of no use. Her husband was waiting at the foot of the gallows with a swift horse to take her home again, and heartbroken, she acquiesced.

Exhausted by this ordeal, Mary Dyer became ill, and her recovery was slow. When she finally regained her strength she again left home to preach the Word, this time on Long Island, where her friend Anne Hutchinson had met her death. By now she belonged more to heaven than to earth, and her face showed it. A contemporary described her as "a comely woman and a grave matron...who shined in the image of God."

All along she had felt that she must return to Boston, "to look their bloody laws in the face." In May of 1660 she set out with two fellow Quakers. She was immediately arrested and brought once more before Governor Endicott, who once more sentenced her to death.

Her husband Will Dyer wrote the governor a humble letter, pleading for her life, but Endicott refused to grant it, and Mary Dyer refused to recant. On June 1, 1660, she once more mounted the gallows. Again she was offered her life and again refused it. "Nay, I cannot, for in obedience to the will of the Lord I came, and in his will I abide faithfully to my death." With a serene smile on her lips, she met her death.

"Look, she hangs there like a flag," someone in the crowd said, half in jest.

But it was true. Mary Dyer's lifeless body became an image of religious freedom. Although one more Quaker was hung in March of 1661, the magistrates were forced to abandon the death penalty as a means of controlling the Quakers. Much as they hated Quaker heresy, the public would not allow such brutality. In addition,, the English Quakers appealed to King Charles II who sent a missive to Endicott demanding that the hangings be stopped. Some persecution of Quakers continued for another twenty years, but public opinion swung more and more strongly against it, and Mary Dyer's famous words on the occasion of her first trip to the gallows were remembered.

"But if one of us must die that the others may live, let me be the one, for if my life were freely granted by you, I could not accept it as long as my sisters suffered and my brothers died. For what is life compared to the witness of Truth?"

Margaret Hope Bacon is an author and lecturer who has written frequently about Quaker women. Among her books are *Valiant Friend: The Life of Lucretia Mott* and *Mothers of Feminism: The Story of Quaker Women in America.* She worked for twenty-two years for the American Friends Service Committee and is active in peace concerns, civil rights and women's rights.

From: AN APOLOGY FOR THE TRUE CHRISTIAN DIVINITY (1678)

Robert Barclay

A QUAKER CONVERT, BARCLAY (1648-1690) was the nominal governor of what is today western New Jersey. Remaining in England, he governed the predominantly Quaker settlement from 1682-1688 through a deputy and there is some disagreement if and when he actually visited the Colonies. Barclay is, in a sense, a transitional writer between the old world and the new. While governing from afar, he clearly set a nonviolent tone as the following excerpt from his 1678 *Apology* will show. He lays out here his understanding of the roots of Christian nonviolence.

Barclay's nonresistance was not solely theoretical nor war related. When a pistol-wielding highwayman in England demanded Barclay's money, he looked his attacker in the face and firmly but gently assured him that he was not his enemy. He was, rather, a friend, willing to help if needed, but not intimidated by his weapon. Barclay informed the man that he did not fear death because he believed in immortality. He asked his would-be attacker if he could actually shed the blood of one who had no enmity for him and who was willing to befriend him. The robber became confused, the hand holding the pistol fell to his side and he fled.

THE LAST THING TO be considered is *Revenge* and *War*, an Evil as opposite and contrary to the Spirit and Doctrine of Christ as *Light* to *Darkness*. For, as is manifest by what is said, through contempt of Christ's Law, the whole World is filled with various *Oaths, Cursings, blasphemous Profanations,* and *horrid Perjuries;* so likewise through contempt of the same Law, the World is filled with *Violence, Oppression, Murders, Ravishing of Women* and *Virgins, Spoilings, Depradations, Burnings, Devastations,* and all manner of

Lasciviousness and *Cruelty:* so that it is strange that Men, made after the Image of God, should have so much degenerated that they rather bear the Image and Nature of Roaring Lions, Tearing Tigers, Devouring Wolves, and Raging Boars, than Rational Creatures endowed with Reason. And is it not yet much more admirable that this *horrid Monster* should find place, and be fomented among those Men, that profess themselves *Disciples* of our *Peaceable Lord* and *Master Jesus Christ,* who by *Excellency* is called *Prince of Peace,* and hath expressly prohibited his Children all Violence; and on the contrary, commanded them that according to his Example, they should follow Patience, Charity, Forbearance and other Virtues worthy of a Christian?

Hear then what this great Prophet saith, whom every Soul is commanded to hear, under the pain of being cut off, *Matthew 5,* from verse 38 to the end of the Chapter. For thus he saith: "Ye have heard that it hath been said, An eye for an eye, and a tooth: But I say unto you, That ye resist no evil; but whosoever shall smite thee on thy right cheek, turn to him the other also. And if any man will sue thee at the law, and take away thy coat, let him have thy cloke also. And whosoever shall compell thee to go a mile, go with him twain. Give to him that asketh thee, and from him that would borrow of thee turn not thou away. Ye have heard that it hath been said, Thou shalt love thy neighbour, and hate thine enemy. But I say unto you, Love your enemies, bless them that curse you, do good to them that hate you, and pray for them which despitefully use you and persecute you; That ye may be the children of your Father which is in Heaven: for he maketh his sun to rise on the evil and on the good, and sendeth rain on the just and the unjust. For if ye love them which love you, what reward have ye? do not even the publicans the same? And if ye salute your brethren only, what do ye more than others? Do not the publicans so? Be ye therefore perfect, even as your Father which is in heaven is perfect."

These words, with a respect to *Revenge,* as the former in the case of *Swearing,* do forbid some things which were formerly lawful to the *Jews,* considering their Condition and Dispensation; and Command unto such as will be the Disciples of Christ a more perfect, eminent and full Signification of Charity, as also Patience and Suffering than was required of them at that Time, State and Dispensation, by the Law of *Moses.* This is not only the Judgement of most, if not all, the *Ancient Fathers* (so called) of the first Three Hundred Years after Christ, but also of many others; and in general of all those, who have rightly understood and propagated the Law of Christ concerning *Swearing.* . . .

From hence it appears that there is so great a Connection betwixt these two Precepts of *Christ* that as they were uttered and commanded by him at one and the same time, so the same way they were received by Man of all Ages, not only in the first Promulgation, by the little number of the Disciples, but also after the Christians increased in the first Three Hundred Years. Even also in the *Apostasy,* the one was not left and rejected without the other; and not again in the *Restitution,* and renewed Preaching of the *Eternal Gospel,* they are acknowledged as Eternal and Unchangeable Laws, properly belonging to the *Evangelical State* and *Perfection* thereof: from which if any withdraw, he falls short of the Perfection of a *Christian Man.*

And truly, the words are so clear in themselves that (in my Judgement) they need no illustration to explain their Sense: for it is as easy to reconcile the greatest Contradictions as these Laws of our Lord Jesus Christ, with the wicked Practices of *Wars;* for they are plainly inconsistent. Whoever can reconcile this, *Resist not Evil, with Resist Violence by Force;* again, *Give also thy other Cheek* with *Strike again;* also, *Love thine Enemies* with *Spoil them, make a Prey of them, pursue them with Fire and Sword;* or, *Pray for those that persecute you, and those that calumniate you,* with *persecute you by Fines, Imprisonments and Death itself;* and not only such as do not *persecute you,* but *who heartily seek and desire your Eternal and Temporal Welfare:* whoever, I say, can find a Means to reconcile these things, may by supposed also to have found a way to reconcile *God* with the *Devil, Christ* with *Antichrist, Light* with *Darkness,* and *Good* with *Evil.* But if this be impossible, as indeed it is, so will also the other be impossible; and Men do but deceive themselves and others while they boldly adventure to establish such absurd and impossible things.

FIRST LETTER TO THE DELAWARE INDIANS (1681)

William Penn

*B*ORN *IN ENGLAND, PENN (1644-1718) was the son of an English* Admiral. He was jailed several times under the restoration laws for his Quaker philosophy and preaching, and increasingly looked to America as a refuge for himself and his fellow Quakers. In 1681, due in large part to Penn's friendships among the English royalty, the King gave him proprietorship over the province which would become Pennsylvania. Before he left for America he sent a letter to the Native Americans via the Commissioner who preceeded him. The attitude expressed in his letter opened the way for Penn's peaceful relations with the Native Americans and the eventual treaty (or treaties) which helped sustain good relations between them and settlers of Pennsylvania, the only colony in the new land where such a rapport existed. Native American tradition holds this time as a bright moment in their relationship with the settlers. While it is not known if there was one treaty or many, the principle points have not been forgotten, in Native American tradition at least: 1) that all paths should be open and free to both Christians and Native Americans; 2) that the doors of the Christians' houses should be open to the Native Americans, and their homes open to the Christians, and they should make each other welcome as friends; 3) that the Christians should not believe any false rumors or reports of the Native Americans, nor the Native Americans believe any such rumors or reports of the Christians, but should first come as brethren to inquire of each other.

London, 18th of 8th Month, 1681

*M*Y FRIENDS——THERE IS one great God and power that hath made the world and all things therein, to whom you and I, and all people owe their being and well-being, and to whom you and I must one day give an account for all that we do in the world; this great God hath written his law in our hearts, by which we are taught and commanded to love and help, and do good to one another, and not to do harm and mischief one to another. Now this great God hath been pleased to make me concerned in your parts of the world, and the king of the country where I live hath given unto me a great province, but I desire to enjoy it with your love and consent, that we may always live together as neighbors and friends; else what would the great God say to us, who hath made us not to devour and destroy one another, but live soberly and kindly together in the world? Now I would have you well observe, that I am very sensible of the unkindness and injustice that hath been too much exercised toward you by the people of these parts of the world, who sought themselves, and to make great advantages by you, rather than be examples of justice and goodness unto you, which I hear hath been a matter of trouble to you, and caused great grudgings and animosities, sometimes to the shedding of blood, which hath made the great God angry. But I am not such a man, as is well known in my own country; I have great love and regard toward you, and I desire to win and gain your love and friendship, by a kind, just and peaceable life, and the people I send are of the same mind, and shall in all things behave themselves accordingly; and if in anything any shall offend you or your people, you shall have a full and speedy satisfaction for the same, by an equal number of just men on both sides, that by no means you may have just occasion of being offended against them. I shall shortly come to you myself, at what time we may more largely and freely confer and discourse of these matters. In the meantime, I have sent my commissioners to treat with you about the land, and a firm league of peace. Let me desire you to be kind to them and the people, and receive these presents and tokens which I have sent to you, as a testimony of my good will to you, and my resolution to live justly, peaceably, and friendly with you.

I am your loving friend,

William Penn

GERMANTOWN FRIENDS' PROTEST AGAINST SLAVERY (1688)

*T*HE EARLIEST PACIFISTS IN *the New World were probably Dutch* Mennonites, living in Manhattan in the early 1640's. It wasn't until later, however, that the first permanent settlement of Mennonites occurred, just north of the newly founded Philadelphia. A mixture of Mennonites and Quaker families from Mennonite backgrounds left Germany and settled in the township of Germantown. The writing of this earliest protest of slaveholding by Quakers was due more to this Mennonite influence than to the Quakers themselves—especially since most Germantown Quakers were of Mennonite origins.

In the Germantown Protest, the impossibility of sustaining slavery, except through violence, was presented as a challenge to Quakers who had renounced violence itself. How would the Quakers respond should the slaves organize and revolt? It was a strange inconsistency that the very people who so ardently upheld the humanity of the Indian would only come to see the inhumanity of slavery much later. It was not until the efforts of John Woolman that the movement for abolition of slavery among Quakers began in earnest.

This is to ye Monthly Meeting Held at Richard Worrell's

*T*HESE ARE THE REASONS why we are against traffick of men-body, as followeth. Is there any that would be done or handled in this manner? viz., to be sold or made a slave for all the time of his life? How fearful and faint-hearted are many on sea, when they see a strange vessel,—being afraid it should be a Turk, and they should be taken, and sold for slaves into Turkey. Now what is this better done, as Turks doe? Yea, rather is it worse for them, which say they are Christians; for we hear that ye most part of such negers are brought hither against their will and consent, and that many of them are stolen. Now, tho they are black, we can not conceive there is more liberty to have them slaves, as it is to have other white ones. There is a saying, that we shall doe

21

to all men like as we will be done ourselves; making no difference of what generation, descent or colour they are. And those who steal or robb men, and those who buy or purchase them, are they not all alike? Here is liberty of conscience, wch is right and reasonable; here ought to be likewise liberty of ye body, except of evil doers, wch is an other case. But to bring men hither, or to rob and sell them against their will, we stand against. In Europe there are many oppressed for conscience sake; and here there are those oppressed who are of a black colour. And we who know that men must not comitt adultery,— some do committ adultery, in others, separating wives from their husbands and giving them to others; and some sell the children of these poor creatures to other men. Ah! doe consider well this thing, you who doe it, if you would be done at this manner? and if it is done according to Christianity? You surpass Holland and Germany in this thing. This makes an ill report in all those countries of Europe, where they hear off, that ye Quakers doe here handel men as they handel there ye cattle. And for that reason some have no mind or inclination to come hither. And who shall maintain this your cause, or pleid for it? Truly we can not do so, except you shall inform us better hereof, viz., that Christians have liberty to practise these things. Pray, what thing in the world can be done worse towards us, than if men should rob or steal us away, and sell us for slaves to strange countries; separating husbands from their wives and children. Being now this is not done in the manner we would be done at therefore we contradict and are against this traffic of men-body. And we who profess that it is not lawful to steal, must likewise, avoid to purchase such things as are stolen, but rather help to stop this robbing and stealing if possible. And such men ought to be delivered out of ye hands of ye robbers, and set free as well as in Europe. Then is Pennsylvania to have a good report, instead it hath now a bad one for this sake in other countries. Especially whereas ye Europeans are desirous to know in what manner ye Quakers doe rule in their province;—and most of them doe look upon us with an envious eye. But if this is done well, what shall we say is done evil?

If once these slaves (wch they say are so wicked and stubbern men) should joint themselves,—fight for their freedom,—and handel their masters and mastrisses as they did handel them before; will these masters and mastrisses take the sword at hand and warr against these poor slaves, licke, we are able to believe, some will not refuse to doe; or have these negers not as much right to fight for their freedom, as you have to keep them slaves?

Now consider well this thing, if it is good or bad? And in case you find it to be good to handel these blacks at that manner, we desire and require you hereby lovingly, that you may inform us herein, which at this time never was done, viz., that Christians have such a liberty to do so. To the end we shall be satisfied in this point, and satisfie likewise our good friends and acquaintances in our natif country, to whose it is a terror, or fairful thing, that men should be handeld so in Pennsylvania.

This is from our meeting at Germantown, held ye 18 of the 2 month, 1688, to be delivered to the Monthly Meeting at Richard Worrel's.

Garret henderich
derick up de graeff
Francis daniell Pastorius
Abraham up Den graef

CONSIDERATIONS ON THE PAYMENT OF A TAX LAID FOR CARRYING ON THE WAR AGAINST THE INDIANS (1755)

John Woolman

*A*T AGE 21, JOHN WOOLMAN (1720-1772) decided to limit his business activities in order to pursue his true calling as a "recommended minister," one of those Friends whose spoken "testimonies" during the otherwise silent Quaker meetings for worship were unusually powerful and uplifting. Often these ministers were sent with a "travelling minute" (letter of introduction) to visit other meetings as unpaid, itinerant preachers. This Woolman did for the rest of his life. What he observed of slave holding during these travels shocked and grieved him so much that his missionary witness became largely a plea against slavery. Still, his best known journey is probably his 1762 visit to the Indians at Wyalusing, Pennsylvania. The trip was prompted by a desire to ". . . feel and understand their life and the spirit they live in, if haply I might receive some instruction from them or they be in any degree helped forward by my following the leading of Truth amongst them."

At thirty-six he started writing his *Journal* and his essays, the two most notable of which are sampled in this collection. While his main concern was slavery, Woolman also opposed war and war taxes, lived a life of voluntary simplicity, and insisted on social and economic justice, as manifested in his pleading for a more just land policy for the Indians. His methods of implementing these concerns included confronting slave owners face to face whenever possible, and rousing his fellow Quakers through his inspired verbal

25

messages. He showed as much concern for the slave owners as for the slaves, trying to show the former that they would benefit as much as their slaves if they ceased being embroiled in the morally wrong slavery system. Personal example was another method. Woolman abstained from using any product connected with the slave trade. He always examined his own practice before trying to influence others. Thus before visiting the Indian settlement, as he notes in his *Journal,* he probed within himself to learn whether he had "kept clear of all things which tended to stir up or were connected with wars..." His concern for economic and social justice expressed itself in constant vigilance lest humans exploit the labor of others, lest they indulge in luxuries at the expense of others, lest they become involved in profit making to the detriment of their spiritual and moral values.

A FEW YEARS PAST, money being made current in our province for carrying on wars, and to be sunk by taxes laid on the inhabitants, my mind was often affected with the thoughts of paying such taxes, and I believe it right for me to preserve a memorandum concerning it. I was told that Friends in England frequently paid taxes when the money was applied to such purposes. I had conference with several noted Friends on the subject, who all favoured the payment of such taxes, some of whom I preferred before myself; and this made me easier for a time. Yet there was in the deeps of my mind a scruple which I never could get over, and at certain times I was greatly distressed on that account.

I all along believed that there were some upright-hearted men who paid such taxes, but could not see that their example was a sufficient reason for me to do so, while I believed that the spirit of Truth required of me as an individual to suffer patiently the distress of goods rather than pay actively.

To refuse the active payment of a tax which our Society generally paid was exceeding disagreeable, but to do a thing contrary to my conscience appeared yet more dreadful.

When this exercise came upon me, I knew of none under the like difficulty, and in my distress I besought the Lord to enable me to give up all, that so I might follow him wheresoever he was pleased to lead me. And under this exercise I went to our Yearly Meeting at Philadelphia in 1755, at which a committee was appointed, some from each Quarter, to correspond with the Meeting for Sufferings in London, and another to visit our Monthly and Quarterly Meetings. And after their appointment, before the last adjournment of the meeting, it was agreed on in the meeting that these two committees should meet together in Friend's schoolhouse in the city, at a time when the meeting stood adjourned, to consider some things in which the cause of Truth was concerned; and these committees meeting together had a weighty conference in the fear of the Lord, at which time I perceived there were many Friends under a scruple like that before-mentioned. . . .

As scrupling to pay a tax on account of the application hath seldom been heard of heretofore, even amongst men of integrity who have steadily borne their testimony against outward wars in their time, I may here note some things which have occurred to my mind as I have been inwardly exercised on that account.

From the steady opposition which faithful Friends in early times made to wrong things then approved of, they were hated and persecuted by men living in the spirit of this world, and suffering with firmness they were made a blessing to the church, and the work prospered. It equally concerns men in every age to take heed to their own spirit, and in comparing their situation with ours, it looks to me there was less danger of their being infected with the spirit of this world, in paying their taxes, than there is of us now. They had little or no share in civil government, and many of them declared they were through the power of God separated from the spirit in which wars were; and being afflicted by the rulers on account of their testimony, there was less likelihood of uniting in spirit with them in things inconsistent with the purity of Truth. We, from the first settlement of this land, have known little or no troubles of that sort. The profession which for a time was accounted reproachful, at length the uprightness of our predecessors being understood by the rulers and their innocent sufferings moving them, the way of worship was tolerated, and many of our members in these colonies become active in civil government. Being thus tried with favour and prosperity, this world hath appeared inviting. Our minds have been turned to the improvement of our country, to merchandise and sciences, amongst which are many things useful, being followed in pure wisdom; but in our present condition, that a carnal mind is gaining upon us I believe will not be denied.

Some of our members who are officers in civil government are in one case or other called upon in their respective stations to assist in things relative to the wars. Such being in doubt whether to act or crave to be excused from their office, seeing their brethren united in the payment of a tax to carry on the said wars, might think their case not much different and so quench the tender movings of the Holy Spirit in their minds. And thus by small degrees there might be an approach toward that of fighting, till we come so near it as that the distinction would be little else but the name of a peaceable people.

It requires a great self-denial and resignation of ourselves to God to attain that state wherein we can freely cease from fighting when wrongfully invaded, if by our fighting there were a probability of overcoming the invaders. Whoever rightly attains to it does in some degree feel that spirit in which our Redeemer gave his life for us, and through divine goodness many of our predecessors and many now living have learned this blessed lesson. But many others, having their religion chiefly by education and not being enough acquainted with that cross which crucifies to the world, do manifest a temper distinguishable from that of an entire trust in God.

. . . Some time after the Yearly Meeting, a day being appointed and letters wrote to distant members, the said committees met at Philadelphia and by adjournments continued several days. The calamities of war were now increasing. The frontier inhabitants of Pennsylvania were frequently surprised, some slain and many taken captive by the Indians; and while these committees sat, the corpse of one so slain was brought in a wagon and taken through the streets of the city in his bloody garments to alarm the people and rouse them up to war.

Friends thus met were not at all of one mind in relation to the tax, which to such who scrupled it made the way more difficult. To refuse an active payment at such a time might be construed an act of disloyalty and appeared likely to displease the rulers, not only here but in England. Still there was a scruple so fastened upon the minds of many Friends that nothing moved it. It was a conference the most weighty that ever I was at, and the hearts of many were bowed in reverence before the Most High. Some Friends of the said committees who appeared easy to pay the tax, after several adjournments withdrew; others of them continued till the last. At length an epistle was drawn up by some Friends concerned on that account, and being read several times and corrected was then signed by such who were free to sign it, which is as follows:

An Epistle of Tender Love and Caution to Friends in Pennsylvania

Philadelphia, 16th day, 12th month, 1755

... And being painfully apprehensive that the large sum granted by the late Act of Assembly for the king's use is principally intended for purposes inconsistent with our peaceable testimony, we therefore think that as we cannot be concerned in wars and fightings, so neither ought we to contribute thereto by paying the tax directed by the said Act, though suffering be the consequence of our refusal, which we hope to be enabled to bear with patience.

And (we take this position even) though some part of the money to be raised by the said Act is said to be for such benevolent purposes as supporting our friendship with our Indian neighbours and relieving the distress of our fellow subjects who have suffered in the present calamities, for whom our hearts are deeply pained; and we affectionately and with bowels of tenderness sympathize with them therein. And we could most cheerfully contribute to those purposes if they were not so mixed that we cannot in the manner proposed show our hearty concurrence therewith without at the same time assenting to, or allowing ourselves in, practices which we apprehend contrary to the testimony which the Lord hath given us to bear for his name and Truth's sake. And having the health and prosperity of the Society at heart, we earnestly exhort Friends to wait for the appearing of the true Light and stand in the council of God, that we may know him to be the rock of our salvation and place of our refuge forever. . . .

And as our fidelity to the present government and our willingly paying all taxes for purposes which do not interfere with our consciences may justly exempt us from the imputation of disloyalty, so we earnestly desire that all who by a deep and quiet seeking for direction from the Holy Spirit are, or shall be, convinced that he calls us as a people to this testimony may dwell under the guidance of the same divine Spirit, and manifest by the meekness and humility of their conversation that they are really under the influence, and therein may know true fortitude and patience to bear that and every other testimony committed to them faithfully and uniformly, and that all Friends may know their spirits clothed with true charity, the bond of Christian fellowship, wherein we again salute you and remain your friends and brethren.

From: A PLEA FOR THE POOR (c.1763)

John Woolman

Section I.

WEALTH DESIRED FOR ITS own sake obstructs the increase of virtue, and large possessions in the hands of selfish men have a bad tendency, for by their means too small a number of people are employed in things useful; and therefore they, or some of them, are necessitated to labor too hard, while others would want business to earn their bread were not employments invented which, having no real usefulness, serve only to please the vain mind. . . .

Section V.

. . .We may reflect on the condition of a poor, innocent man, who by his labor contributes toward supporting one of his own species more wealthy than himself, on whom the rich man, from a desire after wealth and luxuries lays heavy burdens. When this laborer looks over the means of his heavy load, and considers that this great toil and fatigue is laid on him to support that which hath no foundation in pure wisdom, we may well suppose that there ariseth an uneasiness in his mind toward those who might without any inconvenience deal more favorably with him. When he considers that by his industry his fellow creature is benefited, and sees that this man who hath much wealth is not satisfied with being supported in a plain way—but to gratify a wrong desire and conform to wrong customs, increaseth to an extreme the labors of those who occupy his estate—we may reasonably judge that he will think himself unkindly used.

When he considers that the proceedings of the wealthy are agreeable to the customs of the times, and sees no means of redress in this world, how would the sighing of an innocent person ascend to the throne of that great, good Being who created us all and hath a constant care over his creatures? By candidly

31

considering these things, we may have some sense of the condition of innocent people overloaded by the wealthy. But he who toils one year after another to furnish others with wealth and superfluities and who labors and thinks, and thinks and labors, til by overmuch labor he is wearied and oppressed, such a one understands the meaning of that language, "Ye know the heart of a stranger, seeing ye were strangers in the land of Egypt."

As many at this day who know not the heart of a stranger indulge themselves in ways of life which occasion more labor in the world than Infinite Goodness intends for man, and yet are compassionate toward such in distresses who comes directly under their observation, were these to change circumstances awhile with some who labor for them, were they to pass regularly through the means of knowing the heart of a stranger and come to a feeling knowledge of the straits and hardships which many poor, innocent people pass through in a hidden obscure life, were these who now fare sumptuously every day to act the other part of the scene til seven times had passed over them and return again to their former states, I believe many of them would embrace a way of life less expensive and lighten the heavy burdens of some who now labor out of their sight to support them and pass through straits with which they are but little acquainted.

To see our fellow-creatures under difficulties to which we are in no degree accessory tends to awaken tenderness in the minds of all reasonable people, but if we consider the condition of such who are depressed in answering our demands, who labor out of our sight and are often toiling for us while we pass our time in fullness, if we consider also that much less than we demand would supply us with things really needful, what heart will not relent, or what reasonable man can refrain from mitigating that grief of which he himself is the cause of, when he may do it without inconvenience?

Section X.

The way of carrying on wars, common in the world, is so far distinguishable from the purity of Christ's religion that many scruple to join in them. Those who are so redeemed from the love of the world as to possess nothing in a selfish spirit have their "life hid with Christ in God" (Col.3:3), and he preserves them in resignedness, even in times of commotion. As they possess nothing but what pertains to his family, anxious thoughts about wealth or dominion have little or nothing in them to work upon, and they learn contentment in being disposed of according to His will who, being omnipotent and always mindful of his children, causeth all things to work for their good. But when that spirit which loves riches works, and in its working gathers wealth and cleaves to customs which have their root in self-pleasing, this spirit, thus separating from universal love, seeks help from that power which stands in the separation; and whatever name it hath it still desires to defend the treasures thus gotten. This is like a chain in which the end of one link encloseth the end of another. The rising up of a desire to obtain wealth is the beginning. This desire being cherished moves to action, and riches thus gotten please self, and while self hath a life in them it desires to have them defended.

Wealth is attended with power, by which bargains and proceedings contrary to universal righteousness are supported; and hence oppression, carried on with worldly policy and order, clothes itself with the name of justice and becomes like a seed of discord in the soil; and as this spirit which wanders from the pure habitation prevails, so the seed of war swells and sprouts and grows and becomes strong until much fruit is ripened. Then cometh the harvest spoken of by the prophet, which "is a heap in the day of grief and desperate sorrow." O that we who declare against wars, and acknowledge our trust to be in God only, may walk in the light, and therein examine our foundation and motives in holding great estates! May we look upon our treasures, the furniture of our houses, and our garments, and try whether the seeds of war have nourishment in these our possessions. Holding treasures in the self-pleasing spirit is a strong plant, the fruit whereof ripens fast. A day of outward distress is coming, and Divine love calls to prepare against it. . . .

WAR INCONSISTENT WITH THE DOCTRINE AND EXAMPLE OF JESUS CHRIST (c.1782)

Job Scott

*A*N AMERICAN QUAKER MINISTER and mystic, Job Scott (1751-1793) based his religion and anti-war witness on his personal experience of God. Like many other Quakers during the Revolutionary period he struggled against the militarization of the effort for independence and suffered greatly as a result. Perhaps at no other time in our history has the nonviolent stance been less understood or faced greater public opposition as during the Revolutionary period. Scott refused to cooperate with the test oath or the pledge of allegiance to the revolutionary effort, and refused to use the continental paper currency which had been issued to finance the war. He fought hard for a clear Quaker condemnation of the payment of any taxes which supported the war. His pamphlet *War Inconsistent with the Doctrine and Example of Jesus Christ* was written as a letter to a friend.

DEAR SIR,

When I saw you lately, you may remember a part of our conversation turned on war—and perhaps you thought me singular in some of my sentiments, as controverting the received opinion of men in general. I have therefore devoted an hour or two to state further to you my particular views on this subject.

It is really astonishing to observe with how much composure mankind, and many persons acknowledged to be among the best men living, admit the propriety of war; and while they in general terms deplore the misery of it, maintain its necessity in some shape or other; for the most part, in that of defense. Under this mask, the great adversary of men has so imposed on them that they do not even think of discussing the lawfulness of war in any case, though they profess to act on Christian principles. For my own part, I cannot help wishing to see it become a subject of universal discussion, till the renunciation of the tenet shall spread itself as wide as the misery it has produced.

War, however dreadful in its progress, and awful in its consequences, has always been pleaded for as necessary. Time would be lost in endeavoring to prove what scarcely anyone will deny, namely, "the unlawfulness of *offensive wars*," even on moral, much less on Christian principles. The most thorough-paced politician to the existence of whose power and domination war is necessary, will always produce acts of aggression on the part of his adversaries, and justify his measures as defensive, on the ground of necessity. How liable such reasoning is to objection will be evident when it is considered that under this plea, the most ambitious and arbitrary tyrants have justified their vilest atrocities; and if war be convenient, and promise a partial gain, an argument in justification will always be too readily found, although one certain consequence of war is a *"general loss"*—the gain only accruing to an inconsiderable number of individuals.

In these sentiments, then, I have not merely to contend with men who oppose all the order of society, by committing depredation and offense universally; but with those also who interweave the system of bloodshed with the profession of Christianity.

And here it is necessary to observe that all war, even admitting an aggression, goes on the principle of rendering evil for evil. And how difficult is it, even politically, to decide where the aggression begins , or how one nation possesses a right to call in question what to another nation seems an equal right of theirs; yet in questions of this kind frequently originate the most bloody, destructive and unnatural wars. And even admitting the case to be clearly made out, how often does the retaliation of the injured party exceed the offense! In which case, in a moral point of view, they certainly change ground, and the original aggressors become the injured party. Many instances of this kind might be stated, but I shall name one only—the late contest between Great Britain and America. America had chartered rights, which she supposed were infringed by the parent state; she remonstrated and petitioned; the parent state resisted, and refused her demands. America resisted again. Great Britain exercised coercion and sent over an army. America raised a counter army to defend her rights, and was finally successful. And yet how often in that contest did the parties change ground, and each act offensively as well as defensively? And who can state precisely where the act of aggression began, or where retaliation ought to have ceased? Indeed, the subject seems involved in all this intricacy and these evil consequences, as if, by a special intervention of Providence, the rash steps of man should be restrained from going to the extreme bounds of right, lest they should overleap those bounds and enter upon the territory of wrong. In some cases the right will seem more clear; and perhaps on certain principles, may be made out; but as the question is, not whether morality, but whether Christianity allow of war on such occasions, I am bound no further than to the consideration of the latter part of the question. I therefore state the following proposition, as a truth intimately connected with the nature of Christianity, and as a sentiment which will finally prevail.

> That war in every shape is incompatible with the nature of Christianity; and that no persons professing that religion, and under the full and proper influence of the temper and mind of Christ, can adopt, pursue or plead for it . . . .

I have sometimes given scope to my imagination and fancied myself engaged in war, in the defense of the best cause for which the sword was ever drawn—civil liberty, and the deliverance of the oppressed from the hand of tyranny; and have, for the moment, supposed it to be lawful; I have anticipated the sound of the trumpet leading on to the charge, and then have plunged amidst the roaring of cannon, or the clangor of arms in the heat of action—either leading on or led, my bosom swelling with the importance of the cause, my heart beating high, I looked on death with defiance, and on my foes with disdain, determining to conquer or perish in the attempt. All fresh from this bloody scene, I have brought my temper, my bosom, my heart, to the great Exemplar of Christian perfection, and shame has covered me. What trait of the mind of Christ did I follow when I defied death? Did I do it as a Christian? Ah, no! Could my hopes of endless glory be certain during the eventful and bloody scene? Did the spirit of the Christian religion, or the pattern of the holy Jesus, inspire me with disdain for my enemies, while piercing their vitals, and sending their souls into the shades of death? No; he commanded me to love my enemies, but I have been destroying them: he has enjoined submission and suffering, but I have sought for superiority, victory and conquest. On the whole, let that man stand forth, if earth can produce him, who can say he goes into action and engages in the heat of war in that spirit which he is conscious will be approved and owned by the Judge of all the earth, when all our subterfuges and self-impositions must be renounced; and if such a one should arise, and declare that he could do so, I for my own part should infer that a depraved heart had perverted his judgement. But if it be admitted that the temper of mind necessary for the action of war is inconsistent with Christianity, I have all I ask; and those who argue for war have to support an allowed indefensible scheme. But let professing Christians beware how they support it, for in proportion as they give their aid to it, they impede the real progress of Christ's religion.

From: THE MEDIATOR'S KINGDOM NOT OF THIS WORLD: BUT SPIRITUAL (1809)

By An Inquirer,
David Low Dodge

*T*HE MEDIATOR'S KINGDOM WAS *David Low Dodge's (1774-1852) first* war-related pamhlet. It sold nearly a thousand copies within two weeks and began a controversy which caused the first serious examination in America outside the traditional peace churches of the lawfulness of war by Christians. A critical response entitled, "The Duty of a Christian in a Trying Situation" written by three authors who felt themselves as equally committed to peace as Dodge, challenged his belief that the Gospel extends so far as to outlaw even defensive wars. They believed that while aggressive wars were condemned by the Gospel, defensive wars were allowed. Dodge, who came to be known as the father of the modern peace movement, remarked at the time, "Some who were favorable to the doctrines of peace judged that, with a bold hand, I had carried the subject too far." These two strains of thought eventually provided the basis for the creation of the first secular peace organizations in the United States.

... As IT IS A MATTER of great practical consequence to know whether the subjects of the Prince of Peace are authorized in any case under the gospel dispensation to use carnal weapons or not, we propose in this inference to be a little more particular. . . .

In Christ's Sermon on the Mount he quoted a passage from Exodus, "Ye have heard that it hath been said, An eye for an eye, and a tooth for a tooth: but I say unto you, That *ye resist not evil:* but whosoever shall smite thee on thy right cheek, turn to him the other also." The force of this passage has generally been obviated by saying that we are not to take all the words of our Lord literally. Although this is admitted, yet we are absolutely bound to take the spirit of every word, if we can understand them, by comparing the Scriptures with the Scriptures. That the spirit of this passage is directly opposed to the one our Lord quoted from Exodus, we think cannot fairly be denied; and, of course, it disannulled it, for he who had power to make laws under one dispensation had power to abrogate them under another.

The blessed Mediator did, in the most explicit manner, command his subjects to love their enemies and render good for evil. This command we are of the opinion is totally incompatible with resisting them with carnal weapons. He says, "But I say unto you which hear, Love your enemies, do good to them which hate you, and pray for them which despitefully use you." Let us for one moment compare this precept with defensive war and see if it can consistently be put into practice. Suppose our country is invaded and a professed disciple of the Prince of Peace buckles on the harness and takes the field to repel by the point of the sword his enemy. He advances amidst the lamentations of the wounded and the shrieks of the dying to meet his foe in arms. He sees his wrath kindled and his spear uplifted, and in this trying moment he hears his Lord say, "Love your enemy and render to him good for evil"; and his kindness to him is like Joab's to Amasa; he thrusts him through the heart and hurries him to the awful tribunal of his Judge, probably unprepared. Dear brethren, be not deceived; for God is not mocked. Who amongst our fellow-men would receive the thrust of a sword as an act of kindness? Only let conscience do its office, and there will be no difficulty in deciding whether defensive war is inconsistent with the gospel dispensation or not. Carnal and spiritual weapons will no more unite under the gospel dispensation than iron and miry clay.

Our very salvation depends on being possessed of a spirit of forgiveness to enemies. "If ye forgive not men their trespasses, neither will your Father forgive your trespasses." If men invade our rights and trespass upon our privileges, is it forgiveness to repel them at the point of the bayonet? The honest Christian will find no difficulty in conscientiously deciding this question, notwithstanding he may be slow of heart in believing all that is written.

All the conduct of our Lord had meaning to it, and much of it was with an express view to teach his disciples by way of example. A little before he was betrayed, he ordered his disciples to take swords. The object of this must have been either to use them for defense, or for some other purpose. The event proves that they were not taken for self-defense. The question then is, For what were they taken? The event appears fully to answer the question, viz.: To prohibit, by way of example, the use of them for self-defense in the most trying situation possible. If any situation would justify self-defense with carnal weapons, it must have been the situation in which our Lord and his disciples were placed at the time he was betrayed. They were in a public garden, and they were assaulted by a mob, contrary to the statutes of the Romans and the laws of the Jews; and the object was to take his life. This the disciples knew, and Peter judged it a proper time for defense, and drew his sword and smote a servant of the High Priest and cut off his ear. As our Lord's kingdom was not of this world, he would not suffer his subjects to use the weapons of this world in any situation. He therefore healed the wound they made and rebuked Peter for his mistaken zeal. "Then said Jesus unto him, Put up again thy sword into his place: for all they that take the sword shall perish with the sword. Thinkest thou that I cannot pray to my Father, and he would presently send me more than twelve legions of angels?" Here we see that our Lord not only forbade his disciples to use the sword in self-defense, but added a dreadful penalty to transgressors,—"all they that take the sword shall perish with the sword." The disciples did not then fully understand that his kingdom was not of this world. As soon as they were prohibited using the weapons of the world they forsook him and fled.

...It is said that government is an ordinance of God which exists throughout his vast dominion. . . .all powers are ordained by God. . . . It has been often said that he who refuses to comply with the commands of the magistrate resists the powers that be, resists the ordinance of God and will receive to himself damnation. And, further, as all powers are the ordinance of God they ought to be supported, and if they cannot without, they must be even at the point of, the sword. Here the subject of the Mediator must make a distinction between resisting the "powers that be" by force of arms and refusing to obey their unlawful commands. It is not supposed that in one case he would obey and that in the other he would disobey the commands of his Master. No martyr ever considered himself as violating this precept in refusing to sacrifice to an idol at the command of an earthly power; neither will any subject of the Mediator view himself as violating it by refusing to use carnal weapons while he believes that his Lord has utterly forbidden his using them. It is apprehended that if this proves anything upon the principles of war, that it will prove too much for its advocates. The command is to obey the powers that be and not the powers that ought to be. If it is taken in an unlimited sense, it must prohibit resisting even tyrannical powers, and would, of course condemn every Christian who engaged in the American Revolution. To say that all power is in the hands of the people, and, of course, it is the people who are the powers that be, is thought to be but a quibble. We will suppose a very possible case,—that a foreign power completely overturns the government of the people and disannuls their laws and gives a new code; in that case, the command to obey the powers that be would not be annihilated. The precept originally was given while the disciples were in the midst of tyrannical governments. It is thought that it is so far from tolerating defensive war that it is opposed to it. The precepts of the gospel cannot be dependent upon the convulsions of the nations. If Christians are bound to aid with carnal weapons in suppressing a rebellion, then, if the opposing power gains the predominance, they must turn directly about and fight the very power they were before supporting. Such conduct would not become the citizen of Zion. If it is said the powers that be are Christian rulers, then we say, let them govern only by the laws of the Mediator's kingdom, and we will bow with reverence before them, and not teach for commandments the doctrines of men, as we cannot receive human laws for divine precepts.

From: A SOLEMN REVIEW OF THE CUSTOMS OF WAR (1814)

Noah Worcester

*Q*UITE SEPARATELY FROM DODGE *and his friends, Noah Worcester* (1758-1837), a Congregational minister in Massachusetts, was considering the formation of a peace society. The first meeting of his Massachusetts Peace Society was held on December 26, 1815, just four months after the August meeting of Dodge's New York Peace Society. Worcester's group rejected the possibility of Christian participation in wars of aggression but generally accepted the need for defensive wars. Dodge and the New York Peace Society, on the other hand, took a more nonresistant stand, calling for the eradication of all forms of violence. Worcester is honored as the first person in the U.S. to publicly promote the ideas of a world court and arbitration as nonviolent alternatives to war. He was also an early believer in peace education. In *A Solemn Review of the Customs of War*, published on Christmas Day, 1814, Worcester urges Christians to take up the task of creating alternatives to war.

W E REGARD WITH HORROR the custom of the ancient heathens in offering their children as a sacrifice to idols. We are shocked with the customs of the Hindoos in prostrating themselves before the car of an idol to be crushed to death; in burning women alive on the funeral piles of their husbands; in casting their children, a monthly sacrifice, into the Ganges to be drowned. We read with astonishment of the sacrifices made in Papal crusades, and in Mahometan and Hindoo pilgrimages. But that which is fashionable and popular in any country is esteemed right and honorable, whatever may be its nature in the views of men better informed.

But while we look back, with a mixture of wonder, indignation and pity, on many of the customs of former ages, are we careful to inquire whether some customs which we deem honorable are not the effects of popular delusion? Is

43

it not a fact that one of the most horrid customs of savage men is now popular in every nation in Christendom? What custom of the most barbarous nations is more repugnant to the feelings of piety, humanity and justice, than that of deciding controversies between nations by the edge of the sword, by powder and ball, or the point of the bayonet?

War has been so long fashionable amongst all nations that its enormity is little regarded; or, when thought of at all, it is usually considered as an evil necessary and unavoidable; but cannot the state of society and the views of civilized men be so changed as to abolish so barbarous a custom and render wars unnecessary and avoidable?

Some may be ready to exclaim, "None but God can produce such an effect as the abolition of war, and we must wait for the millennial day." We admit that God only can produce the necessary change in the state of society and the views of men, but God works by human agency and human means. None but God could have produced such a change in the views of the British nation as to abolish the slave trade, yet the event was brought about by a long course of persevering and honorable exertions of benevolent men. When the thing was first proposed it probably appeared to the majority of the people as an unavailing and chimerical project; but God raised up powerful advocates, gave them the spirit of perseverance, and finally crowned their efforts with glorious success.

As to waiting for the millennium to put an end to war without any exertions on our own part, it is like the sinner's waiting God's time for conversion, while he pursues his course of vice and impiety. If ever there shall be a millennium in which the sword will cease to devour, it will probably be effected by the blessing of God on the benevolent exertions of enlightened men. Perhaps no one thing is now a greater obstacle in the way of this wished-for state of the church than the spirit and custom of war which is maintained by Christians themselves. Is it not, then that efforts should be made to enlighten the minds of Christians on a subject of such infinite importance to the happiness of the human race?

The whole amount of property in the United States is probably of far less values than what has been expended and destroyed within two centuries by wars in Christendom. Suppose, then, that one-fifth of this amount had been judiciously laid out by peace associations in the different states and nations in cultivating the spirit and arts of peace, and in exciting a just abhorrence of war, would not the other four-fifths have been in a great measure saved, besides many millions of lives and an immense portion of misery? Had the whole value of what has been expended in wars been appropriated to the promotion of peace, how laudable would have been the appropriation and how blessed the consequences!

Let us glance at the pleas in favor of war. . . . "The Israelites were permitted and even commanded, to make war on the inhabitants of Canaan." To this it may be answered that the Giver and Arbiter of life had a right, if he pleased, to make use of the savage customs of the age for punishing guilty nations. If any government of the present day should receive a commission to make war as the Israelites did, let the order be obeyed; but until they have such a commission, let it not be imagined that they can innocently make war. God has, moreover, given encouragement that under the reign of the Messiah there shall be such a time of peace "that nation shall not lift up sword against nation, neither shall they learn war any more." If this prediction shall ever be fulfilled, the present delusion in favor of war must be done away. How is it to be fulfilled? Probably not by miraculous agency, but by the blessing of God on the benevolent exertions of individuals to open the eyes of their fellow-mortals in respect to the evils and delusions of war and the blessings of peace.

A second plea may be this, that war is an advantage to a nation, as it usually takes off many vicious and dangerous characters. But does not war make two such characters for every one it removes? Is it not, in fact, the greatest school of depravity and the greatest source of mischievous and dangerous characters that ever existed among men? Does not a state of war lower down the standard of morality in a nation, so that a vast portion of common vice is scarcely observed as evil? Besides, is it not awful to think of sending vicious men beyond the means of reformation and the hope of repentance? When they are sent into the army, what is this but consigning them to a state where they will rapidly fill up the measures of their iniquity, and become "fitted to destruction"?

It will be pleaded, thirdly, that no substitute for war can be devised which will insure to a nation a redress of wrongs. . . . But is it common for a nation to obtain a redress of wrongs by war? As to redress, do not the wars of nations resemble boxing at a tavern, when both the combatants receive a terrible bruising, then drink together and make peace, each, however, bearing for a long time the marks of his folly and madness? A redress of wrongs by war is so uncommon that, unless revenge is redress, and multiplied injuries satisfaction, we should suppose that none but madmen would run the hazard.

But if the eyes of people could be opened in regard to the evils and delusions of war, would it not be easy to form a confederacy of nations, and organize a high court of equity to decide national controversies? Why might not such a court be composed of some of the most eminent characters from each nation, and a compliance with its decisions be made a point of national honor, to prevent the effusion of blood and to preserve the blessings of peace? Can any considerate person say that the probability of obtaining right in such a court would be less than by an appeal to arms? When an individual appeals to a court of justice for the redress of wrongs it is not always the case that he obtains his right. Still such an appeal is more honorable, more safe, and more certain, as well as more benevolent, than for the individual to attempt to obtain redress by his pistol or his sword. And are not the reasons for avoiding an appeal to the sword for the redress of wrongs always great in proportion to the calamities which such an appeal must naturally involve? If this be a fact, then there is infinitely greater reason why two nations should avoid an appeal to arms than usually exists against a bloody combat between two contending individuals.

The Spirit of War Compared With The Temper of Jesus

Let every Christian seriously consider the malignant nature of that spirit which war-makers evidently wish to excite, and compare it with the temper of Jesus; and where is the Christian who would not shudder at the thought of dying in the exercise of the common war-spirit, and also at the thought of being the instrument of exciting such a spirit in his fellow-men? Any custom which cannot be supported but by exciting in men the very temper of the devil ought surely to be banished from the Christian world.

The impression that aggressive war is murderous is general among Christians, if not universal. The justness of the impression seems to be admitted by almost every government in going to war. For this reason each of two governments endeavors to fix on the other the charge of aggression, and to assume to itself the ground of defending some right or avenging some wrong. Thus each excuses itself and charges the other with all the blood and misery which result from the contest. But these facts, so far from affording a plea in favor of war, afford a weighty reason for its abolition. If the aggressor is a murderer and answerable for the blood shed in war; if one or the other must be viewed by God as the aggressor, and if such is the delusion attending war that each party is liable to consider the other as the aggressor,—surely there most be serious danger of a nation's being involved in the guilt of murder while they imagine they have a cause which may be justified.

So prone are men to be blinded by their passions, their prejudices and their interests, that in most private quarrels each of two individuals persuades himself that he is in the right and his neighbor in the wrong. Hence the propriety of arbitrations, references and appeals to courts of justice, that persons more disinterested may judge and prevent that injustice and desolation which would result from deciding private disputes by single combats or acts of violence.

But rulers of nations are as liable to be misled by their passions and interests as other men; and when misled, they are very sure to mislead those of their subjects who have confidence in their wisdom and integrity. Hence it is highly important that the custom of war should be abolished and some other mode adopted to settle disputes between nations. In private disputes there may be cause of complaint on each side, while neither has reason to shed the blood of the other, much less to shed the blood of innocent family connections, neighbors and friends. So, of two nations each may have cause of complaint, while neither can be justified in making war and much less in shedding the blood of innocent people who have had no hand in giving the offense.

War Involves The Innocent With The Guilty

It is an awful feature in the character of war, and a strong reason why it should not be countenanced, that it involves the innocent with the guilty in the calamities it inflicts, and often falls with the greatest vengeance on those who have had no concern in the management of national affairs. It surely is not a crime to be born in a country which is afterwards invaded; yet in how many instances do war-makers punish or destroy for no other crime than being a native or resident of an invaded territory! A mode of revenge or redress which makes no distinction between the innocent and the guilty ought to be discountenanced by every friend to justice and humanity. Besides, as the rulers of a nation are as liable as other people to be governed by passion and prejudice, there is as little prospect of justice in permitting war for the decision of national disputes as there would be in permitting an incensed individual to be, in his own cause, complainant, witness, judge, jury and executioner. In what point of view then is war not to be regarded with horror?

That wars have been so overruled by God as to be the occasion of some benefits to mankind will not be denied; for the same may be said of every custom that ever was popular among men. War may have been the occasion of advancing useful arts and sciences, and even of spreading the gospel; but we are not to do evil that good may come, nor to countenance evil because God may overrule it for good.

"But war gives opportunity for the display of extraordinary talents, of daring enterprise and intrepidity." True, but let robbery and piracy become as popular as war has been, and will not these customs give as great opportunity for the display of the same talents and qualities of mind? Shall we therefore encourage robbery and piracy? Indeed, it may be asked, do we *not* encourage these crimes? For what is modern warfare but a popular, refined and legalized mode of robbery, piracy, preceded by a proclamation giving notice of the purpose of the war-maker? The answer of a pirate to Alexander the Great was as just as it was severe. "By what right," said the king, "do you infest the seas?" The pirate replied, "By the same that you infest the universe. But because I do it in a small ship, I am called a robber; and because you do the same acts with a great fleet you are called a conqueror!". . . .

. . . Is it not, then, time for Christians to learn not to attach glory to guilt, or to praise actions which God will condemn? Murder and robbery are not the less criminal for being perpetrated by a king or a mighty warrior. . . .

How The State Of Society May Be Changed

An important question now occurs. Is it not possible to produce such a change in the state of society and the views of Christian nations that every ruler shall feel his honor, safety and happiness to depend on his displaying a pacific spirit and forbearing to engage in war? Cannot peace societies be extended through Christendom to support its government and secure the nation from war? In these societies we may hope to engage every true minister of the Prince of Peace and every Christian who possesses his temper. . . . Let every land be filled with newspapers, tracts, and periodical works to excite a just abhorrence of war in every breast. The object so perfectly harmonious with the gospel might be frequently the subject of discussion in the pulpit, of Sabbath and everyday conversation, and of our daily prayers to God.

Especially should early education in families, common schools, academies and universities be made everywhere subservient to this object. "Train up a child in the way he should go, and when he is old he will not depart from it." The power of education has been tried to make children of a ferocious, bloodthirsty character; let it now have a fair chance to see what it will do towards making mild, friendly and peaceful citizens. . . .

Christians Should No Longer Hold Their Peace

Can Christians hold their peace while this custom is sweeping off myriads of their brethren into eternity by violence and murder? Can they forbear to exert themselves to put an end to this voluntary plague? If war is opposed to our religion and God designs to put an end to this scourge by the influence of the gospel, can we still sleep on without an effort to secure this promised and expected result? It can come only from the efforts of Christians, and so long as they acquiesce in the custom this desirable event will be delayed. Christianity itself is not an intelligent agent, neither a God, an angel nor a man. It is only a system of divine instructions to be used by men for their own benefits, the benefit of each other and the honor of its author. Like all other instructions, they are of no use any further than they are reduced to practice.

In what way, then, can Christianity ever put an end to war but by enlightening the minds of men on the subject? Can war cease while Christians themselves are its advocates? If men are to be saved by the preaching of the gospel, the gospel must be preached; and so, if this world is to be delivered from war by the gospel, it must be applied for the purpose. Its pacific tendencies must be illustrated, its opposition to war displayed in the lives of Christians, and men influenced by its motives to cease from destroying one another.

THE ORATORS IN PETTICOATS: ANGELINA AND SARAH GRIMKE

Mary McGlone

T HE NOTORIOUS ABOLITIONISTS, SARAH (1792-1873) and Angelina Grimke (1805-1879), were born into high society in Charleston, South Carolina at the turn of the 19th Century. Their father, John Faucheraud Grimke, was a Revolutionary War veteran and a prominent judge who educated his children well. He expected them to live up to their social status and fulfill their obligations as staunch Episcopalians. When Angelina, the fourteenth child, was born in 1805, her twelve year old sister Sarah begged to be named her godmother. This relationship and the difference in their ages created a maternal role for Sarah which she would always maintain.

The life of the Grimke family was typical for their social set. Winters were spent on their plantation and summers were spent in the city in order to escape the heat and swampy countryside which was considered unfit for white people. The family was served by a full retinue of domestic slaves while more than a hundred other slaves worked the country plantation. The Grimke children were educated at home and in private schools until the time came for the men to go away to the university and the women to enter the social life of teas, dances and church activities.

An unconventional, questioning streak rose and fell in Sarah during her childhood. She had to be taught that it was not her place to question the abuse of slaves. When she was caught teaching her own slave to read she was severely reprimanded and the slave was taken from her. She even went to the docks at one point to ask a ship's captain to take her away to a place where there were no slaves. With the same convictions and love of learning that led her to risk teaching her slave, she asked to study Latin with her brother Thomas so that she too could eventually study law. Permission was refused. Thomas went to Yale in 1807 and two years later Sarah made her debut in society.

When Judge Grimke became ill in 1816 Sarah accompanied him north to Philadelphia in search of a cure. Unable to find help, they took lodging with a Quaker family and Sarah cared for him there until he died. Her experience in Philadelphia was significant in many ways. Away from the milieu of slavery for the first time, she reassessed the lifestyle she had known, recalling questions about slavery that had been buried within her since her childhood attempts to conform to family ethos and social convention. At the same time, she had her first close contact with Quakers. She was attracted by their teachings against slavery and by the simplicity of their worship and lifestyle. Moreover, at the Arch Street Quaker meeting which Sarah later joined, women were as able as men to speak out in and take part in the ministry (not all Quaker meetings accepted women as equals, however).

When Sarah returned to Charleston a few months after her father's death she immersed herself in Quaker teachings. Within a year she was no longer able to conform herself to the Southern lifestyle. She returned to Philadelphia and in 1823 she became a formal member of the small, conservative Quaker group known as the Arch Street Community. So total was her dedication to the faith that when Israel Morris, a widower, proposed marriage to her she regarded her feelings toward him as a temptation and turned him down, "lest any earthly creature intervene between her and her God."

Whereas Sarah was self-effacing and scrupulous, Angelina was more verbal and critical of the religious options presented to her. Strength of character and brutal honesty, traits which were sometimes construed as pride, provided the driving force that allowed her to break with convention and consistently act on her convictions. As long as she believed that she was doing the will of God, Angelina was unconstrained in her actions, regardless of the disapproval of respectable voices that might try to dissuade her. As one who had questioned slavery since her childhood, she found it increasingly difficult to participate in a slave owning society.

When Sarah came home to Charleston in 1827 she found her twenty-two year old sister restless and ready to explore the Quaker message. Given Sarah's example and invitation, Angelina formally resigned from the Presbyterian congregation which she had joined in 1826 and from which she had separated herself in protest over the unwillingness of the church elders, all slaveholders, to dencounce slavery. When Angelina adopted the simple Quaker dress and style and began to attend Quaker meetings in Charleston, the Presbyterian elders tried her for unorthodoxy and formally expelled her from the congregation. Her May 29, 1829 summons to appear before the elders accuses her of neglect of public worship and, "neglect of the means of grace and ordinance of the Gospel."

Angelina remained in Charleston sensing a mission to denounce slavery in the South. When she went to tea with other women of her class she would make use of every opportunity to turn the topic of conversation to slavery and its evil effects. At home she chided her mother and strongly criticized her brother Henry's treatment of slaves. Neither her family nor her friends were open to her message. Some went so far as to question her mental health. After more than a year of this she acknowledged that her efforts were futile and, in October of 1829, with the wholehearted blessing of her mother, she left to join her sister in Philadelphia.

In the freer atmosphere of the North, Angelina's social analysis led her to the conviction that slavery was as dehumanizing to the oppressor as to the oppressed. She saw that it brutalized both owner and slave. She pointed out to her family that it broke down family relations because one member could not attend the needs of another for fear of doing "servants' work." Delighted by the sight of northern workers, black and white, who could take pride in the work of their hands, she realized that the designation of all manual activity to slaves took away from the dignity and creativity of labor. She thoroughly enjoyed the opportunity she now had to go to market for herself, choose her food and begin to learn domestic arts.

In 1835 Angelina made her first break with the restrictions of the Arch Street Community and went to hear the English abolitionist George Thompson, a known "incendiary" and "agent of a foreign government." Angelina was so impressed by Thompson that she joined the Philadelphia Female Anti-Slavery Society which had been founded in 1833 as an auxiliary to the all male American Anti-Slavery Society. She refused to consult her Quaker meeting about the decision because she felt that to do so would be dishonest, having already made up her mind. Involvement with the Anti-Slavery Society educated Angelina to the ideals and methodology of the abolition movement which was, among other nonviolent works, fostering various attempts to boycott all slave-produced goods. Abolitionists even refused to buy the freedom of slaves because the act of such a purchase gave a tinge of legality to the abhorrent system.

Angelina's first truly public and "scandalous" act came in 1835 when she wrote a letter of support to William Lloyd Garrison and told him that his stance on nonviolence and abolition gave her courage. "The ground upon which you stand is Holy ground," she said, " never—never surrender it. If you surrender it the hope of the slave is extinguished." She also reminded him that he would have to be prepared to withstand the scorn and reproach of many. It is certain that Garrison was well aware of this. The letter was Angelina Grimke's coming of age and reflected more her own firm stance when confronted by those who would sway or silence her.

When Garrison published the letter in his widely circulated paper "The Liberator" there was an outraged response. Many Quakers were angered not only by the message, but especially because she had reflected open discord with the tenets of her Quaker faith. Even her sister Sarah joined the chorus of critics who tried to persuade Angelina to retract the letter.

Due to this uproar, Angelina left Philadelphia to reflect on her position and allow the dust to settle. Instead of recanting she was inspired to write what was to become her most famous tract, *An Appeal To The Christian Women Of The South*. The Appeal, a unique document, reflects an educated interpretation of Scripture and sound social analysis. The fact that it was addressed to Southern women by one of their own made it a new addition to abolition literature.

The *Appeal* was a forerunner of the feminist perspective that Angelina and Sarah would eventually articulate, and which neither the Quakers nor the Abolitionists were ready for. Some could accept their anti-slavery position. Some could accept their women's rights position. Few could accept both or see the connections between them.

Angelina encouraged women, helping them to realize that they were not as powerless as they might think. Included among the actions she proposed were the use of boycotts and the freeing of slaves. All of this in a cultural atmosphere where even the likes of Garrison were proposing that the role of woman in the world was to "compensate for the harshness around her, softening the character of man and rewarding him with her love."

The letter published by Garrison had made Angelina famous beyond her imagining. Even before she had finished writing the Appeal she was invited to give a series of talks to women in New York. All of this was highly unacceptable to her Quaker companions who neither shared Angelina's anti-slavery sentiment nor her belief in the role of women in addressing the issue. Sarah was sent to admonish her but found Angelina's position firm. Angelina explained that she would "prefer to be disowned by the Quakers than to be self disowned" for not fulfilling the mission to which she was sure God was calling her. Sarah then decided to accompany Angelina to New York and to assume part of the task herself.

The two sisters began a round of speaking tours in which their message would reach at least 50,000 people. In the middle of the nineteenth century lectures, debates and meetings of all kinds were frequent events which not only served to promoted serious causes but were also the common entertainment of the day. While it was common for women to speak to ladies' parlor groups, a tour on the scale of the Grimke's was highly criticized. It was considered unacceptable for women to speak publicly before audiences that included men and the opponents of abolition vociferously questioned the morality of women who would speak to "promiscuous (male and female) audiences."

Then in July of 1837 came the height of Angelina's notoriety. Two Northern men challenged her to a debate in Amesbury, Massachusetts. While the debate was touted by the abolitionist press as a resounding victory, the local press refused to report the arguments offered because Miss Grimke had broached immoral topics. She had, among other things, decried the sexual abuse of slave women by plantation owners and the resulting chaos in family relations.

Due to the pressure of churches and mainline press, the National Anti-Slavery Society tried to limit the Grimkes' activities to feminine audiences but the sisters refused to capitulate to these demands. Angelina would address her audiences directly on anti-slavery issues, neglecting even to mention, much less defend, her position as a woman involved in public speaking. As far as she was concerned her actions were sufficient public statement about the proper place of women.

While Angelina spoke, Sarah wrote a series of articles published in the abolitionist press. The sisters shared the same sentiments. As Angelina wrote to a friend: "Whatever is morally right for a man to do is morally right for a woman to do. I recognize no rights but human rights. . . . This is part of the great doctrine of human rights and can no more be separated from Emancipation than the light from the heat of the sun; the rights of the slave and woman blend like colors of the rainbow."

The peak of Angelina's speaking career came in February, 1838 when she was invited to speak to the Massachusetts State Legislature. It was the first time that an "Orator in Petticoats," as the Boston press called her, had addressed that governing body for whose members she had no right to vote.

Just before her speech, Theodore D. Weld, one of the country's leading abolitionists, asked Angelina to marry him. The wedding, in May of 1838, was simple and unconventional. The guest list was racially integrated. Selected friends witnessed the ceremony in lieu of a minister because Angelina's Quaker sect would not recognize marriage to a Presbyterian, nor would Weld's Presbyterian church countenance a Quaker ceremony. The vow formula expressed the couple's belief in the equality of man and woman.

Unfortunately, marriage weighed Angelina down. Her public career came to a halt. She fell under scathing "fraternal correction" from both her husband and Sarah who lived with them. Weld and Sarah felt it their duty to purge Angelina of what they called her "willfulness and pride"—their assessment of those qualities which had drawn Sarah to accompany her and had originally attracted Weld's attention and demanded his respect.

For ten years Angelina apparently succumbed to the pressures exerted on her. She seemed to reawaken in 1848 when she read the documents of the Seneca Falls Convention and saw that many of her former co-workers were counted among the first to call a convention and make a declaration of the rights of women.

The Grimke sisters spent their later years in Hyde Park, Massachusetts. There they participated in local movements for women's rights. Sarah died in 1873 and Angelina in 1879. Angelina's funeral was a reunion of many who had given their youth to the causes of abolition and women's rights. Lucy Stone, Wendell Phillips and Elizur Wright were among those who came together one last time to remember and eulogize the work of the "orator in petticoats."

Mary McGlone is a Sister of St. Joseph of Corondolet, a Catholic women's religious community. She recently spent six years as a pastoral minister in indigenous base communities in the Southern Andes of Peru and Bolivia. Currently Mary is studying for her doctorate in Theology at St. Louis University.

APPEAL TO THE CHRISTIAN WOMEN OF THE SOUTH (1836)

Angelina Emily Grimke

... WE HAVE SEEN THAT the code of laws framed by Moses with regard to servants was designed to *protect them as men and women,* to secure to them their *rights as human beings,* to guard them from oppression and defend them from violence of every kind. Let us now turn to the Slave laws of the South and West and examine them too. I will give you the substance only, because I fear I shall trespass too much on your time, were I to quote them at length.

1. *Slavery* is hereditary and perpetual, to the last moment of the slave's earthly existence, and to all his descendants to the latest posterity.

2. The labor of the slave is compulsory and uncompensated; while the kind of labor, the amount of toil, the time allowed for rest, are dictated solely by the master. No bargain is made, no wages given. A pure despotism governs the human brute; and even his covering and provender, both as to quantity and quality, depend entirely on the master's discretion.

3. The slave being considered a personal chattel may be sold or pledged, or leased at the will of his master. He may be exchanged for marketable commodities, or taken in execution for the debts or taxes either of a living or dead master. Sold at auction, either individually, or in lots to suit the purchaser, he may remain with his family, or be separated from them for ever.

4. Slaves can make no contracts and have no *legal* right to any property, real or personal. Their own honest earnings and the legacies of friends belong in point of law to their masters.

5. Neither a slave nor a free colored person can be a witness against any *white*, or free person, in a court of justice, however atrocious may have been the crimes they have seen him commit, if such testimony would be for the benefit of a *slave;* but they may give testimony *against a fellow slave,* or free colored man, even in cases affecting life, if the *master* is to reap the advantage of it.

6. The slave may be punished at his master's discretion—without trial—without any means of legal redress; whether his offence be real or imaginary; and the master can transfer the same despotic power to any person or persons, he may choose to appoint.

7. The slave is not allowed to resist any free man under *any* circumstances, *his* only safety consists in the fact that his *owner* may bring suit and recover the price of his body, in case his life is taken, or his limbs rendered unfit for labor.

8. Slaves cannot redeem themselves, or obtain a change of masters, though cruel treatment may have rendered such a change necessary for their personal safety.

9. The slave is entirely unprotected in his domestic relations.

10. The laws greatly obstruct the manumission of slaves, even where the master is willing to enfranchise them.

11. The operation of the laws tends to deprive slaves of religious instruction and consolation.

12. The whole power of the laws is exerted to keep slaves in a state of the lowest ignorance.

13. There is in this country a monstrous inequality of law and right. What is a trifling fault in the *white* man, is considered highly criminal in the *slave*; the same offences which cost a white man a few dollars only, are punished in the negro with death.

14. The laws operate most oppressively upon free people of color. Shall I ask you now my friends, to draw the *parallel* between Jewish *servitude* and American *slavery*? No! For there is *no likeness* in the two systems; I ask you rather to mark the contrast. The laws of Moses *protected servants* in their rights as *men and women*, guarded them from oppression and defended them from wrong. The Code Noir of the South *robs the slave of all his rights* as a *man*, reduces him to a chattel personal, and defends the *master* in the exercise of the most unnatural and unwarrantable power over his slave. They each bear the impress of the hand which formed them. The attributes of justice and mercy are shadowed out in the Hebrew code; those of injustice and cruelty, in the Code Noir of America. Truly it was wise in the slaveholders of the South to declare their slaves to be "chattels personal," for before they could be robbed of wages, wives, children, and friends, it was absolutely necessary to deny they were human beings. It is wise in them, to keep them in abject ignorance, for the strong man armed must be bound before we can spoil his house—the powerful intellect of man must be bound down with the iron chains of nescience before we can rob him of his rights as a man; we must reduce him to a *thing* before we can claim the right to set our feet upon his neck, because it was only *all things* which were originally *put under the feet of man* by the Almighty and Beneficent Father of all, who has declared himself to be *no respecter* of persons, whether red, white or black. . . .

But perhaps you will be ready to query, why appeal to *women* on this subject? We do not make the laws which perpetuate slavery. No legislative power is vested in *us*; *we* can do nothing to overthrow the system, even if we wished to do so. To this I reply, I know you do not make the laws, but I also know that *you are the wives and mothers, the sisters and daughters of those who do*; and if you really suppose *you* can do nothing to overthrow slavery, you are greatly mistaken. You can do much in every way: four things I will name. 1st. You can read on this subject. 2d. You can pray over this subject. 3d. You can speak on this subject. 4th. You can *act* on this subject. . . .

But you will perhaps say, such a course of conduct would inevitably expose us to great suffering. Yes! my Christian friends, I believe it would, but this will *not* excuse you or any one else from the neglect of *duty*. . . . But you may say we are *women*, how can *our* hearts endure persecution? And why not? Have not *women* stood up in all the dignity and strength of moral courage to be the leaders of the people, and to bear a faithful testimony for the truth whenever the providence of God has called them to do so? Are there no *women* in that noble army of martyrs who are now singing the song of Moses and the Lamb? Who led out the women of Israel from the house of bondage, striking the timbrel, and singing the song of deliverance on the banks of that sea whose waters stood up like walls of crystal to open a passage for their escape? It was a *woman*; Miriam, the prophetess, the sister of Moses and Aaron. Who went up with Barak to Kadesh to fight against Jabin, King of Canaan, into whose hand Israel had been sold because of their iniquities? It was a *woman*! Deborah the wife of Lapidoth, the judge, as well as the prophetess of that backsliding people; Judges iv, 9. Into whose hands was Sisera, the captain of Jabin's host delivered? Into the hands of a *woman*. Jael the wife of Heber! Judges vi, 21. Who dared to *speak the truth* concerning those judgements which were coming upon Judea, when Josiah, alarmed at finding that his people "had not kept the word of the Lord to do after all what was written in the book of the Law," sent to enquire of the Lord concerning these things? It was a *woman*. Huldah the prophetess, the wife of Shallum; 2 Chron. xxiv, 22. Who was chosen to deliver the whole Jewish nation from that murderous decree of Persia's King, which wicked Haman had obtained by calumny and fraud? It was a *woman*; Esther the Queen; yes, *a weak and trembling woman* was the instrument appointed by God, to reverse the bloody mandate of the eastern monarch, and save the *whole visible church* from destruction. What human voice first proclaimed to Mary that she should be the mother of our Lord? It was a *woman*. Elizabeth, the wife of Zacharias; Luke i, 42,43. Who united with the good old Simeon in giving thanks publicly in the temple, when the child, Jesus, was presented there by his parents, "and spake of him to all them that looked for redemption in Jerusalem?" It was a *woman*! Anna the prophetess. Who first proclaimed Christ as the true Messiah in the streets of Samaria, once the capital of the ten tribes? It was a *woman*! Who ministered to the Son of God whilst on earth, a despised and persecuted Reformer, in the humble garb of a carpenter? They were *women*! Who followed the rejected

King of Israel, as his fainting footsteps trod the road to Calvary? "A great company of people and of *women*"; and it is remarkable that to *them alone*, he turned and addressed the pathetic language, "Daughters of Jerusalem, weep not for me, but weep for yourselves and your children." Ah! who sent unto the Roman Governor when he was set down on the judgement seat, saying unto him, "Have thou nothing to do with that just man, for I have suffered many things this day in a dream because of him?" It was a *woman!*— the wife of Pilate. Although *"he knew* that for envy the Jews had delivered Christ," yet *he* consented to surrender the Son of God into the hands of a brutal soldiery, after having himself scourged his naked body. Had the *wife* of Pilate sat upon that judgement seat, what would have been the result of the trial of this "just person?" . . . .

And what, I would ask in conclusion, have *women* done for the great and glorious cause of Emancipation? . . . . Already are there sixty female Anti-Slavery Societies in operation. These are doing just what the English women did, telling the story of the colored man's wrongs, praying for his deliverance, and presenting his kneeling image constantly before the public eye on bags and needle-books, card-racks, pen-wipers, pin-cushions, &c. Even the children of the north are inscribing on their handy work, "May the points of our needles prick the slaveholder's conscience."

. . . The Ladies' Anti-Slavery Society of Boston was called last fall, to a severe trial of their faith and constancy. They were mobbed by "the gentlemen of property and standing," in that city at their anniversary meeting, and their lives were jeopardized by an infuriated crowd; but their conduct on that occasion did credit to our sex, and affords a full assurance that they will *never* abandon the cause of the slave. The pamphlet, Right and Wrong in Boston, issued by them in which a particular account is given of that "mob of broad cloth in broad day," does equal credit to the head and the heart of her who wrote it. I wish my Southern sisters could read it; they would then understand that the women of the North have engaged in this work from a sense of *religious duty*, and that nothing will ever induce them to take their hands from it until it is fully accomplished. They feel no hostility to you, no bitterness or wrath; they rather sympathize in your trials and difficulties; but they well know that the first thing to be done to help you, is to pour in the light of truth on your minds, to urge you to reflect on, and pray over the subject. This is all *they* can do for you, *you* must work out your own deliverance with fear and trembling, and with the direction and blessing of God, *you can do it.*

DECLARATION OF SENTIMENTS (1838)

William Lloyd Garrison

*T*HE *MASSACHUSETTS AND NEW YORK* Peace Societies, *mentioned* earlier, joined with other secular peace groups in 1828 to form the American Peace Society, for which Noah Worcester wrote the constitution. The official position of the Society increasingly emphasized issues related only to wars of aggression. It avoided comment on the Civil War altogether. By 1838, when the American Peace Society was unable to alter its ambiguous stand on nonresistance in the face of personal and state violence, the radical wing left to form the New England Non-Resistance Society. The new society, under the leadership of Adin Ballou and William Lloyd Garrison (1805-1879), was to become the boldest pacifist organization in the nineteenth century. It organized direct actions against railroad segregation and assisted in the freeing of slaves, among other activities. Yet initially the issue of women's rights was a stumbling block. At the organizing convention, the more conservative gentlemen left when women were given full membership. Garrison later wrote their Constitution and the *Declaration of Sentiments*, reprinted here, which was also the declaration of Abolitionist principles of nonresistance. As one of the staunchest Abolitionists, Garrison called for the end of capital punishment, abstention from politics and abolition of all war, as well as the emancipation of the slaves. He was instrumental in convincing the Abolitionists to adopt a nonviolent methodology. Later, after the Fugitive Slave Law was passed in 1850, Garrison came to believe that nonviolence was not adequate to ending slavery in the United States. He eventually supported the Civil War.

A SSEMBLED IN CONVENTION, FROM various sections of the American Union, for the promotion of peace on earth and good will among men, we, the undersigned, regard it as due to ourselves, to the cause which we love, to the country in which we live, and to the world, to publish a Declaration, expressive of the principles we cherish, the purposes we aim to accomplish, and the measures we shall adopt to carry forward the work of peaceful and universal reformation.

We cannot acknowledge allegiance to any human government; neither can we recognize any such government by a resort of physical force. We recognize but one King and Lawgiver, one Judge and Ruler of mankind. We are bound by the laws of a kingdom which is not of this world; the subjects of which are forbidden to fight; in which Mercy and Truth are met together, and Righteousness and Peace have kissed each other; which has no state lines, no national partitions, no geographical boundaries; in which there is no distinction or rank, or division of caste, or inequality of sex; the officers of which are Peace, its exactors Righteousness, its walls Salvation, and its gates Praise; and which is destined to break in pieces and consume all other kingdoms.

Our country is the world, our countrymen are all mankind. We love the land of our nativity, only as we love all other lands. The interests, rights, and liberties of American citizens are no more dear to us than are those of the whole human race. Hence, we can allow no appeal to patriotism, to revenge any national insult or injury. The Prince of Peace, under whose stainless banner we rally, came not to destroy, but to save, even the worst of enemies. He has left us an example, that we should follow his steps. "God commandeth his love toward us, in that while we were yet sinners, Christ died for us."

We conceive that as a nation has no right to defend itself against foreign enemies, or to punish its invaders, no individual possesses that right in his own case. The unit cannot be of greater importance than the aggregate. If one man may take life, to obtain or defend his rights, the same license must necessarily be granted to communities, states, and nations. If he may use a dagger or a pistol, they may employ cannon, bomb-shells, land and naval forces. The means of self-preservation must be in proportion to the magnitude of interests at stake, and the number of lives exposed to destruction. But if a rapacious and blood-thirsty soldiery, thronging these shores from abroad, with intent to commit rapine and destroy life, may not be resisted by the people or magistracy, then ought no resistance to be offered to domestic troublers of the public peace, or of private security. No obligation can rest upon Americans to regard foreigners as more sacred in their persons than themselves, or give them a monopoly of wrong-doing with impunity.

The dogma that all the governments of the world are approvingly ordained of God, and that the powers that be in the United States, in Russia, in Turkey, are in accordance with His will, is no less absurd than impious. It makes the impartial Author of human freedom and equality, unequal and tyrannical. It cannot be affirmed that the powers that be, in any nation, are actuated by the spirit, or guided by the example of Christ, in the treatment of enemies; therefore, they cannot be agreeable to the will of God; and, therefore, their overthrow, by a spiritual regeneration of their subjects, is inevitable.

We register our testimony, not only against all wars, whether offensive or defensive, but all preparations for war; against every naval ship, every arsenal, every fortification; against the militia system and a standing army; against all military chieftains and soldiers; against all monuments commemorative of victory over a foreign foe, all trophies won in battle, all celebrations in honor of military or naval exploits; against all appropriations for the defense of a nation by force and arms on the part of any legislative body; against every edict of government, requiring of its subjects military service. Hence, we deem it unlawful to bear arms, or to hold a military office.

As every human government is upheld by physical strength, and its laws are enforced virtually at the point of the bayonet, we cannot hold any office which imposes upon its incumbent the obligation to do right, on pain of imprisonment or death. We therefore voluntarily exclude ourselves from every legislative and judicial body, and repudiate all human politics, wordly honors, and stations of authority. If *we* cannot occupy a seat in the legislature, or on the bench, neither can we elect *others* to act as our substitutes in any such capacity.

It follows that we cannot sue any man at law, to compel him by force to restore any thing which he may have wrongfully taken from us or others; but, if he has seized our coat, we shall surrender up our cloak, rather than subject him to punishment.

We believe that the penal code of the old covenant, an eye for an eye, and a tooth for a tooth, has been abrogated by Jesus Christ; and that, under the new covenant, the forgiveness instead of the punishment of enemies has been enjoined upon all his disciples, in all cases whatsoever. To extort money from enemies, or set them upon a pillory, or cast them into prison, or hang them upon a gallows, is obviously not to forgive, but to take retribution. "Vengeance is mine—I will repay, saith the Lord."

The history of mankind is crowded with evidences, proving that physical coercion is not adapted to moral regeneration; that the sinful disposition of man can be subdued only by love; that evil can be exterminated from the earth only by goodness; that it is not safe to rely upon an arm of flesh, upon man, whose breath is in his nostrils, to preserve us from harm; that there is great security in being gentle, harmless, long-suffering, and abundant in mercy; that it is only the meek who shall inherit the earth, for the violent, who resort to the sword, shall perish with the sword. Hence, as a measure of sound policy, of safety to property, life, and liberty, of public quietude and private enjoyment, as well as on the ground of allegiance to Him who is King of kings, and Lord of lords, we cordially adopt the non-resistance principle, being confident that it provides for all possible consequences, will ensure all things needful to us, is armed with omnipotent power, and must ultimately triumph over every assailing force.

We advocate no jacobinal doctrines. The spirit of jacobinism is the spirit of retaliation, violence and murder. It neither fears God, nor regards man. We would be filled with the spirit of Christ. If we abide by our principles, it is impossible for us to be disorderly, or plot treason, or participate in any evil work: we shall submit to every ordinance of man, for the Lord's sake; obey all the requirements of government, except such as we deem contrary to the commands of the Gospel; and in no wise resist the operation of law, except by meekly submitting to the penalty of disobedience.

But, while we shall adhere to the doctrines of non-resistance and passive submission to enemies, we purpose, in a moral and spiritual sense, to speak and act boldly in the cause of God; to assail iniquity in high places and in low places; to apply our principles to all existing civil, political, legal, and ecclesiastical institutions; and to hasten the time when the kingdoms of this world shall become the kingdoms of our Lord and of his Christ, and he shall reign forever.

It appears to us as a self-evident truth that, whatever the Gospel is designed to destroy at any period of the world, being contrary to it, ought now to be abandoned. If, then, the time is predicted when swords shall be beaten into plough-shares, and spears into pruninghooks, and men shall not learn the art of war any more, it follows that all who manufacture, sell, or wield those deadly weapons, do thus array themselves against the peaceful dominion of the Son of God on earth.

Having thus briefly, but frankly, stated our principles and purposes, we proceed to specify the measures we propose to adopt in carrying our object into effect.

We expect to prevail through the foolishness of preaching—striving to commend ourselves unto every man's conscience, in the sight of God. From the press, we shall promulgate our sentiments as widely as practicable. We shall endeavor to secure the cooperation of all persons, of whatever name or sect. The triumphant progress of the cause of Temperance and of Abolition in our land, through the instrumentality of benevolent and voluntary associations, encourages us to combine our own means and efforts for the promotion of a still greater cause. Hence we shall employ lecturers, circulate tracts and publications, form societies, and petition our state and national governments in relation to the subject of Universal Peace. It will be our leading object to devise ways and means for effecting a radical change in the views, feelings and practices of society respecting the sinfulness of war, and the treatment of enemies.

In entering upon the great work before us, we are not unmindful that, in its prosecution, we may be called to test our sincerity, even as in a fiery ordeal. It may subject us to insult, outrage, suffering, yea, even death itself. We anticipate no small amount of misconception, misrepresentation, calumny. Tumults may arise against us. The ungodly and violent, the proud and pharisaical, the ambitious and tyrannical, principalities and powers, and spiritual wickedness in high places, may combine to crush us. So they treated the Messiah, whose example we are humbly striving to imitate. If we suffer with him, we know that we shall reign with him.

Firmly relying upon the certain and universal triumph of the sentiments contained in this Declaration, however formidable may be the opposition arrayed against them, in solemn testimony of our faith in their divine origin, we hereby afix our signatures to it, commending it to the reason and conscience of mankind, giving ourselves no anxiety as to what may befall us, and resolving, in the strength of the Lord God, calmly and meekly to abide the issue.

EVILS OF THE REVOLUTIONARY WAR (1839)

Charles K. Whipple

*C*HARLES WHIPPLE (1808-1900) WAS a Bostonian pacifist and member of the Bowdoin Street Young Men's Peace Society, a local affiliate of the American Peace Society. As with other nonresistants who lived in a world where slavery and revolution were well known, Whipple questioned the relationship between pacifism and the struggle for independence. In *Evils of the Revolutionary War*, Whipple challenges the assumption that the war itself was necessary given the nonviolent struggle for independence which had already begun. Clearly, Whipple felt that violent revolution was not the only means to rid the colonies from British domination. He saw it as enslaving the new republic to cruelty and revenge rather than setting it free. Lest we consider this naive, we should note that several modern British and United States historians have raised the same question. In as recent a publication as the 1985 publication *Resistance, Politics And The American Struggle For Independence, 1765-1775*, for example, the editors argue that the nonviolent approach to the American Revolution would have been sufficient in attaining independence. Whipple describes here several nonviolent strategies for freedom which are amazingly similar to those suggested by Gandhi decades later.

W HAT, ALL WAR WRONG?

Yes, says the Peace man.

Then the war which gained American Independence, our glorious Revolutionary war, was wrong!

It was.

Then, sir, tell me this if you can. Where would our great, prosperous, and happy country have been at this moment, but for that war?

I will tell you. It would have been more prosperous, more moral, and happier than it now is.

You cannot surely believe such an absurdity. Wonderfully prosperous and happy we should be, no doubt, remaining to this hour under the tyranny of Great Britain!

There is your mistake, my friend. You take it for granted, without examination, that we could never have freed ourselves from British domination, except by war. Now, I say, that we should have attained independence as effectually, as speedily, as honorably, and under very much more favorable circumstances, if we had not resorted to arms.

Very well: now show me how it could have been done.

Our fathers might have accomplished this object, great as it was, merely by taking the course which the society of Friends took to maintain their rights, and by which, though a small and despised body of men, they compelled the English and American governments to recognize and protect those rights. This course consisted of three things. 1st, a steady and quiet refusal to comply with unjust requisitions; 2d, public declarations of their grievances, and demands for redress; and 3d, patient endurance of whatever violence was used to compel their submission.

We have every reason to expect that steady perseverance in a course like this will ultimately succeed, wherever the cause is just. Because 'moral might is always on the side of right,' and because governments are composed of men, and not of brutes.

Let us suppose, for a moment, that our fathers had acted in the manner I have mentioned, and see what the various stages of the process would have been. In every part of the contest, they strictly adhere to the principles above stated. They carefully refrain from violence, constantly remonstrate against the oppressive acts, and persevere in passive resistance. When the taxed tea is brought to their shores, they universally abstain from the use of it. It lies undemanded in the ware-houses, and thus the plan of taxation, as far as that article goes, is as completely defeated as it could have been by violence and robbery. When the stamped paper is taxed, they carry on their business without it. This involves great difficulty, inconvienence, and embarrassment of business. No matter! They are patriots, and willing to suffer for their country; and the evils thus endured are infinitely less than the calamities of war. If direct taxes are laid upon them, they quietly, but universally, refuse payment. Their property is seized and sold to raise the tax. They patiently submit to this evil, for their country's sake, and rejoice that it is so slight in comparison with war. Imprisonment, insult, and abuse of every kind, are added to enforce the oppressive acts of parliament. Still no violence is used, either for defence or retaliation; but petitions, remonstrances, delegations are multiplied as the occasions for them recur. When all these measures are found to fail of success, they unite in solemn assembly to make to the world a declaration of their wrongs, and pronounce their formal separation from, and independence of the

British nation. This movement excites new and more violent demonstrations of hostility on the part of the British functionaries. The signers of the Declaration of Independence, and the officers of the new government, are seized and sent to England to take their trial for high treason. No opposition is made, no defence attempted by the patriot leaders. They are ready to lay down their lives in support of the liberty of their country, and they rejoice to meet the danger of this form, in which they can explain and defend their principles, rather than submit their cause to the decision of brute force on the battle-field, where their own fall would involve the destruction of thousands of their countrymen. They are tried by the constituted authorities of England, and calmly avow and defend their revolutionary measures. They are found guilty, sentenced to death, and (for we will suppose the worst) actually executed as traitors. But their defence, their bold and clear explanation of the principles of liberty, their new views of the relative rights and duties of a government and its subjects, are in the mean time eagerly read and pondered by all the British nation. And while this good seed is taking root in the hearts of the people, the source of power, let us turn to the United States, and see what the revolutionists, thus suddenly deprived of their leaders, are doing.

As soon as that noble band of pioneers is taken from them, they choose others to administer the affairs of the new nation. These, too, are seized as rebels. They immediately elect more. What shall the colonial officers do against such pertinacious, yet unresisting opponents? The whole population avow their determination to be free. The whole population offer themselves for punishment. The prisons are filled to overflowing with rebels; yet they have accomplished nothing, for every man they meet is a rebel. What is to be done? Shall they send for an army? That is needless, for their present force is unresisted. But suppose an army comes. They can do nothing but take prisoners and destroy property, and perhaps execute a few persons; for I take it for granted that they would not attempt to put to death the great mass of the population. All that they do to enforce obedience renders them more odious to the people, and nothing is effected towards destroying the principles of liberty. Intelligence arrives of the death of their leaders in England. This adds fuel to the fire. Their determination, before strong, is now irrevocable. On the other hand, the news of their measures, their pertinacity, and non-resistance, is constantly going to the people of England, a people already moved to sympathy by the constancy and heroism of the patriot leaders, and already half persuaded by the arguments of those leaders that their cause is just. Can it be imagined, is it consistent with the attributes of human nature to suppose, that such a persevering and undaunted defence of principles so just would fail of working conviction in the hearts of a people like the English? Even were it possible for parliament to persevere in the attempt to subjugate such opponents by force, the whole English people, the whole civilized world, indeed, would cry out shame upon them, and force them to abandon the design, and finally to recognize the independence of the Americans.

It follows as a necessary inference from the principles before alluded to, namely, that moral might is always on the side of justice, and that governors and legislators are never destitute of the feelings and sympathies of men, that firm perseverance in such a course as I have described *must* have resulted in the acknowledgment of American Independence; and probably that result would have occurred in much less time than was occupied by the revolutionary war. This will be made perfectly clear by looking for a moment, at the reason why Great Britain at last gave up the contest. Did we conquer that mighty nation? Not at all! Still less did they conquer us! Why then, did not the war continue? Simply and solely because Great Britain was tired of fighting! Absolutely wearied out by contention and its necessary consequences! Would not a similar pertinacity in time produce the same effect without the use of physical force? I say, we should *certainly* in this way have attained our Independence.

We will now suppose this object effected. Let us see what evils the pacific course has produced, in comparison with the evils actually resulting from the revolutionary war.

1st. LOSS OF LIFE. We will make a liberal estimate, and allow that one thousand persons have been executed as traitors, after deliberate trial and sentence; and that ten thousand (men, women, and children) have been slain, unresisting, by the exasperated British soldiers. Upon this enormously exaggerated supposition we have eleven thousand lives lost. But it is computed that a hundred thousand Americans perished during the eight years of the revolutionary war. We have, then a direct saving of eighty-nine thousand lives of American citizens by pacific measures. This alone should decide the question in favor of peace. But we have other considerations.

2d. EXPENSE, DIRECT AND INDIRECT. Commerce, trade, and manufacturing have been to a great extent suspended, and a large amount of property has been wantonly destroyed by the devastations of the enemy. But all this would have happened to a still greater extent in war; and the non-resisting policy has saved us the enormous expense of supporting an army and navy, and of building and equipping fortifications. The direct expense of the revolutionary war to our country is estimated, by Pitkin, at $135,000,000. The same author has stated the direct expense of our military operations *since* that war, to be more than $300,000,000. All this at least $435,000,000, we should have saved by the pacific policy.

3d. THE INTERESTS OF MORALITY AND RELIGION. If a whole people have such a sense of their duty to God as to refuse to protect themselves by means which he has forbidden, they will not be likely to neglect either to recognize his hand or implore his protection, throughout the struggle. The Sabbath has been strictly observed, and the supplications of the nation have arisen more ardently than ever to Him who holds the hearts of kings in his hand. The mass of the people having their minds intently fixed on the great struggle between liberty and oppression, and anxiously watching the contest of faith, love, patience and hope, against carnal weapons, have been strongly withheld both from trifling amusements and vicious indulgences. At the close of the struggle, therefore, the interests of religion and morality are more flourishing than at its commencement. . . .

The loss of $400,000,000 and even the destruction of 100,000 lives, appear but trifling evils, in comparison with the enormous depravation of moral habits and religious principles which the revolutionary war has produced in this nation.

The considerations above mentioned entirely satisfy me not only that we should have gained our independence, but that we should have been more prosperous, better and happier than we now are, had there been no revolutionary war.

So much for *positive* results of the non-resistance plan. It may now be well to look at the subject in another aspect, and see what results *would not have taken place*, had our ancestors been magnanimous enough, honorable enough, CHRISTIAN enough, to refuse to fight with Great Britain.

Having gained their independence in the mode above mentioned, most assuredly THEY WOULD NOT HAVE CONTINUED TO HOLD THEIR FELLOW CREATURES IN SLAVERY.

Upon this point we cannot be mistaken. Men who had been led by Christian principles to regard the rights and abstain from the destruction of their *enemies,* could not have deliberately pursued a system of oppression and fraud against their former fellow-sufferers. Men who had so strongly demonstrated their belief in the doctrine that the whole human race are alike entitled to life, liberty and the pursuit of happiness could not have systematically manufactured and used whips, chains, handcuffs and branding-irons. They would not have kept back the hire of the laborer; they would not have taken away the key of knowledge; they would neither have denied the theory nor shrunk from the practice of immediate emancipation. They would certainly have been, in truth as well as in pretence, a free people.

Again. They would not have proceeded to defraud, corrupt, and exterminate the original inhabitants of this country. They would neither have deprived the Indians of their lands, nor supplied them with liquid fire, nor broken their faith plighted in solemn treaties, nor expended the revenues of the country in making war upon them. How much treasure, how much blood, how many precious lives, how many immortal souls, might they have saved!

Lastly. They would not have admitted the system of violence and retaliation as a constituent part of their own government. Having forgiven their foreign foes, they would have pursued the like Christian course towards every domestic enemy. Having conquered by suffering in the great contest between nations, they would have trusted to the same means for overcoming all minor evils. So far from depending on the gallows, the prison, the stocks, the whipping-post, for peace and quietness, they would utterly have rejected all such barbarous instruments, and substituted for them love, joy, peace, long-suffering, gentleness, goodness, faith, hope, patience, meekness. And, doing thus, they would have found the word of God a sure reliance; the whole armor of God a safe protection.

HAS THE DUTY OF OBEYING GOVERNMENT NO BOUNDS? (1841)

William Ellery Channing

*W*ILLIAM CHANNING *(1780-1842) HAS been credited with attempting* "the conversion of the Christian church to Christian principles." The following selection shows with what vehemence he analyzed the ability of modern governments to declare and wage "just wars," and of modern Christians to blindly follow. He continually counseled Christians to take responsibility for their personal decisions about the justice of any war. Channing was a Unitarian minister and a contemporary of Noah Worcester, with whom he co-founded the Massachusetts Peace Society. He emphasized the changes needed in society in order to reduce the likelihood of war, and the Christian's responsibility for those changes. Greatly influenced by the New Testament as well as the Eighteenth Century "Enlightenment" philosophers of France and England, Channing believed in the dignity and goodness of humanity and had tremendous faith in the human potential for progress. In the last part of this selection, he addresses the perennial objection raised by proponents of a non-questioning stance toward the decrees of government: that if one law can be resisted, what will stop the resistance of all law and the ultimate fall of government?

I KNOW IT WILL be asked, "And is not the citizen bound to fight at the call of his government? Does not his commission absolve him from the charge of murder or enormous crime? Is not obedience to the sovereign power the very foundation on which society rests?" I answer, "Has the duty of obeying government no bounds? Is the human sovereign a God? Is his sovereignty absolute? If he command you to slay a parent, must you obey? If he forbid you to worship God, must you obey? Have you no right to judge his acts?

71

Have you no self-direction? Is there no unchangeable right which the ruler cannot touch? Is there no higher standard than human law?" These questions answer themselves. A declaration of war cannot sanction wrong, or turn murder into a virtuous deed. Undoubtedly, as a general rule, the citizen is bound to obey the authorities under which he lives. No difference of opinion as to the mere expedience of measures will warrant opposition. Even in cases of doubtful right he may submit his judgement to the law. But when called to do what his conscience clearly pronounces wrong, he must not waver. No outward law is so sacred as the voice of God in his own breast. He cannot devolve on rulers an act so solemn as the destruction of fellow beings convicted of no offense. For no act will more solemn inquisition be made at the bar of God.

I maintain that the citizen, before fighting, is bound to inquire into the justice of the cause which he is called to maintain with blood, and bound to withhold his hand, if his conscience condemn the cause. On this point he is able to judge. No political question, indeed, can be determined so easily as this of war. War can be justified only by plain, palpable necessity; by unquestionable wrongs, which, as patient trial has proved, can in no other way be redressed; by the obstinate, persevering invasion of solemn and unquestionable rights. The justice of war is not a mystery for cabinets to solve. It is not a state secret which he must take on trust. It lies within our reach. We are bound to examine it.

We are especially bound to this examination because there is always a presumption against the justice of war; always reason to fear that it is condemned by impartial conscience and God. This solemn truth has peculiar claims on attention. It takes away the plea that we may innocently fight because our rulers have decreed war. It strips off the most specious disguise from the horrors and crimes of national hostilities. If hostilities were, as a general rule, necessary and just, if an unjust war were a solitary exception, then the citizen might extenuate his share in the atrocities of military life by urging his obligation to the state. But if there is always reason to apprehend the existence of wrong on the part of rulers, then he is bound to pause and ponder well his path. Then he advances at his peril, and must answer for the crimes of the unjust, unnecessary wars in which he shares.

The presumption is always against the justice and necessity of war. This we learn from the spirit of all rulers and nations toward foreign states. It is partial, unjust. Individuals may be disinterested, but nations have no feeling of the tie of brotherhood to their race. A base selfishness is the principle on which the affairs of nations are commonly conducted. A statesman is expected to take advantage of the weaknesses and wants of other countries. How loose a morality governs the intercourse of states! What falsehoods and intrigues are licensed diplomacy! What nation regards another with true friendship? What nation makes sacrifices to another's good? What nation is as anxious to perform its duties as to assert its rights? What nation chooses to suffer wrong rather than to inflict it? What nation lays down the everlasting law of right, casts itself fearlessly on its principles, and chooses to be poor or to perish rather than to do wrong?

Can communities so selfish, so unfriendly, so unprincipled, so unjust, be expected to wage righteous wars? Especially if with this selfishness are joined national prejudices, antipathies and exasperated passions, what else can be expected in the public policy but inhumanity and crime? An individual, we know, cannot be trusted, in his own cause, to measure his own claims, to avenge his own wrongs; and the civil magistrate, an impartial umpire, has been substituted as the only means of justice. But nations are often more unfit than individuals to judge in their own cause; more prone to push their rights to excess, and to trample on the rights of others; because nations are crowds, and crowds are unawed by opinion, and more easily inflamed by sympathy into madness. Is there not, then, always a presumption against the justice of war?

This presumption is increased when we consider the false notions of patriotism and honor which prevail in nations. Men think it a virtuous patriotism to throw a mantle, as they call it, over their country's infirmities, to wink at her errors, to assert her most doubtful rights, to look jealously and angrily on the prosperity of rival states; and they place her honor not in unflatering adherence to the right, but in a fiery spirit, in quick resentment, in martial courage, and especially in victory; and can a good man hold himself bound and stand prepared to engage in war at the dictate of such a state?

The citizen or subject, you say, may innocently fight at the call of his rulers; and I ask, who are his rulers? Perhaps an absolute sovereign, looking down on his people as another race, as created to toil for his pleasure, to fight for new provinces, to bleed for his renown. There are indeed republican governments. But were not the republics of antiquity as greedy of conquest, as prodigal of human life, as steeled against the cries of humanity, as any despots who ever lived? And if we come down to modern republics, are they to be trusted with our consciences? What does the Congress of these United States represent? Not so much the virtue of the country as a vicious principle, the spirit of party. It acts not so much for the people as for the parties; and are parties upright? Are parties merciful? Are the wars to which party commits a country generally just?

Unhappily, public men under all governments are, of all moral guides, the most unsafe, the last for a Christian to follow. Public life is thought to absolve men from the strict obligation of truth and justice. To wrong an adverse party or another country is not reprobated as are wrongs in private life. Thus duty is dethroned; thus the majesty of virtue insulted in the administration of nations. Public men are expected to think more of their own elevation than of their country. Is the city of Washington the most virtuous spot in this republic? Is it the school of incorruptible men? The hall of Congress, disgraced by so many brawls, swayed by local interest and party intrigues, in which the right of petition is trodden under foot, is this the oracle from which the responses of justice come forth? Public bodies want conscience. Men acting in masses shift off responsibility on one another. Multitudes never blush. If these things be true, then, I maintain that the Christian has not a right to take part in war blindly, confidingly, at the call of his rulers. To shed the blood of fellow creatures is too solemn a work to be engaged in lightly. Let him not put himself, a tool, into wicked hands. Let him not meet on the field his brother man, his brother Christian, in a cause on which heaven frowns. Let him bear witness against unholy wars as his country's greatest crimes. If called to take part in them, let him deliberately refuse. If martial law seize him, let him submit. If hurried to prison, let him submit. If brought thence to be shot, let him submit. There must be martyrs to peace as truly as to other principles of our religion. The first Christians chose to die rather than obey the laws of the state which commanded them to renounce their Lord. "Death rather than crime"; such is the good man's watchword, such the Christian's vow. Let him be faithful unto death.

Undoubtedly it will be objected that if one law of the state may in any way be resisted, then all may be, and so government must fall. This is precisely the argument on which the doctrine of passive obedience to the worst tyrannies rests. The absolutist says, "If one government may be overturned, none can stand." Your right of revolution is nothing but the same. Extreme cases speak for themselves. We must put confidence in the common sense of men, and suppose them capable of distinguishing between reasonable laws and those which require them to commit manifest crimes. The objection which we are considering rests on the supposition that a declaration of war is a common act of legislation, bearing no strong marks of distinction from other laws, and consequently to be obeyed as implicitly as all. But it is broadly distinguished. A declaration of war sends us forth to destroy our fellow creatures, to carry fire, sword, famine, bereavement, want and woe into the fields and habitations of our brethren; whilst Christianity, conscience and all the pure affections of our nature call us to love our brethren, and to die, if need be, for their good.

And from whence comes this declaration of war? From men who would rather die than engage in unjust or unnecessary conflict? Too probably, from men to whom Christianity is a name, whose highest law is honor, who are used to avenging their private wrongs and defending their reputations by shedding blood, and who, in public as in private life, defy the laws of God. Whoever, at such men's dictation, engages in war without solemnly consulting conscience, and inquiring into the justice of the cause, contracts great guilt, nor can the "right of war," which such men claim as rulers, absolve him from the crimes and woes of the conflict in which he shares.

From: CHRISTIAN NON-RESISTANCE IN ALL ITS IMPORTANT BEARINGS (1846)

Adin Ballou

ADIN BALLOU (1803-1890), AN early nineteenth century reformer, Abolitionist, and American Universalist Clergyman, founded one of the first utopian communities in the United States in Hopedale, Massachusetts. Of all the Abolitionists, Ballou did the most to further nonviolence theory. Ballou struggled against the idea that nonresistance was passive. He believed that moral resistance included physical intervention such as non-injurious restraint of criminals and bodily interpositioning between violent people. He provided the synthesis of two seemingly antithetical interpretations of Gospel nonviolence, one calling on Christians to withdraw from evil and the structures of evil in the name of witnessing to the need for social change, the other promoting social change through participation rather than withdrawal. Ballou believed that through extreme withdrawal people do in fact engage the power structures and force change to happen. Thus, for example, Ballou supported boycotts of slave-made products, boycotts of churches which did not oppose slavery, sit-ins, walk-alongs (in which a black person and a white person would walk along the street arm in arm, having withdrawn their allegiance to the prohibition of racial mixing), the underground railroad, and many other forms of nonviolent protest. All of these tactics created pressure for change by withdrawing participation from an immoral law or practice. Leo Tolstoy, in Russia, and Mahatma Gandhi, in India, studied Ballou's works and used his synthesis in forming their own theories of nonviolent action. The following sections are excerpted from his book, *Christian Non-Resistance, in All Its Important Bearings, Illustrated and Defended,* which contains a longer description of the various types of nonresistance.

What A Christian Non-Resistant Cannot Consistently Do:

IT WILL APPEAR FROM the foregoing exposition, that a true Christian non-resistant *cannot,* with deliberate intent, knowledge or conscious voluntariness, compromit his principles by either (any) of the following acts.

1. He cannot kill, maim or otherwise *absolutely injure* any human being, in personal self-defense, or for the sake of his family, or any thing he holds dear.

2. He cannot participate in any lawless conspiracy, mob, riotous assembly, or disorderly combination of individuals, to cause or countenance the commission of any such absolute personal injury.

3. He cannot be a member of any voluntary association, however orderly, respectable or allowable by law and general consent, *which declaratively* holds as *fundamental truth,* or claims as an essential right, or distinctly inculcates as sound doctrine, or approves as commendable in practice, *war, capital* punishment, or any other absolute personal injury.

4. He cannot be an *officer* or *private,* chaplain or retainer, in the army, navy or militia of any nation, state, or chieftain.

5. He cannot be an officer, elector, agent, legal prosecutor, passive constituent, or approver of any government, as a sworn or otherwise pledged supporter thereof, whose civil constitution and fundamental laws, require, authorize or tolerate war, slavery, capital punishment, or the infliction of any absolute personal injury.

6. He cannot be a member of any chartered corporation, or body politic, whose articles of compact oblige or authorize its official functionaries to resort for compulsory aid, in the conducting of its affairs, to a government of constitutional violence.

7. Finally, he cannot do any act, either in person or by proxy; nor abet or encourage any act in others, nor demand, petition for, request, advise or approve the doing of any act, by an individual, association or government, *which* act would inflict, *threaten* to inflict, or *necessarily* cause to *be* inflicted *any absolute personal injury,* as herein before defined.

Such are the necessary bearings, limitations and applications of the doctrine of Christian non-resistance. Let the reader be careful not to misunderstand the positions laid down. The platform of principle and action has been carefully founded, and its essential peculiarities plainly delineated. Let it not be said that the doctrine goes against all religion, government, social organization, constitutions, laws, order, rules and regulations. It goes against none of those things, *per se.* It goes for them, in the highest and best sense. It goes only against *such* religion, government, social organization, constitutions, laws, order, rules, regulations and restraints, as are unequivocally contrary to the law of Christ; as sanction taking "life for life, eye for eye, tooth for tooth"; as are based on the assumption, that it is *right* to resist *injury with injury, evil with evil. . . .*

Self-Preservation the First Law of Nature

It is reiterated that "self-preservation is the first law of nature." I grant it, and then what follows? "Self-defence against whatever threatens destruction or injury," says the opponent. I grant it, and what next follows? "Generally mutual personal conflict, injury, and in the extremities, *death*." Hence there are justifiable homicides, wars, injuries and penal inflictions. Nature impels them. The law of self-preservation necessitates them. They are *right* in the very nature of things; and therefore nonresistance must be *wrong*, as it is impracticable. It is contrary to nature and cannot be brought into practice.

What Is the True Method of Self-Preservation?

For it remains to be seen whether this general method of self-preservation be the *true* method. Whether it be not a very bad method. Whether it be not a method which absolutely defeats its own designed object. Let us inquire. If it be the true method, it must on the whole work well. It must preserve human life and secure mankind against injury, more certainly and effectually than any other possible method. Has it done this? I do not admit it. How happens it that, according to the lowest probable estimate, some fourteen thousand millions of human beings have been slain by human means, in war and otherwise? Here are enough to people eighteen planets like the earth with its present population. What inconceivable miseries must have been endured by these worlds of people and their friends, in the process of those murderous conflicts which extinguished their earthly existence! Could all their dying groans be heard and their expiring throes be witnessed at once, ... would it be deemed conclusive evidence that mankind had practised the true method of self-preservation!! Would it encourage us still to confide in and pursue the same method? Would it suggest no inquiries, whether there were not "a more excellent way?" Should we not be impelled to conclude that this method was the offspring of a purblind instinct—the cherished salvo of ignorance—the fatal charm of deluded credulity—the *supposed preserver*, but the *real destroyer* of the human family? If this long-trusted method of self-preservation be indeed the best which nature affords to her children, their lot is most deplorable. To preserve what life has been preserved at such a cost, renders life itself a thing of doubtful value. If only a few thousands, or even a few millions, had perished by the two-edged sword; if innocence and justice and right had uniformly triumphed; if aggression, injustice, violence, injury and insult, after a few dreadful experiences, had been overawed; if gradually the world had come into wholesome order—a state of truthfulness, justice and peace; if the sword of self-defence had frightened the sword of aggression into its scabbard, there to consume in its rust; then might we admit that the common method of self-preservation was the true one. But now we have ample demonstration that *they who take the sword, perish with the sword.* Is it supposable that if no injured person or party, since the days of Abel, had lifted up a deadly weapon, or threatened an injury against an offending party, there would have been a thousandth part of the murders and miseries which have actually taken place on our earth? Take the worst possible view; resolve all the assailed and injured into the most passive non-resistants imaginable, and let the offenders have unlimited scope to commit all the robberies, cruelties and murders they pleased; would as many lives have been sacrificed, or as much real misery have been experienced by the human race, as have actually resulted from the general method of self-preservation, by personal conflict, and resistance of injury with injury? He must be a bold man who affirms it. The truth is, man has stood in his own light. He has frustrated his own wishes. He has been deceived, deluded, betrayed, and all but destroyed, by his own self-conceited, evil imagination. He would not be taught of God. He would have his own way. He would be a fool, a spendthrift, a murderer and a suicide. Yet his Father still calls after him. He offers to make him wise, good and happy. He offers to teach him the true method of self-preservation. It is found in the non-resistance of Jesus Christ. But he is wretchedly wedded to his old idols, and will scarcely hear the voice of his only true friend. When he will hear, he shall live. . . .

HARRIET TUBMAN: LIBERATOR

Maggie Fisher

A RARE ENTRY UNDER "Tubman, Harriet," (c. 1820-1913) in the *Reader's Guide to Periodical Literature* notes that in 1986 the editors of *Ladies Home Journal* honored her as one of the twenty-five most important women in the United States. This less than radical magazine had chosen these women for possessing "extraordinary vigor and drive" and for having "lived productive lives well past 70, often into their 80's." When spoken about the life of the woman born Araminta Ross, these characteristics gravely understate the marvels of her person and accomplishments. It even understates the length of her full life; she died in 1913, between the age of 93 and 98, her birth as a Dorchester County, Maryland slave child having been unrecorded.

Childhood experiences of the brutality of owners and overseers roused in her a determination to be free, as well as marked her physically with a husky voice and a susceptibility to coma-like episodes. Her intense desire for freedom was heightened by a series of visions: "I seemed to see a line, and on the other side of that line were green fields, and lovely flowers, and beautiful white ladies, who stretched out their arms to me over the line, but I couldn't reach them nohow. I always fell before I got to the line."

When she was young, Harriet's father, "Old Ben," had given her an intimate knowledge and love of nature. Both he and she knew that the skills he taught her might well be used at times of extreme danger. Old Ben, who was renowned for his understanding of the forests and fields, taught her to move silently, unobtrusively and with grace, even in darkness. Her apprenticeship was complete on the occasion when she touched his shoulder without his having perceived her approach.

Illiterate but brilliant and passionate, Araminta Ross escaped to freedom on a solitary journey in 1849 guided by a star, her brothers William and Robert having turned back in fear. Her husband, whom she married in 1849, was unwilling to risk that first trip and threatened to report her to the master.

After leaving "Egypt" behind and arriving in Pennsylvania, she "looked at my hands to see if I was the same person. There was such a glory over everything; the sun came like gold through the trees and over the fields, and I felt like I was in Heaven." Then, she realized her loneliness, "I had crossed the line. I was FREE; but there was no one to welcome me to the land of freedom. I was a stranger in a strange land; and my home, after all, was down in Maryland. . . But I was free and THEY should be free. I would make a home in the North and bring them there, God helping me."

Despite her husband's threatened betrayal, she returned after her own escape to take him North, only to find that he had remarried and settled into a new life. Since he was not interested in leaving, she gathered a group and led them to freedom.

She was to return to "Pharaoh's Land" nineteen times in the next twelve years and to bring out at least 300 slaves including her parents "Old Rit" (Harriet) Greene, and "Old Ben" Ross. These return trips to the South were arduous, uncertain, and extremely dangerous. Days were usually spent hiding, whether in fields, potato holes, forests, haystacks, or in the homes of sympathetic persons, white and Black and frequently Quakers. She followed the Underground Railroad through Maryland, Delaware, Pennsylvania, New Jersey, New York, and Massachusetts, and after the passage of the Fugitive Slave Law in 1850, into Canada.

The Underground Railroad system had already become tightly organized with stationmasters, junctions, regular routes, engineers, impressive systems of communications and fund-raisers. Escapes were made on foot, by wagons and even on the overground trains.

The mysterious darkness of night with the paradoxical brightness of the night sky became Harriet Tubman's enduring symbols. Frederick Douglass once wrote to her that the night sky and silent stars were witnesses of her devotion and heroism. They were also cover and guide as she led persons of all ages, including infants, to safety, the smallest children often drugged with opium or paregoric lest their cries reveal the presence of the fugitives. By night Harriet and her bands crossed streams and rivers, climbed mountains and sometimes were able to follow roads and trails. At one point a man who had previously housed groups of fleeing slaves was arrested. Unknown to Harriet, his house had been given to a less friendly person. Discovering this only upon knocking at the door, she withdrew quickly, changed course and devised an alternative. On another trip she sensed danger, altered her direction and took her followers to an island. It was necessary to cross a stream, and all waited to see that she made it safely before venturing to follow her. The next day she learned that a group of slave-hunters had indeed been on the road she had left. Still another time, upon reaching the Wilmington, Delaware bridge, she found it heavily guarded. The man in town with whom her group was to stay realized the delay. He hired and sent across the bridge several wagonloads of bricklayers. After some hours they made their way back to town, having hidden the fugitives under the bricks.

The South was becoming inexorably more and more an armed camp. "Wanted" posters were everywhere with descriptions of fleeing slaves, above all of "Moses," the one who led out so many bands and who was believed by slave-owners to be a man. Harriet usually disguised herself by dressing as a man. She had gained the needed physical stength and stamina during years as a field hand when masters gladly allowed her her preference of field work over house work—and thus got a field hand labor for a woman's wages. But those in that male-dominated world who knew her best often compared her to Joan of Arc. Steadily withdrawing the slaves from her Bucktown, Maryland home area, Harriet caused the value of slaves in markets there to drop dramatically. Owners refused to pay large amounts, knowing there was little certainty of keeping the slaves. The rewards offered for the capture or death of Moses was set at a total of $40,000. Harriet Tubman is considered to have been the most successful of the underground engineers. Only the most committed, usually Blacks, were willing to take on this dangerous role. Of the other engineers, many were captured and imprisoned, killed, or emotionally scarred if they survived. Her strength of spirit and ability to encourage and inspire those who followed her, her depth and richness of personality remain a source of wonder. She drew on dreams, visions and intuitions. Upon meeting John Brown, she identified him as a man she had seen in a dream. Twice she went to an Abolitionist who recieved money for her from European supporters and told him how much he was holding and that she had come to collect it. Three years before the Emancipation Proclamation she had a vision of the freedom of her people. Then at the time of its pronouncement she said, "I rejoiced all I could then; I can't rejoice no more." Harriet attributed these dreams, warnings, and the like, to God. Her unshakable confidence and faith in God's love and providence were manifested often along the railroad and later during the War between the States. In both circumstances she was certain of God's care, she believed that she would die only at the appointed and right moment, then to be welcomed by God. When asked how she could go back into danger knowing the price on her head, she answered, "Why, don't I tell you, 'twasn't me 'twas THE LORD. I always told him, 'I trust to you. I don't know where to go or what to do, but I expect you to lead me,' and he always did."

After word reached her of a meeting of slaveholders in Maryland, at which additional money was pledged for her capture and more torture devised for her, friends begged her not to endanger herself further. She responded that St. John had seen Paradise with four gates, one of which was on the south, "and I reckon if they kill me down there, I'll get into one of them gates, don't you?"

In her early life at home, Harriet and her people had been forbidden to sing such songs as "Go down, Moses/ Way down in Egypt's land/ Tell old Pharaoh/ Let my people go!" Leaving for her first trip guided by the North Star, Harriet had sung her farewell to family and friends, knowing that after her departure they would understand. On her many returns to Egypt's land, she signaled her arrival and the time for gathering by singing, her husky voice immediately recognized in the slave's quarters. Certain stanzas communicated a delay, others immediate departure. On the road, some words indicated the need to separate, and others that it was safe to come together again.

Between trips Harriet did domestic work in hotels and inns, now being paid for what was called "free work," work which as a slave she had disliked. She also gardened and sold her produce to earn money for the expenses of her journeys and to support her parents, as well as those who came to her for refuge and nursing.

The Maryland slave child became a respected friend of Abolitionists, of authors, and of northern government officials. She was sought after for lectures, for salons, for house meetings. Throughout the years, she had understood the value of initiating whites into her people's culture, so when she sang and danced, it was not just to entertain.

Soon after the beginning of the Civil War, Harriet was asked by Governor Andrew of Massachusetts to become scout, spy and nurse for the Union troops. She spent several years chiefly in South Carolina, but also at times in Virginia. In one capacity she gained information and in another shielded raiding parties. Through careful nursing and the use of native and natural remedies learned from Old Rit, she saved the lives of Union and Confederate soldiers as well as her own people.

She was moved by the plight of the freed Blacks, who were, she said, nearly naked and possessing nothing. To change this situation she taught and encouraged women in the conflict areas to set up ways of helping themselves and their families. She helped organize wash services and the making and selling of articles needed by the soldiers.

She approved of the tactics of John Brown. She is known to have led raiding parties, one of which was remarkably successful and became a model for a Union strategy. She combined nonviolent methods as in the Underground Railroad and in her nursing with decisions and actions she considered necessary to end slavery. No evidence or hint exists of any adherence to theoretical nonviolence on her part, nor of her having injured or killed anyone. Her greatest risks and the heritage she has passed on lie clearly within the realm of respecting and protecting life. Her capacity for forgiveness and her greatness of soul are revealed, for example, in her sympathy for Jefferson Davis and her hope that after the war he would find peace. She showed her compassionate insight into humanity when she stated, "I think there's many a slaveholder will get to Heaven. They don't know no better. They acts up to the light they have. You take that sweet little child (pointing to a lovely baby)—appears more like an angel than anything else—take her down there, let her never know nothing about niggers but they was made to be whipped, and she'll grow up to use the whip on them just like the rest. No, Missus, it's because they don't know no better."

When the war ended, Harriet returned to Auburn, New York, where she had a small home. She was ill, exhausted, penniless, and wounded in body and spirit. A train conductor had refused to recognize her pass, certain that a Negro would not validly carry one, and had physically thrown her into a baggage car for another solitary trip North. Despite her services to the nation and the insistent efforts of Secretary of State William Seward, she was never given the pension she earned through her work for the Union. It is unclear whether this was due to bureaucratic inefficiency or racism or sexism. In 1869, Sarah H. Bradford, a white woman who loved and admired Harriet, printed largely at her own expense *SCENES OF THE LIFE OF HARRIET TUBMAN* in order to raise funds for Harriet. Still Harriet continued to organize, this time in the temperance and suffrage movements.

She died in Auburn in 1913. At her service Booker T. Washington praised her, as did many others, saying, "She brought the two races closer together and made it possible for the white race to place a higher estimate upon the black race."

Araminta Ross, who came to be known as Harriet Tubman, still leads on many roads those who seek to open up life and freedom to the oppressed. She integrated a life of faith, understanding and action. When slaves she was leading by the North Star out of Egypt's Land wished to turn back, Harriet reminded them of her own deepest conviction, that she and they had two choices, freedom or death. She was willing to risk one for the sake of the other—for herself, her family, her people, her country.

Maggie Fisher has been involved in a variety of justice issues including women in church and society, migrant farm workers, disarmament, and Central American concerns. She currently coordinates the Interfaith Committee on Latin America in St. Louis, Missouri.

I ASK NO FAVOR FOR MY SEX: LUCRETIA MOTT AND NON-RESISTANCE

Margaret Hope Bacon

W HEN SHE DIED IN 1880, *The New York Times* called Lucretia Mott (1793-1880) "One of the greatest fighters of the world." She fought most of her long life for an end to slavery and racial discrimination; for the rights of women, Native Americans, workers; for freedom of thought and religion. To her the impulse to struggle for justice and to use the methods of "moral suasion" in that struggle were identical. When people suggested to her that she drop one cause to concentrate upon another she was perplexed. The Inner Light demanded that she oppose injustice wherever she encountered it and to oppose it always with the weapons of love.

Lucretia grew up with a hot temper and a warm heart; early stories of the capture of slaves and their transportation to the Caribbean upset her and converted her to the antislavery position. Later, at boarding school in New York State, she learned that women teachers were paid less than half the salaries that men commanded and determined that she must do something also about the rights of women.

At eighteen Lucretia married a fellow teacher, James Mott, in Philadelphia, and here she spent the rest of her life. Although she was soon busy with a family of six children, she was independent and active, teaching school for some years after she was married, struggling against the growing conservatism in the Religious Society of Friends, and pushing the movement against the use of the products of slavery, an early form of boycott.

In 1833 when Lucretia was forty, William Lloyd Garrison came to Philadelphia to organize the American Antislavery Society which pledged to "use no carnal weapons for deliverance of those in bondage." The Society was made up of men only, as was the social custom of the day. Four days later Lucretia helped to organize the Philadelphia Female Antislavery Society, the

85

first national active political organization of women, the launching pad for the women's rights movement and the marriage of nonviolence and feminism.

The women of the Antislavery Society circulated petitions, organized meetings, distributed literature and raised money. As they uncovered their own abilities, they began to question the rule that they could not speak before public meetings in which men were present or participate in all-male organizations.

The controversy came to a climax in May of 1838 when the First Annual Convention of Antislavery Women met in Philadelphia in newly dedicated Pennsylvania Hall. A mob formed around the building, angry that Black and white women were meeting together and angrier yet when it was decided to permit women to address a mixed male and female or "promiscuous" audience. On the night of May 17th the mob, with the tacit permission of the mayor and his police, burned the new structure to the ground. They then prepared to attack the nearby home of the Motts, until a friend shouting, "On to the Motts," led them in the wrong direction.

Although Lucretia Mott had been raised as a Quaker pacifist and was an advocate of the boycott, the events of the burning of Pennsylvania Hall began her lifelong practice of personal nonviolence. On the afternoon before the burning of the hall, she had shepherded the women to safety by asking them to walk with linked arms, one Black woman with one white woman, and to ignore provocations.

When the women's convention met in Philadelphia the following year, Lucretia held a series of animated conferences with the mayor who wanted to provide police protection and who urged her to prevent Black and white women from walking together in the streets. Lucretia insisted that the women needed no such advice and were prepared to protect themselves.

Lucretia herself practiced both nonviolence and democracy in her home life. All the Motts, everyone, male or female, had his or her chore so that housework did not fall too heavily on any one member. Her marriage to James was a unique one of mutual support. She frequently urged newly-wed couples to follow her example. Her motto, often repeated at weddings, was "In the true marriage relationship, the independence of husband and wife is equal, their dependence mutual, and their obligations reciprocal."

The antislavery movement at this time was split over the issue of nonresistance as well as the Woman Question. Some conservative abolitionists, particularly clergymen, objected to the inclusion of these "divisive" issues in the antislavery crusade. A series of schisms climaxed in May of 1840 while Lucretia Mott was on the high seas on her way to London to represent the Pennsylvania Antislavery Society at the World Antislavery Convention. She and her followers had succeeded in obtaining equal rights in the Pennsylvania Society eighteen months earlier, and the New England Antislavery Society was also sending women. She was nevertheless denied a seat; the British had not yet faced the Woman Question, and members of the New Organization, formed in the United States as a result of the May schism, were present to spread rumors about her as a heretic.

Lucretia returned to the U.S. to do battle on a whole series of issues. She lectured vigorously against slavery, making a trip into the South, addressing Congressmen, and meeting with the President to express her feelings; and she became involved in an across-the-seas women to women exchange during the crisis between the United States and Great Britain over the Oregon territory, 54-40 Or Fight. She was also struggling within the Society of Friends for equal rights for women in the business of the church, and for a time she had to defend herself against efforts to have her disowned from the Society because of her radical views.

Mott had met Elizabeth Cady Stanton at the London Convention, and the two had pledged to hold a convention for the rights of women. In July of 1848 they had tea in upstate New York and decided to organize that gathering. Hastily called, the Seneca Falls Convention was a success, winning advocates and critics as well. At the Convention, and for many years thereafter, Lucretia was recognized as the guiding spirit of women's rights, giving counsel and direction to the younger women. As the Woman Question became more and more controversial and angry mobs circled the national conventions, she was often called upon to chair the meetings in order to use her unique presence to keep order. She still had her sharp tongue, but she combined it with a warm spirit and was able to use wit and sarcasm delicately to put hecklers into place without offending them.

In her speeches at the women's conventions Lucretia frequently referred to the links between women's rights, nonresistance and peace. She often said it was actually human rights, not just women's rights, that they must try to achieve: "It has sometimes been said that if women were associated with men in their efforts, there would be not as much immorality as now exists in Congress, for instance, and other places. But we ought, I think to claim no more for woman than for man; we ought to put woman on a par with man, not invest her with power, or call for her superiority over her brother. If we do, she is just as likely to become a tyrant as man is, as with Catherine the Second. It is always unsafe to invest man with power over his fellow being. 'Call no man master. . .' is a true doctrine. But be sure that there would be a better rule than now; the elements which belong to woman as such and to man as such, would be beautifully and harmoniously blended. It is to be hoped that there would be less war, injustice, and intolerance in the world than now."

In 1853, when the Woman's Rights Convention was held in New York City, the Rynder gang, a group of toughs, were determined to break up the meeting. They jeered the speakers, including Sojourner Truth and William Lloyd Garrison. During the second night the violence began to escalate. The crowd panicked as the Rynder gang began shoving the woman nearest the door while other gang members seemed to be waiting outside to beat up the leaders. As chair, Lucretia refused to call for police protection. Instead she persuaded the women to leave the hall with dignity, each with an escort. When asked who was to escort her, she calmly tucked her hand under the arm of Captain Rynders himself and said, "This man will see me through." Stunned by this expectation of courtesy, Rynders complied.

During the turbulent 1850's she continued to practice nonviolence, helping with several slave rescues and making a daring trip into the South to preach against slavery. While many of her abolitionist colleagues were beginning to question nonresistance, and to support John Brown and his followers in their idea of encouraging an armed slave revolt, she remained faithful to the superiority of moral weapons. Following the tragic events at Harpers Ferry she wrote movingly of her belief in the power of nonresistance: "For it is not John Brown the soldier we praise, it is John Brown the moral hero; John Brown the noble confessor and patient martyr we honor, and whom we think it proper to honor in his day when men are carried away by the corrupt and proslavery clamour against him." On another occasion she said, " Our weapons were drawn only from the armory of Truth; they were those of faith and love. They were those of moral indignation, strongly expressed against any wrong. Robert Purvis has said that I was 'The most belligerent Non-Resistant he ever saw.' I accept the character he gives me; and I glory in it. I have no idea because I am a Non-Resister of submitting tamely to injustice inflicted either on me or on the slave. I will oppose it with all the moral power with which I am endowed. I am no advocate of passivity. Quakerism as I understand it does not mean quietism. The early Friends were agitators, disturbers of the peace, and were more obnoxious in their day to charges which are now so freely made than we are."

From: DISCOURSE ON WOMAN (1849)

Delivered at the Assembly Buildings, Philadelphia, PA
Being a Full Phonographic Report, Revised By The Author

Lucretia Mott

LIKE SO MANY WOMEN of her time — and of all times — Lucretia Mott (1793-1880) did not write theoretical treatises on nonviolence. She wrote of her vision and the struggle it would take to achieve it. Yet her writings reveal such a complete integration of the concepts of nonviolence with, that vision and struggle that her understanding of nonviolence is clear. In *The Discourse On Woman*, it is seen in her invitation to the women of her day to take power, not by overcoming others but by becoming fully themselves. The *Discourse* is an exquisite cry against the violence of exclusion. It is a teaching on the structural "weapons" that give sexism its force. At the same time it also cries out to woman to awaken to her "highest destinies and holiest hopes," to prepare herself to meet the weapons of sexism with the power of her self, her scripture, and her social story.

IN THE BEGINNING, man and woman were created equal. "Male and female created he them, and blessed them, and called their name Adam." He gave dominion to both over the lower animals, but not to one over the other.

> "Man o'er woman
> He made not lord, such title to himself
> Reserving, human left from human free."

The cause of the subjection of woman to man, was early ascribed to disobedience to the command of God. This would seem to show that she was then regarded as not occupying her true and rightful position in society.

The laws given on Mount Sinai for the government of man and woman were equal, the precepts of Jesus make no distinction. Those who read the Scriptures, and judge for themselves not resting satisfied with the perverted application of the text, do not find the distinction, that theology and ecclesiastical authorities have made, in the condition of the sexes. In the early ages, Miriam and Deborah, conjointly with Aaron and Barak, enlisted themselves on the side which they regarded the right, unitedly going up to their battles, and singing their songs of victory. We regard these with veneration. Deborah judged Israel many years—she went up with Barak against their enemies, with an army of 10,000, assuring him that the honor of the battle should not be to him, but to a woman. Revolting as were the circumstances of their success, the acts of a semi-barbarous people, yet we read with reverence the song of Deborah: "Blessed above woman shall Jael, the wife of Heeber, the Kenite be; blessed shall she be above women in the tent. . . . She put her hand to the nail, and her right hand to the workman's hammer; she smote Sisera through his temples. At her feet he bowed, he fell, he lay down dead." (Judges: 5:24, 26-7) This circumstance, revolting to Christianity, is recognized as an act befitting woman in that day. Deborah, Huldah, and other honorable women, were looked up to and consulted in times of exigency, and their counsel was received. In that Eastern country, with all the customs tending to degrade woman, some were called to fill great and important stations in society. There were also false prophetesses as well as true. The denunciations of Ezekiel were upon those women who would "prophesy out of their own heart, and sew pillows to all armholes," &c.

Coming down to later times, we find Anna, a prophetess of four-score years, in the temple day and night, speaking of Christ to all them who looked for redemption in Jerusalem. Numbers of women were the companions of Jesus,—one going to the men of the city, saying, "Come, see a man who told me all things that ever I did; is not this the Christ?" Another, "Whatsoever he saith unto you, do it." Philip had four daughters who did prophesy. Tryphena and Tryphosa were co-workers with the apostles in their mission, to whom they sent special messages of regard and acknowledgment of their labors in the gospel. A learned Jew, mighty in the Scriptures, was by Priscilla instructed in the way of the Lord more perfectly. Phebe is mentioned as a *servant* of Christ, and commended as such to the brethren. It is worthy of note, that the word *servant*, when applied to Tychicus, is rendered *minister*. *Women* professing godliness, should be translated *preaching*.

The first announcement, on the day of Pentecost, was the fulfillment of ancient prophecy, that God's spirit should be poured out upon *daughters* as well as sons, and they should prophesy. It is important that we be familiar with these facts, because woman has been so long circumscribed in her influence by the perverted application of the text, rendering it improper for her to speak in the assemblies of the people, "to edification, to exhortation, and to comfort."

If these scriptures were read intelligently, we should not so learn Christ, as to exclude any from a position, where they might exert an influence for good to their fellow-beings.   The epistle to the Corinthian church, where the supposed apostolic prohibition of women's preaching is found, contains express directions how woman shall appear, when she prayeth or prophesyeth. Judge then whether this admonition, relative to *speaking* and asking questions, in the excited state of that church, should be regarded as a standing injunction on woman's *preaching,* when that word was not used by the apostle.   Where is the Scripture authority for the advice given to the early church, under peculiar circumstances, being binding on the church of the present day? Ecclesiastical history informs us, that for two or three hundred years, female ministers suffered martyrdom, on company with their brethren.

These things are too much lost sight of.   They should be known, in order that we may be prepared to meet the assertion, so often made, that woman is stepping out of her appropriate sphere, when she shall attempt to instruct public assemblies.   The present time particularly demands such investigation.   It requires also, that "of yourselves ye should judge what is right," that you should know the ground whereon you stand.   This age is notable for its works of mercy and benevolence—for the efforts that are made to reform the inebriate and the degraded, to relieve the oppressed and the suffering.   Women as well as men are interested in these works of justice and mercy.   They are efficient co-workers, their talents are called into profitable exercise, their labors are effective in each department of reform.   The blessing to the merciful, to the peacemaker is equal to man and to woman.   It is greatly to be deplored, now that she is increasingly qualified for usefulness, that any view should be presented, calculated to retard her labors of love.

Why should not woman seek to be a reformer?   If she is to shrink from being such an iconoclast as shall "break the image of man's lower worship," as so long held up to view; if she is to fear to exercise her reason, and her noblest powers, lest she should be thought to "attempt to act the man," and not "acknowledge his supremacy"; if she is to be satisfied with the narrow sphere assigned her by man, nor aspire to a higher, lest she should transcend the bounds of female delicacy; truly it is a mournful prospect for woman.   We would admit all the difference, that our great and beneficent Creator has made, in the relation of man and woman, nor would we seek to disturb this relation; but we deny that the present position of woman, is her true sphere of usefulness; nor will she attain to this sphere, until the disabilities and disadvantages, religious, civil, and social, which impede her progress, are removed out of her way.   These restrictions have enervated her mind and paralyzed her powers.   While man assumes, that the present is the original state designed for woman, that the existing "differences are not arbitrary nor the result of accident," but grounded in nature; she will not make the necessary effort to obtain her just rights, lest it should subject her to the kind of scorn and contemptuous manner in which she has been spoken of. . . .

The question is often asked, "What does woman want, more than she enjoys?   What is she seeking to obtain?   Of what rights is she deprived?   What privileges are withheld from her?" I answer, she asks nothing as favor, but as right, she wants to be acknowledged a moral, responsible being. She is seeking not to be governed by laws, in the making of which she has no voice. She is deprived of almost every right in civil society, and is a cypher in the nation, except in the right of presenting petition. In religious society her disabilities, as already pointed out, have greatly retarded her progress. Her exclusion from the pulpit or ministry—her duties marked out for her by her equal brother man, subject to creeds, rules, and disciplines made for her by him—this is unworthy of her true dignity. In marriage, there is assumed superiority, on the part of the husband, and admitted inferiority, with a promise of obedience, on the part of the wife. This subject calls loudly for examination in order that the wrong may be redressed. Customs suited to darker ages in Eastern countries, are not binding upon enlightened society. The solemn covenant of marriage may be entered into without these lordly assumptions, and humiliating concessions and promises.

I tread upon delicate ground in alluding to the institutions of religious association; but the subject is of so much importance, that all which relates to the position of woman, should be examined, apart from the undue veneration which ancient usage receives.

> "Such dupes are men to custom, and so prone
> To reverence what is ancient, and can plead
> A course of long observance for its use,
> That even servitude, the worst of ills,
> Because delivered down from sire to son,
> Is kept and guarded as a sacred thing."

So with woman. She has so long been subject to the disabilities and restrictions, with which her progress has been embarrassed, that she has become enervated, her mind to some extent paralyzed; and, like those still more degraded by personal bondage, she hugs her chains. Liberty is often presented in its true light, but it is liberty for man.

> "Whose freedom is by suffrance, and at will
> Of a superior—he is never free
> Who lives, and is not weary of a life
> Exposed to manacles, deserves them well."

I would not, however, go so far, either as regards the abject slave or woman; for in both cases they may be so degraded by the crushing influences around them, that they may not be sensible of the blessing of Freedom. Liberty is not less a blessing, because oppression has so long darkened the mind that it cannot appreciate it. . . .

Let woman then go on—not asking as favor, but claiming as right, the removal of all the hindrances to her elevation in the scale of being—let her receive encouragement for the proper cultivation of all her powers, so that she may enter profitably into the active business of life; employing her own hands, in ministering to her necessities, strengthening her physical being by proper exercise, and observance of the laws of health. Let her not be ambitious to display a fair hand, and to promenade the fashionable streets of our city, but rather, coveting earnestly the best gifts, let her strive to occupy such walks in society, as will befit her true dignity in all the relations of life. No fear that she will then transcend the proper limits of female delicacy. True modesty will be as fully preserved, in acting out those important vocations to which she may be called, as in the nursery or at fireside, ministering to man's self-indulgence.

Then in the marriage union, the independence of the husband and wife will be equal, their dependence mutual, and their obligations reciprocal.

In conclusion, let me say, "Credit not the old fashioned absurdity, that woman's is a secondary lot, ministering to the necessities of her lord and master! It is a higher destiny I would award you. If your immortality is as complete, and your gift of mind as capable as ours, of increase and elevation, I would put no wisdom of mine against God's evident allotment. I would charge you to water the undying bud, and give it healthy culture, and open its beauty to the sun—and then you may hope, that when your life is bound up with another, you will go on equally, and in a fellowship that shall pervade every earthly interest."

"AIN'T I A WOMAN?"
(1852)
Sojourner Truth

Sojourner Truth, BORN ISABELLA BAUMFREE (1797-1883), is remembered as the first outstanding Afro-American woman to speak out publicly against slavery. Born into slavery in upstate New York, she learned from her mother, Mau Mau Bett, not to be defeated by the injustice and cruelty of the world. She learned to pray and to be tough and then, at nine years of age, she learned what it meant to be sold into slavery and away from her parents. The sale included a flock of sheep which is said to have increased her marketability. In 1810 she was sold a third and last time, at the age of thirteen, to John J. Dumont for $300. After living under the torment of Dumont's wife for sixteen years, she ran away from the household in 1826 when Dumont broke his promise to free her a year before the state law would require.

During her years as a slave, Isabella Baumfree bore five children to a fellow slave, Thomas. Her son Peter was sold and sent to Alabama despite a state law forbidding such a sale. He became emotionally scarred for life due to his master, who systematically beat and abused him. Finally free, but penniless, Isabella's first act was to confront the local court, an unheard of use of the white legal system by a black woman. With the aid of some Quaker friends, and with remarkable perseverance in the face of numerous obstacles, Isabella finally gained the return of her son.

In 1829, as a domestic servant and evangelist in New York City, she began a fourteen-year-long search for her particular idea of justice among the churches and religious sects of the city. Then, in 1843, as a result of a vision, she left New York with twenty-five cents and a new name, Sojourner Truth, to "travel up and down the land" testifying to God and showing the people their sins. Now forty-six years old, she began a pilgrimage throughout New England until she reached the Utopian community called the Northampton Association. There she became an enthusiastic convert to abolition, working with William Lloyd Garrison, Wendell Phillips, Frederick Douglass and David Ruggles, among others.

In 1850, Sojourner Truth learned of the women's rights movement at a conference in Worcester, Massachusetts. Thus began her long friendship with Lucretia Mott, Elizabeth Cady Stanton, and other movement leaders. Sojourner had become famous for her quick wit, remarkable singing, and pithy genius for illuminating controversial issues in her own unschooled language.

In May, 1852, she attended a women's rights convention in Akron, Ohio. By then a known Abolitionist, she had been traveling through the country preaching and lecturing against slavery. A large, generally unsympathetic crowd filled the Universalist church to hear the speakers. Dressed in her long grey garb and white turban covered by a sunbonnet, Sojourner Truth walked up the aisle and sat on the pulpit steps. Comments such as, "An abolition affair. . . Women's rights and niggers, we told you so!. . . Go it, old darkey!" filled the church. Pleas from those in favor of women's rights to Mrs. Gage, the chairwoman, filled the air also. "Don't let her speak, Mrs. Gage! It will ruin us! Every paper in the land will have our cause mixed up with abolition and niggers. . . ." As speakers both pro and con women's rights followed one after another Sojourner sat and listened. Finally, a clergyman rose and claimed superior rights and privileges for man because of man's superior intellect. Another added men were superior because of the manhood of Christ. "If God had desired the equality of women," he said, "he would have given some token of His will through the birth, life, and death, of the Saviour." Sneers of agreement rose in the air. Sojourner rose to her feet and said:

> "Well, chillun, where there's so much racket there must be something out of kilter. I think that 'twixt the niggers of the South and the women at the North all a-talking 'bout rights, the white men will be in a fix pretty soon.
>
> But what's all this here talking about? That man over there say that women needs to be helped into carriages, and lifted over ditches, and to have the best place everywhere. Nobody ever helps me into carriages, or over mud puddles, or gives me any best place—and ain't I a woman?
>
> Look at me! Look at my arm! (And she bared her right arm to the shoulder), I've plowed and planted and agathered into barns, and no man could head me—and ain't I a woman? I could work as much as a man, and eat as much, when I could get it, and bear the lash as well. And ain't I a woman? They talks about this thing in the head—what's this they call it?
>
> (Someone whispered "Intellect.")
>
> That's it, honey. What's that got to do with women's rights or niggers' rights? If my cup won't hold but a pint and your'n holds a quart, wouldn't ye be mean not to let me have my little half-measure full?
>
> Then that little man in black there, he says women can't have as much rights as men 'cause Christ warn't a woman. Where did your Christ come from?
>
> *Where did your Christ come from?* From God and a woman! Man had nothing to do with it!."

From:
NON-RESISTANCE APPLIED TO THE INTERNAL DEFENSE OF A COMMUNITY (1860)

Charles K. Whipple

IN THIS SELECTION, WHIPPLE continues in the same practical strategizing mode of his essay *Evils of the Revolutionary War* written 21 years earlier. He outlines the qualities and effects of a morally acceptable penal system as opposed to one which values revenge and retribution. In many ways, Whipple is applying the arguments offered by Ballou which emphasised intervention rather than withdrawal from aggressive situations. With Adin Ballou, Whipple draws out the gospel value of overcoming evil with goodness rather than trying to avoid or destroy it—both of which are seen as counter-productive, if not impossible. He calls for a police force without weapons, trained in the methods of "non-injurious force." Whipple partially attributes the rehabilitation of criminals to the community's ability to sustain its concern for them But fundamentally, as with Ballou and other nonresistors, Whipple insists that reducing crime depends on the elimination of its social and economic causes.

NON-RESISTANCE OBJECTS, NOT to government, but to an anti-Christian mode of governing; not to physical force, but to injurious force; not to the restraint of malefactors, but to a system which contents itself with punishing, without attempting, or wishing, to reform them. It objects, in short, only to violations of the Golden Rule.

War is a combination of many evils. It confounds the innocent with the guilty, and practises robbery and murder alike upon both. It wastes human life, depraves morals, destroys the products of industry, and discourages all the labors of peaceful life; but its great, its radical vice is, that it seems to give the sanction of legitimate authority to the practice of overcoming evil with evil. It publishes to the world, as a right and just mode of procedure, that, because our neighbor has done us a wrong, we may and will do him one, and if possible greater. It does not, in the least, recognize the Christian principle of overcoming evil with good.

The practice of judicial murder, commonly called capital punishment, that formal elaboration of lynch law which gives it an outward conformity to the manners and customs of civilized life, is a combination of many evils. By it, the State gives an example to the individual of violating the sacredness of human life; by it the anti-Christian doctrine of retaliation is officially and effectually taught; and by it a human being, often a grossly vicious one, is violently thrust out of the position in which his Maker placed him, has his course of reformatory discipline (as far as this world is concerned) prematurely cut short by unauthorized hands, and is prevented from making that reparation for his offences which subsequent reformation might have disposed him to make. But the radical vice of this custom also is, that it seems to give the sanction of legitimate authority to the practice of overcoming evil with evil.

The penalty of imprisonment for crime, as now practised, involves many evils. It places the criminal in a position, and under influences, which, if he be not already hardened to the utmost extent, are likely to make him worse instead of better. It deprives his wife and children of such care and support as he gave them, without attempting, or caring, to make for their bodies and souls such a provision as their welfare, and the welfare of the State, alike demand; and it entirely disregards the fact that a large proportion of discharged convicts are worse men, more likely to repeat their crimes, and more dangerous to the well-being of society when they come out, than when they went in. But the radical vice of this, as of the other customs I have instanced, is that it seems to give the sanction of legitimate authority to the practice of overcoming evil with evil. It neither recognizes the brotherhood of individual men, nor provides, by other than the coarsest temporary make-shifts, for the welfare of the community.

. . . .In commencing any undertaking, our purpose and effort should be twofold; to do the right thing, and to do it in the right manner. But in the matter of criminal jurisprudence, we have not yet even attempted either of these, if the Christian system is admitted to be our proper guide.[1] The object of our penal system is to protect the community by inflicting such vengeance on the transgressor as shall tend to deter him and others from doing the like again, and in effecting this, we not only directly violate the Christian rule of forgiveness of enemies, but we put the bad man into a position whose tendency is to make him worse. The whole proceeding is as selfish as that of the baker who puts up the price of bread when the people are starving; and like all selfishness, it creates more harm than it cures; it palliates the symptoms, but confirms the disease.

The purpose of a well-ordered community will be the welfare of ALL; of the minority as well as of the majority; and none the less when the minority is a minority of one, and that one the worst person in the community. The greater the need, material or spiritual, the greater the obligation resting upon those who can supply that need; and if there be a poverty so extensive, a wickedness so desperate, as to be invincible save by the efforts and resources of the whole community, the removal of that poverty or wickedness should be considered as the very purpose for which God gave to the community strength and wealth, mind and conscience. . . .

. . . But here an obvious difficulty arises. You can help the weak who wishes for strength, and the poor man who is struggling to rise above poverty, but how are you to help the vicious man who rejoices in his depravity and rejects with scorn your offer of the means of improvement? Is he to be helped against his will, and by infringement of his natural liberty?

I answer, if his violations of the rights of others prove too great for patience to bear, and too obstinate for love and the return of good for evil to overcome, after these methods have been fairly and fully tried, he *is* to be helped against his will, and deprived of that liberty which experience has shown him determined to abuse. But this course must not be the abandonment of patience and love, but a prolongation of them under a new form. The offender's own welfare is no more to be lost sight of in restraining him from the opportunity of theft, or drunkenness, or murder, than the welfare of a child is lost sight of by the wise parent who separates him from the brothers with whom he persists in quarreling. The remedy should not be less suited to the real needs of the offending than of the suffering party; and it should be so obviously dictated by real benevolence, so plainly designed as well as suited, and suited as well as designed, to promote the offender's welfare, that he himself shall see this and be grateful for it, whenever he returns to his right mind.

. . .The Christian system accomplishes the welfare of man more thoroughly than any other; but it attains this end only through an extended process of self-discipline, which first prompts its subjects to strive to do right because it is their duty, and as fast as they reduce this duty to practice, shows them that their truest interest, their highest welfare and happiness, are secured by this very allegiance to duty. But before this self-discipline has been attained, while men are seeking happiness with eyes unenlightened by a sense of the supremacy of duty, the requisitions of Christianity sometimes seem directly opposed to their happiness, and hence are disregarded. The miser, who knows no higher pleasure than hoarding his money, shrinks from the precept, "Give to him that asketh thee," and feels a pang for every penny that he bestows; it is not until he has discerned and begun to practise the duty of liberality, that he finds the enjoyment of giving to be far greater than that of hoarding. . . . In like manner the men and the nations which have hitherto contented themselves with applying to malefactors the system of judicial retaliation commonly and erroneously called "justice," are alarmed at the very idea of no longer taking an eye for an eye, a tooth for a tooth, and life for life, and cry out that the very foundations of society are subverted when it is proposed to treat these malefactors by the Christian method of returning good for evil. They do not see that the adoption of the Christian method of overcoming evil with good, and a voluntary acceptance of the temporary evils of a change of system, would ultimately insure to them not only a far higher measure of security than they now enjoy, but a decrease, in geometrical ratio, in every department of crime....

. . .The system called (for shortness) "Non-Resistance," is not an inert and merely harmless thing, but it proposes to execute the two duties expressed in the Christian precept—"Overcome evil with good." It *purposes* constant aggression against evil and sin, and also to conduct this aggression invariably by right means. It *purposes* to *overcome* evil; it is equally resolute to overcome it *with good*.

---

[1] The words *Christian* and *Christianity* have been so extensively and so variously misused by sectarians, and are so generally misapplied in common speech and writing—the word Christian being used as if it meant merely church-member, and Christianity being held to include those things (and no more) which cause a man to be admitted to church-membership—that I must define the sense in which I use them.

By Christianity, I mean the rule of living which Jesus of Nazareth summed up in these two provisions—TO LOVE GOD WITH THE WHOLE HEART, AND OUR NEIGHBOR AS OURSELVES; defining our neighbor to be any one who is in need that we can relieve, without regard to color, creed, country or condition—illustrating the nature of love by showing that it should be *practical* in its operation, and should include even our enemies—further explaining that this love must have a constant and active energy in reforming the world, *overcoming* its evil, and overcoming it *with good*—and emphatically enjoining that all good shall be cherished and all evil overcome in each man's own heart and life, as well as in the world around him.

This rule of living is what I mean by Christianity; I hold it to be the *right* rule; and I so decide because it is the *best* I can find, or conceive of. It seems to me perfect, adapted in the most thorough manner to secure the progressive improvement, the welfare, and thus the happiness, of the human race. And the life which constantly strives for conformity to it, I call a *Christian life*.

THE PURPOSE OF JESUS: THE KINGDOM OF GOD (1907)

Walter Rauschenbusch

A TALL, DEAF, BEARDED theologian active in the turbulent 1890's, Walter Rauschenbusch (1861-1918) was a thinker whose name is synonomous with the concept of the *Social Gospel*. His era saw a growing awareness in the industrial United States of the evils of unrestrained capitalism, and Rauschenbusch helped mold the movement to define social justice in Christian terms. He became the foremost prophet of the *Social Gospel* as described in such books as *Christianity and the Social Crisis*. Rauschenbusch's thought marked a turning point in redirecting modern Christian theological explorations toward the social consequences of the Gospel rather than the myopic exclusive focus on God and the individual, an approach which had preoccupied Christian theology for decades. He redefined Christian commitment in social terms. His message summoned Christians to build a new social order in which moral law would replace Darwin's law of the jungle. He confronted church leaders with the differences between the Kingdom which Jesus preached and the church which had come to be. Rauschenbusch attributed the major responsibility for evil in the world not to individuals but to the sinful social structures which affected people's lives. In turn, people could act to effect change in these sinful structures. In this selection, Rauschenbusch talks about the the Kingdom of God, and the methods Jesus gave for helping to build that Kingdom in the midst of a sinful world. The following selection is taken from the second chapter of *Christianity and the Social Crisis*.

J ESUS BEGAN HIS PREACHING with the call: "The time is fulfilled; the kingdom of God is now close at hand; repent and believe in the glad news"

(Mark 1:15). The kingdom of God continued to be the center of all his teaching as recorded by the synoptic gospels. His parables, his moral instructions, and his prophetic predictions all bear on that. . . .

. . .The historical study of our own day has made the first thorough attempt to understand this fundamental thought of Jesus in the sense in which he used it, but the results of this investigation are not all completed. There are a hundred critical difficulties in the way of a sure and consistent interpretation that would be acceptable to all investigators. . . . I shall have to set down my own results with only an occasional reference to the difficulties that beset them.

(We know that) the hope of the Jewish people underwent changes in the course of its history. It took a wider and more universal outlook as the political horizon of the people widened. It became more individual in its blessings. It grew more transcendent, more purely future, more apocalyptic and detached from present events, as the people were deprived of their political autonomy and health. Moreover it was variously understood by the different classes and persons that held it. Because this hope was so comprehensive and all-embracing, every man could select and emphasize that aspect which appealed to him. Some thought chiefly of the expulsion of the Roman power with its despotic officials, its tax-extorters, and its hated symbols. Others dwelt on the complete obedience to the Law which would prevail when all the apostates were cast out and all true Israelites gathered to their own. And some quiet religious souls hoped for a great outflow of grace from God and a revival of true piety; as the hymn of Zacharias expresses it: "that we, being delivered from the hand of our enemies, might serve him without fear, in holiness and righteousness before him all the days" (Luke 1: 74-75). But even in this spiritual ideal the deliverance from the national enemies was a condition of a holy life for the nation. Whatever aspect any man emphasized, it was still a national and collective idea. It involved the restoration of Israel as a nation to outward independence, security, and power, such as it had under the Davidic kings. It involved that social justice, prosperity, and happiness for which the Law and the prophets called, and for which the common people always long. It involved that religious purity and holiness of which the nation had always fallen short. And all this was to come in an ideal degree, such as God alone by direct intervention could bestow.

When Jesus used the phrase "the kingdom of God," it inevitably evoked that whole sphere of thought in the minds of his hearers. If he did not mean by it the substance of what they meant by it, it was a mistake to use the term. If he did not mean the consummation of the theocratic hope, but merely an internal blessedness for individuals with the hope of getting to heaven, why did he use the words around which all the collective hopes clustered? In that case it was not only misleading but a dangerous phrase. It unfettered the political hopes of the crowd; it drew down on him the suspicion of the government; it actually led to his death.

Unless we have clear proof to the contrary, we must assume that in the main the words meant the same thing to him and to his audiences. But it is very possible that he seriously modified and corrected the popular conception. That is in fact the process with every great, creative religious mind: the connection with the past is maintained and the old terms are used, but they are set in new connections and filled with new qualities. In the teaching of Jesus we find that he consciously opposed some features of the popular hope and sought to make it truer.

For one thing he would have nothing to do with bloodshed and violence. When the crowds that were on their way to the Passover gathered around him in the solitude on the Eastern shore of the lake and wanted to make him king and march on the capital, he eluded them by sending his inflammable disciples away in the boat, and himself going up among the rocks to pray till the darkness dispersed the crowd (Matthew 14: 22-23). Alliance with the Messianic force-revolution was one of the temptations which he confronted at the outset and repudiated (Matthew 4:8-10); he would not set up God's kingdom by using the devil's means of hatred and blood. With the glorious idealism of faith and love Jesus threw away the sword and advanced on the entrenchments of wrong with hand out-stretched and heart exposed.

He repudiated not only human violence, he even put aside the force which the common hope expected from heaven. He refused to summon the twelve legions of angels either to save his life or to set up the kingdom by slaying the wicked. John the Baptist had expected the activity of the Messiah to begin with the judgment. The fruitless tree would be hewn down; the chaff would be winnowed out and burned; and there was barely time to escape this (Matthew 3:10-12). Jesus felt no call to that sort of Messiahship. He reversed the programme; the judgment would come at the end and not at the beginning. First the blade, then the ear, and then the full corn in the ear, and at the very last the harvest. Only at the end would the tares be collected; only when the net got to shore would the good fish be separated from the useless creatures of the sea. Thus the divine finale of the judgment was relegated to the distance; the only task calling for present action was to sow the seed.

The popular hope was all for a divine catastrophe. The kingdom of God was to come by a beneficient earthquake. Some day it would come like the blaze of a meteor, "with outward observation," and they would say: "Lo, there it is!" (Luke 17: 20-21). We have seen that the prophetic hope had become catastrophic and apocalyptic when the capacity for political self-help was paralyzed. When the nation was pinned down helplessly by the crushing weight of the oppressors, it had to believe in a divine catastrophe that bore no causal relation to human action. The higher spiritual insight of Jesus reverted to the earlier and nobler prophetic view that the future was to grow out of the present by divine help. While they were waiting for the Messianic cataclysm that would bring the kingdom of God ready-made from heaven, he saw it growing up among them. He took his illustrations of its coming from organic life. It was like the seed scattered by the peasant, growing slowly and silently, night and day, by its own germinating force and the food furnished by the earth. The people had the impatience of the uneducated mind which does not see processes, but clamors for results, big, thunderous, miraculous results. Jesus had the scientific insight which comes to most men only by training, but to the elect few by divine gift. He grasped the substance of that law of organic development in nature and history which our own day at last has begun to elaborate systematically. His parables of the sower, the tares, the net, the mustard-seed, and the leaven are all polemical in character. He was seeking to displace the crude and misleading catastrophic conceptions by a saner theory about the coming of the kingdom. This conception of growth demanded not only a finer insight, but a higher faith. It takes more faith to see God in the little beginnings than in the completed results; more faith to say that God is now working than to say that he will some day work. . . .

A. J. MUSTE REMEMBERED

Tom Cornell

THE OLD MAN SAT in a small office in a warren of offices housing a number of under-financed radical peace groups in Lower Manhattan. A. J.'s knees were long from his body and long from the floor. He was tall and bony. There was a cup of luke-warm coffee on his desk and cigarette ash all over him. He hands shook. He was in his early seventies. His face was plain and his expression alert and friendly, his mouth wide and thin-lipped, his nose long and straight and his eyes wide apart under a high and ample forehead with a large mole over the right eye. A. J. dropped what he was doing to talk to me. Later I noticed that he would drop whatever he was doing for any visitor, elicit views, reason together. Each left a little stronger. A. J. was a great man, and he shared his time with anyone.

Abraham Johannes Muste (1885-1967) was born in 1885, in the Netherlands, and brought as a small child by his parents to Michigan where he was reared in a strict conservative Dutch Calvinist immigrant community. After graduating from Union Theological Seminary in New York City, he was ordained to the ministry of the Reformed Church in America in 1909, married, and became pastor of the Fort Washington Collegiate Church in New York City. From 1914 until 1918 he pastored the Central Congregational Church in Newtonville, Massachusetts. He finally resigned his pulpit because he could not bring himself to give what his congregants required. They considered the American dead from World War I as heroic martyrs in an epic struggle between good and evil. A. J. saw their loss as a tragic waste in a war that should never have been fought. They wanted ever more jingoistic panegyrics. A. J. could give them only Jesus of Nazareth, whom he saw ever more clearly as the nonviolent Christ. Drawn to a small group of Quaker pacifists, he helped organize a Boston chapter of the Fellowship of Reconciliation (FOR), an international organization of Religious pacifists formed at the outset of the war by a German Lutheran pastor and an English Quaker. Later, A. J. signed on

105

as pastor to the Providence Friends Meeting.

During the landmark Lawrence textile strike of 1919, a strike denounced as "revolutionary" by the American Federation of Labor because it aimed at organizing all the workers in an industry rather than just workers in a particular trade, A.J. rose from observer to organizer of the strike's Boston Defense Committee. He then became executive secretary of the strike committee itself.

A.J. resigned his post with the Quaker Meeting to devote his energies to organizing, and never had another congregation, not in the usual sense. But he had a collar and a gift for oratory, and his charismatic leadership was more and more pronounced. As he gathered support for the Massachusetts strikers among textile workers in the Middle Atlantic states a new union formed around him, the Amalgamated Textile Workers of America. A.J. was elected its executive secretary.

Radicals saw the Lawrence strike as pivotal to the future of organizing efforts in the reactionary postwar period, so support came in from leading figures of the day, including Elizabeth Gurley Flynn and Carlo Tresca, making it all the more necessary for the power structure of his day to crush the strike. Despite provocations to violence by company spies and unrestrained police brutality, and in the face of all odds, the strike succeeded just as it was about to collapse. It was the first example of organized, consciously nonviolent labor action led and assisted by members of the religious community as well as the radical Left. A.J. was now in his mid-thirties and suddenly a labor leader, respected by the younger, more progressive elements of the labor movement for his vision, and by the others as a winner. His own union, the Amalgamated Textile Workers, languished, however, and collapsed soon after he left its leadership to join the faculty of Brookwood Labor College in Katonah, New York, in 1921.

The Mustes spent twelve years at Brookwood. A.J. was soon director. The AFL and its member unions funded the training of labor leaders at Katonah, many rising to prominence, like Walter and Victor Ruether of the United Auto Workers. As a leader and a teacher A.J. had proven himself a pragmatist, cutting a deal when necessary to avoid futile confrontation, but he saw the larger picture too, and he judged by moral standards. He concluded that there were irremedial flaws in a system that shut workers out of decisions directly affecting their lives and pitted them against each other. At Brookwood A.J. had time to study and travel to labor hot-spots around the U.S. His heart was moved by the suffering he witnessed, in the unorganized textile mills of the South, for example, where children barely into their teens spat out their lungs in twelve hour shifts of grueling labor in sub-human conditions. Eventually he justified revolutionary violence, if it came to that, to right wrongs. Since he could not square Christian discipleship with violence, he left the church for revolutionary Marxism-Leninism and the comradeship of the followers of Leon Trotsky. Brookwood followed Muste's leftward drift. The AFL didn't and withdrew financial support, and so did most of its affiliates. Brookwood closed in 1937.

During his Trotskyist period A.J. led his own political party, the American Workers Party, known as the Musteites. He may not have thought of himself as a Christian, but Calvinism was in his bone-marrow, with an admixture of Quaker optimism. He never doubted that human nature was capable of transcending self-interest and expediency. He rejected the thesis of Reinhold Niehbur, in *Moral Man, Immoral Society*, that nations can not and ought not to try to act on the same moral principles as individuals, a bedrock principle of the school of so-called "Christian realism" of the neo-Calvanists preparing for World War II.

James P. Cannon, principal historian of the Trotskyist movements in the U.S., reported that Trotsky had great hopes that A.J. would develop, into a "true Bolshevik," and that he might be the last and best hope for an American communist revolution, but Trotsky feared the "terrible flaw" in Muste's background: the religious influence upon his formative years. A.J. and Anna, his wife, went to Norway in 1936, to confer with Trotsky himself. For the first time, A.J. failed to send near-daily communications to his associates at home, but it can be surmised that the topic of his talks with Trotsky over several days was the perennial question, *what is to be done?* Trotsky and his associates were consumed with the betrayal of the Russian revolution by Stalin and with their vision of an alternate Bolshevik International. A.J. focused rather on the gathering clouds of World War II. Averting the war, if possible, had to take top priority. If that was impossible, then mitigating the horrors to come and saving some remnant of the nonviolence at the core of true religion was critical, as Muste understood it. His long silence was broken with a sixteen page single-spaced letter to his Trotskyite comrades, which also broke his political and organizational bond with them. Trotsky's fear was realized; A.J.'s "fatal flaw" asserted itself. A.J. turned back to Christianity and the church. Suddenly, and for the first time in many years, A.J. was a leader with no following, by his own doing.   The Fellowship of Reconciliation, then the principal inter-denominational organization of religious pacifists, created a position for him, industrial secretary. On the eve of World War II he was named executive secretary. He retired as secretary emeritus in 1953.

Popular opposition to U.S. entry into World War II collapsed utterly after the attack on Pearl Harbor, December 7, 1941. In articles, pamphlets and speeches across the country, to dwindling audiences, A.J. attempted to clarify the meaning of Christian discipleship in regard to war as including refusal to participate.   He joined leaders of the "historic peace churches," the Mennonites, Brethren and Quakers, to press the government for the rights of conscientious objectors, and helped establish the Civilian Public Service program. This allowed conscientious objectors recognized by the Selective Service System to serve the public good as civilians under civilian authority in camps established and maintained by their denominations. The work and the locations of the camps were assigned by the government. The men were not compensated for their labor, which turned out to be "make-work" of little or no value, in camps so far removed from population centers that the men felt quarantined; conscientious objectors became prisoners in concentration camps for which their families and churches were forced to pay. It was one of A.J's few mistakes. Many men walked out of the camps, preferring a real prison to a phoney one. They felt resentment toward the peace leadership that collaborated with the state in establishing and running the camps. A.J. and the FOR withdrew from the program toward the end of the war.

Meanwhile, the prisons were serving as graduate schools of nonviolence. Rare men, otherwise scattered across the country, were concentrated; men otherwise preoccupied with work and family suddenly had little else but time and each other. Together they studied nonviolence theory and practice, and America's most dangerous social problem, racism. They concluded that the legal structures of racial segregation had to be dismantled, and that nonviolent direct action could find a testing ground in the struggle.

Two years after the war, in 1947, FOR and the Congress of Racial Equality (CORE) sponsored the first Freedom Ride, a bus trip through the upper South with racially integrated teams consisting almost entirely of graduates of the federal prison system, among them Igal Roodenko, Jim Peck, Conrad Lynn, George Houser, Wally Nelson, Bayard Rustin and David Dellinger. A federal court had banned racial segregation on busses in interstate travel. The Freedom Riders were to test the effectiveness of the court order. They travelled both Greyhound and Trailways, sitting together, black and white, up front, where local and state laws forced blacks to sit in the rear. Many of the Riders did thirty days on segregated chain gangs in North Carolina! It took a few more years before the civil rights movement gained momentum, but the pattern of nonviolent direct action was established.

The Committee for Nonviolent Action (CNVA) was formed at about the same time in the late 50's, and some consider its projects A.J.'s greatest legacy. In 1959, A.J. and fourteen others from CNVA climbed over the fence at Meade Missile Base, the nerve center of the Strategic Air Command (SAC) near Omaha, Nebraska designed to coordinate all-out atomic warfare against the Soviet Union. Each was immediately arrested. The trial brought six month suspended sentences. Repeat "offenders" served their time. A period fertile in direct action began. It was based on a rationale for phased unilateral disarmament, and included the San Francisco to Moscow peace walk, and the Polaris Actions in Groton-New London, Connecticut. Classic Gandhian nonviolence was not only the discipline but the heart of the movement. Authorities were notified in advance of every project and every action. All plans were made by participants themselves with the Committee and its staff by consensus; all meetings were open, so that even if FBI agents wanted to attend they might. Violence was absolutely excluded, in word, manner or deed, including injury to persons or to property. There was never any attempt to avoid prosecution or legal penalties. "Opponents" were always afforded a reasonable and honorable alternative for themselves in any conflict situation so that they might retain their dignity and some form of reconciliation be reached. These elements were seen as essential to nonviolent action, flowing from the conviction that a just and peaceful society can not be brought into being by methods that are other than just and peaceful. "There is no way to peace, peace is the way," A.J. was fond of saying.

The war in Southeast Asia consumed the disarmament movement as well as so much else. By 1965 it was clear to peace activists that the escalating U.S. involvement had to take top priority, and so it did for the next decade. That August an umbrella leadership pulled together by A.J. brought 15,000 people to the Capitol, where the largest mass arrest since the 30's was made. The first draft card burnings also took place that year. Some members of the House and Senate were enraged and introduced a bill to make destruction of draft cards a felony punishable by five years imprisonment. The bill was passed without debate and signed by President Lyndon Johnson. A.J. understood this as an attempt to stifle dissent and to intimidate the young from protest and resistance to the war and concluded that this attempted repression had to be countered. He gladly agreed to join Dorothy Day and the Catholic Worker movement in support of five of us who burned our draft cards publicly in Union Square, New York City. The next few years saw the growth of the most effective anti-war movement in U.S. history built around mass nonviolent action in the streets and organized draft resistance. A.J. had laid the groundwork for both.

In 1966 A.J. recognized that the U.S. administration would not be moved from its disastrous course in Vietnam without mass protest in the streets. It would be necessary to form a coalition of all elements opposed to the war. That meant an opening to the Left, as well as to labor, academic liberals and religious activists. That September in a Howard Johnson's motel in Cleveland, Ohio, A.J. appealed to a gathering of leaders of these circles, including representatives of the Communist Party USA and the Socialist Workers Party (Trotskyites), for a coalition to be based on the simple demand of U.S. withdrawal from the war. The Mobilization against the War in Vietnam ("the Mobe") was born. Operating principles would be non-exclusion and at least tactical nonviolence. By 1969, after organizing ever larger demonstrations, the Mobe, with the Student Moratorium group, brought out the largest public demonstration in U.S. history in Washington. Later, Lyndon Johnson would admit that he was considering the use of nuclear weapons to end the frustration of U.S. military designs in Vietnam, but that his hand was stayed by the masses of people outside his gate on Pennsylvania Avenue. Richard Nixon admitted the same. Only A.J. had the skills to bring such a politically diverse coalition together. He was the only figure in the country who had the respect and the trust of the liberal academic, labor, religious, New and Old Left communities.

On Sunday, February 12, 1967, we were scheduled for brunch at A.J.'s with Robert and Joyce Gilmore, and Dom Helder Camara, Archbishop of Recife in Northeast Brazil, the voice of the poor in Latin America. I was to bring Dorothy Day. What a conversation that would have been! Early Saturday evening Robert Gilmore called me to say that A.J. had died that afternoon of an aneurysm, sick only one day.

A.J. had come to the conclusion that the U.S. was in a pre-revolutionary condition. If violent revolution came, A.J. believed that the nonviolent movement had to be present to the process and involved, to moderate the evils that would come out of violence and to point the way to reconciliation. Events proved the status quo more resilient than that. But events also proved that A.J. was correct in mobilizing a mass nonviolent movement as an expression of democracy to end an unpopular war.

If we are to survive in any measure of dignity we will have to invent the future. A study of A.J.'s career, the principles that guided him and the ways he found to give them life, is a rich source toward that goal.

Tom Cornell joined the Catholic Worker movement in 1953, served as managing editor of *The Catholic Worker* from 1962-1964, and has served as secretary of the Catholic Peace Fellowship since 1965. Tom, Monica Ribar Cornell and their son Tom operate two soup kitchens in Waterbury, Conn. for the local council of churches and live at Guadalupe House, a Catholic Worker community. Daughter Deirdre organizes on race and peace issues at Smith College, Northampton, Mass.

PACIFISM AND CLASS WAR (1928)

A. J. Muste

A. J. MUSTE WROTE *the following essay before his temporary break* with Christianity and affiliation with the Trotskyites. It was during the period of his life which focused most intensely on labor issues. The essay explores commonly held assumptions about the sources of violence in both class and labor struggles. Eight years after writing this essay, Muste would be involved in the Goodyear strike which popularized the sit-in tactic in labor struggles throughout the country. During the winter of 1936, when Goodyear refused to enter into collective bargaining with the union, the tactic was implemented and greatly minimized the violence that management could use against the workers. If the workers remained in the factories, near their machines, management could not risk a physical attack which might lead to the destruction of their machinery.

IT IS EXPECTED PERHAPS that an article dealing with pacifism in relation to class war should consist of an exhortation to labor organizations and radicals to eschew violent methods in the pursuit of their ends, together with an exposition of the use of pacifist methods in labor disputes and social revolutions. If there is such an expectation, this article will be in large measure disappointing. Chiefly, because in my opinion much more time must be spent than has yet been given to clearing away some exceedingly mischievous misconceptions before we can think fruitfully about concrete non-violent methods of social change; and because there are very, very few individuals in the world, including the pacifist groups and churches, who are in a moral position to preach non-resistance to the labor or radical movement.

Practically all our thinking about pacifism in connection with class war starts out at the wrong point. The question raised is how the oppressed, in struggling for freedom and the good life, may be dissuaded from employing

111

"the revolutionary method of violence" and won over to "the peaceful process of evolution." Two erroneous assumptions are concealed in the question put that way. The first is that the oppressed, the radicals, are the ones who are creating the disturbance. To the leaders of Jesus' day, Pharisees, Sadducees, Roman governor, it was Jesus who was upsetting the people, turning the world upside down. In the same way, we speak of the Kuomintang "making a revolution" in China today, seldom by any chance of the Most Christian Powers having made the revolution by almost a hundred years of trickery, oppression, and inhumanity. Similarly, society may permit an utterly impossible situation to develop in an industry like coal, but the workers who finally in desperation put down tools and fold their arms, they are "the strikers," the cause of the breach of the peace. We need to get our thinking focused and to see the rulers of Jewry and Rome, not Jesus; the Powers, not the Chinese Nationalists; selfish employers or a negligent society—not striking workers—as the cause of disturbance in the social order.

A second assumption underlying much of our thinking is that the violence is solely or chiefly committed by the rebels against oppression, and that this violence constitutes the heart of our problem. However, the basic fact is that the economic, social, political order in which we live was built up largely by violence, is now being extended by violence, and is maintained only by violence. A slight knowledge of history, a glimpse at the armies and navies of the Most Christian Powers, at our police and constabulary, at the militaristic fashion in which practically every attempt of workers to organize is greeted, in Nicaragua or China, will suffice to make the point clear to an unbiased mind.

The foremost task, therefore, of the pacifist in connection with class war is to denounce the violence on which the present system is based, and all the evil—material and spiritual—this entails for the masses of men throughout the world; and to exhort all rulers in social, political, industrial life, all who occupy places of privilege, all who are the beneficiaries of the present state of things, to relinquish every attempt to hold on to wealth, position and power by force, to give up the instruments of violence on which they annually spend billions of wealth produced by the sweat and anguish of the toilers. So long as we are not dealing honestly and adequately with this ninety percent of our problem, there is something ludicrous, and perhaps hypocritical, about our concern over the ten percent of violence employed by the rebels against oppression. Can we win the rulers of earth to peaceful methods?

The psychological basis for the use of nonviolent methods is the simple rule that like produces like, kindness provokes kindness, as surely as injustice produces resentment and evil. It is sometimes forgotten by those whose pacifism is a spurious, namby-pamby thing that if one Biblical statement of this rule is "Do good to them that hate you" (an exhortation presumably intended for the capitalist as well as for the laborer), another statement of the same rule is, "They that sow the wind shall reap the whirlwind." You get from the universe what you give, with interest! What if men build a system on violence and injustice, on not doing good to those who hate them nor even to those who meekly obey and toil for them? And persist in this course through centuries of Christian history? And if, then, the oppressed raise the chant:

> Ye who sowed the wind of sorrow,
> Now the whirlwind you must dare,
> As ye face upon the morrow,
> The advancing Proletaire!

In such a day, the pacifist is presumably not absolved from preaching to the rebels that they also shall reap what they sow; but assuredly not in such wise as to leave the oppressors safely entrenched in their position, not at the cost of preaching to them in all sternness that "the judgments of the Lord are true and righteous altogether."

As we are stayed from preaching nonviolence to the underdog, unless and until we have dealt adequately with the dog who is chewing him up, so also are all those who would support a country in war against another country stayed from preaching nonviolence in principle to labor or to radical movements. Much could be said on this point, but it is perhaps unnecessary to dwell on it here. Suffice it to observe in passing that, to one who has had any intimate connection with labor, the flutter occasioned in certain breasts by the occasional violence in connection with strikes seems utterly ridiculous, and will continue to seem so until the possessors of these fluttering breasts have sacrificed a great deal more than they already have in order to banish from the earth the horrible monster of international war.

We are not, to pursue the matter a little further, in a moral position to advocate nonviolent methods to labor while we continue to be beneficiaries of the existing order. They who profit by violence, though it be indirectly, unwillingly and only in a small measure, will always be under suspicion, and rightly so, of seeking to protect their profits, of being selfishly motivated, if they address pious exhortations to those who suffer by that violence.

Nor can anyone really with good conscience advocate abstention from violence to the masses of labor in revolt, unless he is himself identified in spirit with labor and helping it with all his might to achieve its rights and to realize its ideals. In a world built on violence, one must be a revolutionary before one can be a pacifist; in such a world a non-revolutionary pacifist is a contradiction in terms, a monstrosity. During the war, no absolute pacifist in America would have felt justified in exhorting Germany to lay down its arms while saying and doing nothing about America's belligerent activities. We should have recognized instantly the moral absurdity, the implied hypocrisy of such a position. Our duty was to win our own "side" to a "more excellent way." It is a sign of ignorance and lack of realism in our pacifist groups and churches that so many fail to recognize clearly and instantly the same point with regard to the practice of pacifism in social and labor struggles.

Things being as they are, it is fairly certain that if a group of workers goes on strike for better conditions, other methods having failed, they will commit some acts of violence and coercion; some evil passions will be aroused in their breasts. Shall the pacifist who has identified himself with labor's cause therefore seek to dissuade the workers from going on strike? (I am of course confining myself here to a question of principle, leaving out of account questions of the expediency of a strike in given conditions.) My own answer is an emphatic negative, because I am convinced that in these cases the alternative of submission is by far the greater evil. Appearances are deceiving here, and the human heart is deceitful. There is a certain indolence in us, a wish not to be disturbed, which tempts us to think that when things are quiet all is well. Subconsciously, we tend to give the preference to "social peace," though it be only apparent, because our lives and possessions seem then secure. Actually, human beings acquiesce too easily in evil conditions; they rebel far too little and too seldom. There is nothing noble about acquiescence in a cramped life or mere submission to superior force. There is as vast a spiritual difference between such submission of the masses and the glad acceptance of pain by the saint, as there is between the sodden poverty of the urban or rural slum and the voluntary poverty of St. Francis "that walks with God upon the Umbrian hills." No one who has ever inwardly experienced the spiritual exaltation and the intense brotherhood created by a strike, on the one hand, and the sullen submission of hopeless poverty or the dull contentment or "respectability" of those who are too fat and lazy to struggle for freedom, on the other hand, will hesitate for a moment to choose the former, though it involves a measure of violence.

Here it may be well to point out that, as a matter of fact, the amount of violence on the part of workers on strike is usually grossly exaggerated; and that, on the other hand, practically every great strike furnishes inspiring examples of non-resistance under cruel provocation and victory by "soul force" alone—victory through patient endurance of evil and sacrifice, even unto death, for spiritual ends. I have witnessed these things repeatedly. More than once, I have exhorted masses of strikers to fold their arms, not to strike back, to smile at those who beat them and trample them under horses' feet, and the strikers' response has been instantaneous, unreserved, exalted. I have also appealed to police heads to call off violence-provoking extra forces and to employees to discharge labor spies, and have been laughed at for my pains.

Much of what has already been said bears upon the special problem of the Communist, with his frank espousal of terrorism, his conviction that no great and salutary social change can be accomplished without violence and that the workers must therefore be prepared for armed revolt. Our whole focus on this problem also is wrong unless we get it clear that violence inheres first in the system against which the Communist revolts; that they who suffer from social revolt in the main reap what, by positive evildoing or indifference, they have sown; that practically every great revolution begins peacefully and might proceed so, to all appearances, but for the development of violent counter-revolution; that the degree of terrorism employed in such an upheaval as the French or Russian revolution is always directly proportionate to the pressure of foreign attack; that in general the amount of "red" terrorism in human history is a bagatelle compared to the "white" terrorism of reactionaries. The question is pertinent as to whether the "Lord's will" is done by the servant who talks about terrorism and practices very little, or by the servant who talks about law and order and practices a vast deal of terrorism. . . .

. . . All this does not mean that the labor movement is not confronted with a serious problem as to the means to which it will resort to advance its aims. Many times employers, on the one hand, and workers, on the other hand, are approached by the most crude and self-defeating psychological methods. Money is spent on gangsters, for example, that might well net a thousand fold better return if devoted to the education of workers and of the public. Violence begets violence by whomever it is used. War is a dirty business and entails the use of degrading means, whoever wages it.

The labor movement in New York City has recently given a striking illustration of the law, upon which the pacifist so often insists, that the means one uses inevitably incorporate themselves into his ends and, if evil, will defeat him. Some years ago, employers in the garment trades resorted to the practice of employing armed gangsters to attack peaceful picketers. It became impossible to send men and women on the picket line to meet such brutal attacks, so the union also resorted to hiring gangsters. Once you started the practice, you had to hire gangsters in every strike, of course. Thus a group of gangsters came to be a permanent part of the union machinery. Next, it was easy for officers who had employed the gangsters in strikes to use these same gangsters, who were on the pay roll anyway, in union elections to insure continued tenure to the "machine." The next step in the "descent to Avernus" was for the gangsters on whom the administration depended for its tenure of office to make themselves the administration—the union "machine." In the meantime, the union gangsters naturally came to an agreement with those hired by the employer, so that both sides were paying out large sums of money to gangsters no longer doing any decisive work in strikes or lockouts; both sides had likewise to pay graft to the police so that they would not interfere with their private armies; and the rank and file of union members, having come to look to gangsters to do the real picketing, no longer had the desire, courage, or morale to picket peacefully, appeal to strike-breakers to join them, and so on. The whole process, working itself out so fatally, and from the aesthetic viewpoint so beautifully, had not a little to do with the deterioration undergone by these unions in which the bitter left-right factional strife was rather a symptom than a cause.

Those who can bring themselves to renounce wealth, position and power accruing from a social system based on violence and putting a premium on acquisitiveness, and to identify themselves in some real fashion with the struggle of the masses toward the light, may help in a measure—more, doubtless, by life than by words—to devise a more excellent way, a technique of social progress less crude, brutal, costly and slow than mankind has yet evolved.

AN ACTIVE GLOWING FORCE: THE NONVIOLENCE OF DOROTHY DAY

Kathleen De Sutter Jordan

"AREN'T WE DECEIVING OURSELVES? . . . What are we accomplishing anyway for them (those coming in on the souplines, or in need of clothing or shelter), or for the world or for the common good? Are these people being 'rehabilitated'. . .?" According to Dorothy Day (1897-1980), in an April 1964 appeal for funds written in *The Catholic Worker*, these were some of the questions most frequently asked by readers and visitors alike. But the majority, Dorothy continued, would always ask the same question: "How can you see Christ in people?"

If in the Gandhian sense nonviolence, or satyagraha, means literally a "holding on to Truth," perhaps the nonviolence practiced by Dorothy Day can be best understood as flowing out of her experience of being "held onto" by Truth. For Dorothy it was precisely the love of God and the grace to "see Christ in people" that inspired her radical Christian pacifism and life of nonviolence.

A convert to Catholicism, Dorothy Day was born in Brooklyn, New York, shortly before the turn of the century. Her father was a newspaper reporter who worked on various papers across the country. Dorothy, as well as her three brothers, would follow in his footsteps. Her youth was spent searching, at times with a degree of desperation, for some sense of purpose as well as for companionship. In 1919 she had an abortion in a futile attempt to salvage a love affair. Formal religion, for the most part experienced as "tepid," had little substance to offer: "I did not see anyone taking off his coat and giving it to the poor. I didn't see anyone having a banquet and calling in the lame, the halt

117

and the blind." It was rather the fervor and vision of the Socialists and Marxists, the heroic struggles taking place in the American labor movement, her first arrest and jail sentence with the Suffragettes in 1917, and the searing literary portraits drawn by Upton Sinclair and Dostoevski, that focused the lens through which Dorothy viewed the world in her teens and twenties. With a touch of irony, she admitted years later to having completely failed even to notice quotes from *Rerum Novarum,* the great social encyclical of Pope Leo XIII, appearing in the pages of the socialist magazine, *The Masses,* at the very time she was on its editorial staff.

From her early youth on, however, Dorothy also possessed a disposition of openness toward the Holy and a capacity to take genuine delight in its manifestations, grand and subtle alike. It was only fitting, she noted later, that it would be during a period of great "natural happiness," culminating in the birth of her only child, that she finally found herself drawn to conversion. Dorothy was received into the Catholic Church in December 1927. But it would take another six years before she perceived an answer to her plea: "Where were the Catholics?. . . Where were the saints trying to change the social order, not just to minister to the slaves but to do away with slavery?"

The answer arrived, initially rather well-disguised, in the person of Peter Maurin. An itinerant French philosopher, Peter had spent years of study and reflection developing a synthesis of how traditional Catholicism ("so old it looked like new") might address the chaos and social injustices rampant in the early twentieth century. Peter proposed a three-point program: round table discussions for the clarification of thought; houses of hospitality where Christ could be met and served daily through the practice of the Works of Mercy; and farming communes, to provide land and worthwhile work for the unemployed. In Dorothy Day, Peter Maurin found not only a highly receptive audience, but a practical-minded woman who was also a journalist. Together they launched the Catholic Worker Movement—to "make known the expressed and implied teachings of Christ"—with the first issue of *The Catholic Worker* distributed on May 1, 1933. It was a movement that Dorothy herself would lead for almost fifty years, and a movement that has continued to the present; there are currently more than seventy-five Catholic Worker communities throughout the country.

From its inception the Catholic Worker took an explicitly pacifist position in regard to war and the use of force—"We had been pacifist in class war, race war, in the Ethiopian war, in the Spanish Civil war, all through World War II, as we are now during the Korean war," Dorothy wrote in 1952—a position maintained through the Vietnam war years and up through the present.

While this position of radical Christian pacifism would be espoused with a remarkable, prophetic clarity and fidelity, it was also to be "deeply, costingly realized." For example, in taking a stand critical of all warring parties during the Spanish Civil War, Dorothy wrote, "We got it from both sides." The young newspaper's monthly circulation of well over 150,000 dropped by nearly

100,000 by the war's end.

A much harsher test came with World War II when the position of *The Catholic Worker* was certainly not neutral; Catholic Workers had been protesting the rise of Nazism and anti-Semitism since 1935. Yet, after the U.S. entered the war, *The Catholic Worker* continued its pacifist stand: "What shall we say? . . . What shall we print? We will print the words of Christ who is with us always, even to the end of the world. 'Love your enemies, do good to those who hate you, and pray for those who persecute and calumniate you.'" Pledging to "try to be peacemakers," to pray daily, hourly, for an end to the war, readers were encouraged to combine prayer with action; with almsgiving and penance, as well as continuing to perform the Corporal and Spiritual Works of Mercy.

The pacifism of Dorothy Day and the Catholic Worker movement was anything but passive. "We are not talking of passive resistance," Dorothy wrote in 1938. On the contrary, it was based on Christ's revolutionary commandment (not merely a counsel, or recommendation, Dorothy pointed out) that His followers "Love one another as I have loved you." Its manifesto was the Sermon on the Mount; its weapons, the weapons of the Spirit: prayer, fasting, voluntary poverty, refusing to return evil for evil. "Love and prayer are not passive," Dorothy wrote, "but a most active glowing force."

Nor was it a type of quietism or retreat from the world that the Catholic Worker was promoting. Engagement with the joys and sorrows of the world is precisely where Christ is to be found. When Peter Maurin had emphasized the necessity of practicing the Works of Mercy, Dorothy said, he meant all of them. The Corporal Works of Mercy include: To feed the hungry, to give drink to the thirsty, to clothe the naked, to ransom the captive, to harbor the harborless, to visit the sick, to bury the dead. The Spiritual Works of Mercy are: to admonish the sinner, to instruct the ignorant, to counsel the doubtful, to comfort the sorrowful, to bear wrongs patiently, to forgive all injuries, to pray for the living and the dead.

From the first issue, *The Catholic Worker* announced a commitment to work toward "a reconstruction of the social order," based on the teachings of the Gospels and the papal social encyclicals. Peter Maurin was Dorothy's instructor in these matters. At the time of her conversion, she had anguished over the scandal of the Church in respect to the social order: "Plenty of charity but too little justice." Now there was to be launched a newspaper calling attention to the fact that "the Catholic Church has a social program." The Catholic Church, particularly in the thought of Thomas Aquinas, had traditionally emphasized that justice is the basis of a proper social order, and that genuine and lasting peace can only be established in the context of such a social order. That is why from the start *The Catholic Worker* was involved in the struggles of the labor movement, from support of the fledgling seamen and auto workers' unions in the 1930's (the workers raised Dorothy up through a window during the famous Flint strike), to support of the farm workers and woodcutters unions in the later years of Dorothy's life (her final imprisonment was with Cesar Chavez's United Farm Workers union in 1973). The Catholic Worker helped found the Association of Catholic Trade Unionists in 1937 and picketed the Archdiocese of New York in 1949 in support of its striking gravediggers union.

When I think back about Dorothy now, words from her own biography of Therese of Lisieux come to mind: "What was there about her to make such an appeal?. . . What did she do?. . . What stands out in her life?"

Dorothy's own approach to reconstructing the social order and attempting to make visible the peace of Christ was both personal and direct. There was no distinction made between speaking at a peace rally, visiting a dying friend, going to jail to protest air raid drills, or saying evening prayers; not between walking a picket line with migrant farmworkers, fasting during Vatican II in support of a strong peace statement, working for integration in the South, or washing someone's feet. "We find they (the Works of Mercy) all go together," Dorothy reflected.

If she was prophetic in this regard, Dorothy noted wryly that it all just "came about" from attending to what needed to be done. It was the quality of her attention, closely akin to that described by Simone Weil as the very essence of love of God and love of neighbor alike, that enabled Dorothy to "see Christ in people," whether it be an "enemy" nation or a suffering neighbor. It is a reverence, a way of being, we are all called to, and capable of. "We each have our own vocation," Dorothy wrote, "the thing to do is to answer the call."

Besides this quality of attention, what made such an appeal about Dorothy was her own remarkable beauty, and the fact that she encouraged others to "feast on beauty," on God in all God's manifestations. Shortly after I was married I asked Dorothy, with an earnest seriousness, how people can combine voluntary poverty and family life. "The world will be saved by beauty," she reminded me; and that was the heart of the whole mystery.

Her own tastes, while refined, were quite simple. Books were staples, especially Tolstoy and Dostoevski, Dickens and a smattering of good mysteries. She loved music, particularly opera, and would listen to her radio in utter rapture on Saturday afternoons when the Metropolitan Opera was broadcast. Unfailingly grateful for the plainest of meals, she would also comment on the beauty of the very common "golden wheat" patterned plate on which it had been served.

You always knew when Dorothy was in a room. Her presence, modest and deeply courteous, was nonetheless commanding—like the heavy shoes she wore, unassuming but substantial. Reserved with an Anglo-Saxon type of reticence, she loved giving and receiving gifts, often quoting St. Ignatius's dictum that "love is an exchange of gifts." Her humor was delightful, reflecting an inherent sense of irony and a keen eye for incongruity; it came often and unexpectedly. I sensed Dorothy coming to terms with her own aging, for example, when she commented on one occasion that, while she envied others who were going to sign up for an upcoming sit-in protesting arms development, she would probably have been unable to recall for the arresting officer why she had decided to take part in the demonstration.

What Dorothy did, in word and deed, was give us "at least a glimpse of eternity" (Lubac).[1] She reminded us over and over again that we are *all* called to be saints—to put on Christ and joyfully "complete the sufferings of Christ." When we pray in the Psalm, "O Lord, deliver us from fear of our enemies," it is not from our enemy that we are begging to be delivered, Dorothy pointed out, but from our own *fear.*

To "see Christ in other people" requires an act of faith ("an overwhelming act of faith," Dorothy put it). But "we have seen His hands and His feet in the poor around us. He has shown himself to us in them. We start by loving them for Him, and we soon love them for themselves, each a most unique person, most special!" Such is the heart of Dorothy Day's nonviolence, and her invitation to us.

Kathleen De Sutter Jordan was an associate editor of *The Catholic Worker* newspaper from 1969 to 1975, and a long time friend of Dorothy Day. She is an R.N., and for the last several years of Dorothy's life, lived across the path from her house on the beach at Staten Island, New York.

---

[1]The full quote by Lubac, as it appears in an article by Dorothy Day, "Here and Now," in the book *The Third Hour*, published in 1949, is: "It is not the proper duty of Christianity to form leaders — that is, builders of the temporal, although a legion of Christian leaders is infinitely desirable. Christianity must generate saints — that is, witnesses to the eternal. The efficacy of the saint is not that of the leader. The saint does not have to bring about temporal achievements; he is one who succeeds in giving us at least a glimpse of eternity despite the thick opacity of time." This quote, a favorite of Dorothy's, also appears in Robert Ellsberg's *By Little and By Little*, 1983: Alfred A. Knopf, New York.

CATHOLIC WORKER
POSITIONS

According to workers at Mary House, the Catholic Worker House in New York's Lower East Side, where Dorothy lived when in the city, the wording of the Catholic Worker Positions has been in evolution since the 30's. The following version appeared in The Catholic Worker in the 60's. We include it here, although chronologically out of order, to accompany the article on Dorothy Day. It was Dorothy's spirit and insights which guided the evolution of these Positions and which still guides the Catholic Worker movement today as it continues its works of mercy and justice.

THE GENERAL AIM OF the Catholic Worker movement is to realize in the individual and in society the expressed and implied teachings of Christ. It must, therefore, begin with an analysis of our present society to determine whether we already have an order that meets with the requirements of justice and charity of Christ.

The society in which we live and which is generally called capitalist (because of its methods of producing wealth) and bourgeois (because of the prevalent mentality) is not in accord with justice and charity—

IN ECONOMICS—because the guiding principle is production for profit and because production determines needs. A just order would provide the necessities of life for all, and needs would determine what would be produced. From each according to his ability, to each according to his needs. Today, we have a non-producing class which is maintained by the labor of others with the consequence that the laborer is systematically robbed of that wealth which he produces over and above what is needed for his bare maintenance.

IN PSYCHOLOGY—because capitalist society fails to take in the whole nature of man but rather regards him as an economic factor in production. He is an item in the expense sheet of the employer. Profit determines what type of work he shall do. Hence, the deadly routine of assembly lines and the whole mode of factory production. In a just order the question will be whether a certain type of work is in accord with human values, not whether it will bring a profit to the exploiters of labor.

IN MORALS—because capitalism is maintained by class war. Since the aim of the capitalist employer is to obtain labor as cheaply as possible and the aim of labor is to sell itself as dearly as possible and buy the products produced as cheaply as possible, there is an inevitable and persistent conflict which can only be overcome when the capitalist ceases to exist as a class. When there is but one class the members perform different functions but there is no longer an employer/wage-earner relationship.

To Achieve this Society We Advocate:

A complete rejection of the present social order and a nonviolent revolution to establish an order more in accord with Christian values. This can only be done by direct action since political means have failed as a method for bringing about this society. Therefore we advocate a personalism which takes on ourselves responsibility for changing conditions to the extent that we are able to do so. By establishing Houses of Hospitality we can take care of as many of those in need as we can rather than turn them over to the impersonal "charity" of the State. We do not do this in order to patch up the wrecks of the capitalist system but rather because there is always a shared responsibility in these things and the call to minister to our brother transcends any consideration of economics. We feel that what anyone possesses beyond basic needs does not belong to him but rather to the poor who are without it.

We believe in the withdrawal from the capitalist system in so far as each one is able to do so. Toward this end we favor the establishment of a *distributist* economy wherein those who have a vocation to the land will work on the farms surrounding the village itself. In this way we will have a decentralized economy which will dispense with the State as we know it and will be federationist in character as was society during certain periods that preceded the rise of national states.

We believe in worker-ownership of the means of production and distribution, as distinguished from nationalization. This is to be accomplished by decentralized co-operatives and the elimination of a distinct employer class. It is revolution from below and not (as political revolutions are) from above. It calls for widespread and universal ownership of property by all men as a stepping stone to a communism that will be in accord with the Christian teaching of detachment from material goods and which, when realized, will express itself in common ownership. "Property, the more common it is, the more holy it is," St. Gertrude writes.

We believe in the complete equality of all men as brothers under the Fatherhood of God. Racism in any form is blasphemy against God who created all mankind in his image and who offers redemption to all. Man comes to God freely or not at all and it is not the function of any man or institution to force the Faith on anyone. Persecution of any people is therefore a serious sin and denial of free will.

We believe further that the revolution that is to be pursued in ourselves and in society must be pacifist. Otherwise it will proceed by force and use means that are evil and which will never be outgrown, so that they will determine the *end* of the revolution and that end will again be tyranny. We believe that Christ went beyond natural ethics and the Old Dispensation in this matter of force and war and taught nonviolence as a way of life. So that when we fight tyranny and injustice and the class war we must do so by spiritual weapons and by noncooperation. Refusal to pay taxes, refusal to register for conscription, refusal to take part in civil-defense drills, nonviolent strikes, withdrawal from the system are all methods that can be employed in this fight for justice.

We believe that success, as the world determines it, is not the criterion by which a movement should be judged. We must be prepared and ready to face seeing failure. The most important thing is that we adhere to these values which transcend time and for which we will be asked a personal accounting not as to whether they succeeded (though we should hope that they do) but as to whether we remained true to them even though the whole world go otherwise.

IF AMERICA ENTERS THE WAR, WHAT SHALL I DO? (1941)

Ernest Fremont Tittle

*D*R. *ERNEST FREMONT TITTLE (1885-1949), a Methodist Minister,* served in the Methodist Church in Evanston, Illinois for almost thirty years. He was an ardent pacifist, and when he allowed a World War I CO to speak to the church's Sunday night youth group, he was afterward denied the honor of preaching the baccalaureate sermon at Northwestern University in 1924. Here he reflects on the powerlessness of war to solve the problems of aggression and injustice. Even in the face of "scorpions" such as Hitlerism, methods must be used which do not simply kill Hitler, but end Hitlerism. This, Tittle asserts, war can never do. The following article was written in response to a question put to Tittle and nine other Christians by *The Christian Century* magazine on the verge of the United States' entrance into World War II. "If America is drawn into the war," they asked, "Can you, as a Christian, participate in it or support it?"

I_N 1917 I BELIEVED that war was the only means of preserving a humane and civilized culture. In that conviction, I left a wife and three children and went to France. I undertook to promote a fighting morale. I did what little I could, at a first-aid dressing station, to relieve the suffering of wounded men. On the way to the front, I came upon a poem that deeply moved me. It was found on the body of a dead and unidentifiable Australian, who had written:

> Rejoice, whatever anguish rend the heart,
>   That God has given you a priceless dower
> To live in these great times and have your part
>   in freedom's crowning hour,

> That ye may tell your sons, who see the light
> High in the heavens, their heritage to take,
> I saw the powers of darkness put to flight,
> I saw the morning break.

But the powers of darkness were not put to flight. Men were killed, millions of them, including promising young writers and artists and musicians and scientists and philosophers. Women were desolate, multitudes of them. Wealth was destroyed. Hunger stalked and pestilence raged over vast areas of the earth. Thirty million civilians were liquidated. The world was set on the road to an economic debacle. But Justice was not achieved. Liberty was not secured. The rights and liberties of small nations were not guaranteed. Brute force was not banished from international affairs. The world was not made safe for democracy or for morality or for Christianity or for anything else that decent men care for and would be glad to die for. A heritage there was for the sons of the men who died in the First World War, but it was not light "high in the heavens" or anywhere else. It was the descending darkness of the present war.

I am now convinced that war, being, as the Oxford Conference said, "a defiance of the righteousness of God as revealed in Jesus Christ and him crucified," cannot serve the ends of freedom and justice but is certain to defeat them. So, if the United States becomes a belligerent in Europe or in Asia, I shall undertake to contribute in some way to the good of my country, but I shall not "support" the war.

The present war in Europe is not only a clash of imperialism; it is also a conflict of ideologies and ways of life. There is now far more at stake then there was in 1917. Prussianism threatened the world with whips; Hitlerism threatens it with scorpions. It is now all-essential to the welfare and progress of humanity that Hitlerism be overcome. On this point American Christians are agreed. The point on which they are not agreed is the means by which Hitlerism can be overcome. Christian pacifists do not proclaim that tyranny is better than war; they proclaim that tyranny cannot be overcome by war. They believe with the late Lord Lothian that "the triumph of Hitler grew out of the despair that settled on central Europe in the years of war, defeat, inflation and revolutionary propaganda." And they believe that this war is now producing political, economic and psychological conditions that make for the survival and spread of Hitlerism.

1. I believe that war as we now know it cannot pave the way for the doing of good. When the fighting ends, who makes the peace? Not the man who actually fought the war, nor the parsons who blessed it, nor the professors who glorified it. When the fighting ends, the people who make the peace are the same people whose ambitions and practices created the situation which bred the war. It is they who, behind the scenes if not at the peace table, decided what is to be done. It is their interests that are considered, their ideas that prevail. Idealists may fight or bless a war, but they, when the fighting ends, have little

voice in the making of peace. This is inevitable; for war, being what it is, plays into the hands of unreason and reaction. It provides a field day for the munitions industry, for the jingoistic press, for every kind of industry that is antisocial and reckless in the pursuit of private gain. It provides a sounding board for politicians and other persons who have the deadly gifts of the demagogue. Inevitably, war strengthens the forces of darkness and destruction . . .

It has been said of the pacifist that he has "a confidence in human nature that human nature cannot support." As a matter of fact, it is the nonpacifist, not the pacifist, who believes that after a long-drawn-out orgy of indiscriminate killing and wholesale destruction people may be expected to think rationally and act justly. The pacifist has no such confidence in human nature.

2. I believe that war as we now know it cannot even hold evil in check. Total war is itself a most active and destructive evil. It knows no distinction of guilty and innocent or even of conbatant and noncombatant. It has no "reverence for personality." It treats human beings as if they were things. It demands the distortion of truth. It knows no distinction of right and wrong but only military necessity. It requires men to believe that the end for which they are fighting is so important that it justifies the use of any means. It is now persuading men that a food blockade, although it may bring starvation, disease and death to innocent aged pesons and women and children, is justified on the ground that it is essential to the preservation of civilization!

Can war, nevertheless, be made to hold evil in check? I have no confidence in attempts to preserve civilization by means that are themselves a denial and betrayal of everything that is essential to a humane and civilized culture. When men do evil that good may come, what they get is not the good they seek but the evil they do. History joins the New Testament in saying, "Be not deceived; God is not mocked: for whatsoever a man soweth, that he shall also reap". . . .

I am convinced that the doing of good is the only way to put an end to aggression. Under present conditions, aggression may not be wholly unprovoked. It may be provoked by fear of future agression on the part of some other nation. It may be provoked by bitter belief, not wholly unwarranted, that there is now no peaceful way of solving a desperate economic problem. It may be provoked by a stinging sense of inferiority in a world where certain other nations are now in a position to gather wealth from the ends of the earth and to lord it over others. To say this is by no means to condone aggression, which in any case is an infamous thing; it is only to face the fact that, rooted in historical events and psychological situations, aggression is seldom unprovoked. Nations that benefit from a world situation which denies equality of opportunity may view with abhorrence any attempt to change it by force. But if they themselves refuse to consent to peaceful change through discussion and negotiations, their refusal may be as immoral as the aggression it provokes.

In a world that is suffering from injustice piled upon injustice, the immediate overcoming of evil may be impossible. There may be no escape from the wages of sin. The question then is: What course, if faithfully followed, would eventually lead to a better state of affairs? War, I am convinced, is not the answer. War can overcome a dictator; it cannot rid the world of dictatorship. It can stop an aggressor; it cannot put an end to aggression. On the contrary, it can only provide new soil for the growth of dictatorship and aggression. The answer, I believe, is the persistent doing of good. Injustice breeds injustice. Hatred breeds hatred. Cruelty breeds cruelty. War breeds war. And no less does good beget good.

If the United States were invaded I should feel called upon to resist the invader by refusing to become his accomplice in the doing of evil. Both in South Africa and in India this kind of resistance has produced notable results. (To say that it can be effective only when the aggressor is an Anglo-Saxon is to invite the charge of dogmatism, if not of self-righteousness.) It produces a situation which the aggressor is unprepared to handle. Air raid for air raid, blockade for blockade, evil for evil—this he has been taught to expect, and when it occurs he knows what to do. But what is he to do when the pastors of all the Protestant churches of the Netherlands read from their pulpits a vigorous protest, in the name of Christ, against any attempt to force upon their country an anti-Jewish program? Nonviolent resistance forces the aggressor to think, which he can hardly do without a disastrous loss of military morale. It forces him to think because, although it refuses to become his accomplice, it does not seek to hurt him.

Pacifists do not suppose that nonviolent resistance can be offered without risk of arrest, imprisonment and death. There would doubtless be many casualties, just as in war. Yet the end result, pacifists believe, would be far different; for war produces in victor and vanquished alike a state of mind that forbids the making of a just and durable peace, whereas nonviolent resistance, which appeals to the best in the aggressor and calls forth the best in his victim, may hope to be redemptive. Of course, nonviolent resistance to evil is not enough. It must be accompanied by a positive program of good which seeks long-range objectives.

I believe that Christian pacifism has relevance to the relations between nations as well as to the relations of the individual to his fellows. The doing of good is not only the way of life for the individual: it is also the way of life for society. This way the pacifist is obligated both to take for himself and to advocate for his nation.

What would pacifism as our national policy require?. . . As a national policy, pacifism would require the United States to set its own house in order. It would seek a real solution (which peacetime conscription is not) for the problem of unemployment and equality of opportunity for all Americans, including Negroes. It would require the repeal of the Oriental Exclusion Act and the placing of Orientals on the quota basis which now governs immigration from other countries. It would call upon the United States to abrogate its present treaties with China and to establish its relations with China on a basis of complete equality and reciprocity. It would require the United States, in the formation of its domestic policies, to have a lively and continuing regard for the welfare of the rest of mankind... It would lead the United States to become indeed a good neighbor, concerned that all nations should have equal access to raw materials and needed markets for their industrial goods.

In the present crisis, pacifism as a national policy would constrain the United States to announce to the world (1) its readiness to associate itself with other nations in the building of a new world order; (2) its determination in any case to order its own life with a sensitive regard for the well-being of other peoples; (3) its desire to contribute to the relief of human suffering in war-stricken regions, through gifts of food, clothing and medical supplies; (4) its readiness at the war's end to make loans for economic rehabilitation, if convinced of the desirability of the projects for which the money is sought. This foundation of justice being laid, pacifism would constrain the United States to appeal for an armistice and for an earnest attempt through discussion and negotiation to find a fundamental solution of world problems in a just peace.

WAR IN THE ATOMIC AGE (1946)

Kirby Page

*D*ESCRIBED BY THE NEW YORK TIMES as *"an itinerant social evangelist for peace,"* Kirby Page (1890-1957) was ordained a minister of the Disciples of Christ in 1915. In his work with the Y.M.C.A. in the U.S., France and England, and later during World War II as vice-chairperson of the Fellowship of Reconciliation, Page consistently preached the gospel of peace. In the following excerpt from his book, *Now Is the Time to Prevent a Third World War,* published on the eve of the nuclear arms race, he speaks about our willingness to wage atomic war and the eroding effects of nuclear preparedness on the moral health of our society. Page raises the issue of the reverse destruction which the readiness to use violence, in this instance atomic weapons, causes on our own attitudes and perspectives.

A NATION'S PREPAREDNESS TO wage atomic war will have disastrous effects upon its relations with other peoples, through increased suspicion, deeper fear, more bitter enmity, and counterpreparedness to wage atomic war. So long as nations and alliances are frantically preparing to annihilate enemies with atomic energy, mutual aid in the solution of common problems on an adequate scale will be impossible. Effective forms of international government can never be operated so long as nations are preparing to wage war. The international mind and the international heart can never function adequately so long as the race of atomic armaments continues. Preparedness to wage war with these new weapons will perpetuate anarchy among the nations and will surely lead to a suicidal third world war if it is continued. It will be sheer madness to engage in a race of atomic armaments.

A nation's preparedness to wage atomic war will also have devastating consequences upon its own scale of values and code of morals. It will be morally paralyzing for America to prepare for the mass promiscuous killing of millions of human beings in Soviet Russia or in some other land. If we indoctrinate the youth of our land with the idea that they must be ready to kill Russian wives and babies in order to protect their own families, we will thereby destroy the very foundations of high morality. All exalted concepts of morality are based on reverence for human life and recognition of human solidarity. A low estimate of the worth of human life is essential to the training of our young men in the science of human slaughter.

The spiritual effects of preparedness to massacre millions of human beings are even more appalling. Every basic doctrine of Christianity is nullified to the degree that we accept the ideas and practices of atomic war: the fatherhood of God, the brotherhood of man, the inestimable value of human life, the kinship of all peoples, the duty and privilege of sympathy and compassion and affection, the responsibility of the strong to bear the burdens of the weak, the overcoming of evil with goodness, the redemptive power of self-giving forgiving love, the supremacy of spiritual forces over material might. We can take Jesus seriously and strive earnestly to follow him, or we can prepare to wage atomic war, but it is utterly impossible to do both at the same time.

CLARENCE JORDAN: A BIOGRAPHICAL SKETCH

Dallas Lee

Y EARS AGO, BEFORE SOUTHERN churches exhibited such a fear of him, Clarence Jordan (1912-1969) went before a Southern congregation and spoke of the spirit of brotherhood alive in the New Testament.

After the sermon an elderly woman, as crisp with pride as a dead honeysuckle vine, made her way down the aisle, her blazing eyes telegraphing the tone of her response. Clarence braced, and she delivered—straight from the gut level of her culture—:

"I want you to know that my grandfather fought in the Civil War, and I'll never believe a word you say."

Clarence, who was tall and gracious and as Southern as sow belly itself, smiled and replied:

"Ma'am, your choice seems quite clear. It is whether you will follow your granddaddy or Jesus Christ."

Clarence knew, from the pure deep streams of his own heritage, that the ghosts of old Confederate grandfathers still manipulated the spirits of a people, somehow making it possible for them to voice obedience to this radical Jesus on the one hand, and yet cling to a deadening web of tradition on the other.

It was spiritual schizophrenia. But the churches, professing to be the body of Christ, seemed to offer no counsel toward restoration of mental health. A culture had appropriated a religion and the name of its Lord without resistance, and continued daily to establish firmer precedent, justifying its violent existence with the self-proclaimed approval of God.

Clarence grew up in south Georgia and somehow managed to gain the clear vision to perceive this unholy alliance. At the University of Georgia's School of Agriculture and at Southern Baptist Theological Seminary's graduate program in Greek New Testament, he equipped himself to speak to the situation. In 1942 he established Koinonia Farm in south Georgia as an interracial experiment in Christian communal living. The intention was to give

135

flesh as well as voice to the basic ideas of peace and love and sharing—ideas which call men to acknowledge that in Christ the walls of culture, race, and status are down.

Clarence, his wife Florence, and others who joined them sought to be a part of the economic and religious life of the South, and yet remain distinct as committed followers of Jesus. They obviously succeeded in focusing their lives on the sensitive spot in the culture. When the experiment in community began giving visibility to their beliefs (Black people *were* welcomed into the fellowship, possessions *were* relinquished, and men *did* go to prison rather than co-operate with the military), they fell victim to the "race-mixing Communist" epithet and violent hostility. The scandalous affair between the church and the culture had been exposed and threatened. The battle was on.

As the Koinonia community endured physical violence and economic boycott, Clarence's communication grew bolder and more prophetic. He began translating his own *Cotton Patch* versions of the New Testament books with the hope that he could make people feel like participants in the New Testament drama, rather than like spectators. Translating the ideas more than the words of the New Testament, he set the gospel story in twentieth-century Georgia and sought to recount New Testament episodes in ways that would leapfrog the centuries and confront modern-day America with the mind of this man Jesus.

To him, a failure to read the Bible with a sense of participation and imagination helped to explain the great distance that separated the ideas of the New Testament from the activities of the twentieth-century churches. And such cold reading also helped explain what he considered to be the fundamental error of modern American churchism: the constant emphasis on the deity of Jesus to the point of obscuring the humanity of God. Most churchmen, he felt, spent so much energy trying to assure themselves of the deity of Jesus that they in fact denied the humanity of God in the process. And the humanity of God, Clarence believed, was what the incarnation was all about.

All across the country, from 1942 until his death at Koinonia Farm in the fall of 1969, Clarence proclaimed an incarnational faith—a faith that took shape in the life-styles, actions, and attitudes of people. The Scriptures were alive in the man and in his experiences, and the power of his proclamations restored a sense of excitement to thousands whose faith had grown stale.

He seldom spoke from the confines of a written manuscript. Working from a brief outline scribbled on the back of an envelope or on an old purchase order from the farm, or on a sheet of hotel stationery, he would just start rolling, speaking his mind in the context of the moment, staying close to some New Testament text, hoping that the ideas would take root in his listeners and be cultivated in personal ways.

When he spoke, he communicated all over. The message was in his tone, in his motions, in his eyes, in his often deliberate stumbling misuse of words, and most of all in his spirit. His brand of communication was meant to be heard and felt and tasted—in short, experienced. When you heard him you didn't just get new information or a new scholarly angle on some theological issue. You encountered a man—a man who strove to live by what he was talking about; a tall, country man with a big Southern voice, an infectious sense of humor, and a penetrating social compassion that balanced his evangelical warmth with ethical dynamite.

Koinonia Partners grew out of (Clarence's) vision and seeks today to give it expression through, for example, the Fund for Humanity, which is supported by thousands of "partners" across the land as well as by the shared profits of farming and industries at Koinonia.

Through the fund, houses are built and sold to the rural disinherited at cost with no-interest loans; industries are established to provide jobs for the low-skilled; land is provided for farming "by virtue of usership rather than ownership"; and a communication ministry is sustained that is grounded in the idea that incarnational faith—faith rooted in action—is the way for man to rediscover a sense of partnership with God and with his fellow men. The rich and the poor, the educated and uneducated, the skilled and the unskilled are coming together in a spirit of partnership under God.

There was scholarship in his head, the excitement of confrontation in his posture, the integrity of practicing what he preached in his countenance; there was humbleness and gentle love in his spirit. And there was reservoired deep in his soul, like a great valley of water behind a tiny dam, a celebration of life. For all the anger he expressed, for all the grief he shared, for all the thunder he delivered, there was the feeling that he sought to share *good news*: not to keep a wrathful God from condemning someone to eternal fires, but to say, "Here are ideas for life, not death; ideas a loving God has given to us all. We have tried them and found them fulfilling. For God's sake and yours, give them a chance to find expression in your life."

CLARENCE JORDAN'S
SERMONS

*T*HE *FOLLOWING TWO SERMONS are good examples of Clarence* Jordan's *Cotton Patch* style, rich in Southern flavor and brimming with his understanding of the message of Jesus. *The Lesson on The Mount - II* explores the choice between retaliation and reconciliation in light of the Gospels, and Jordan's experience of the South. The second selection, *God Against The Rich,* a commentary on Luke 12:13-21, challenges the assumption that riches are a sign of God's favor. It questions whether people possess or are possessed by wealth and the consequences of such possession for a just economic order. (The exact dates of the sermons are not known. The *Lesson on the Mount* was given sometime between 1959 and 1969, but published in 1972; *God Against the Rich* was published in 1976.)

THE LESSON ON THE MOUNT - II

Clarence Jordan

*Y*OU'VE ALSO HEARD THE saying, "Take an eye for an eye; take a tooth for a tooth." But I'm telling you never respond with evil.

In some translations that is translated "Do not resist him who is evil" or "Do not resist evil." The Greek has three cases, all with the same case ending—the locative, the instrumental, and the dative. The context of the word has to tell you which case it is in. Now, if this word is in the dative case, it should be translated: "Do not resist a person who is evil." But I really can't imagine our Lord saying that, for he surely did resist evil people. He preached with all his heart against them. It could be locative, in which case it should be translated: "Do not resist when you find yourself in the presence of evil." Certainly that does not fit with the context. Or it could be instrumental—that is: "Do not resist with evil." Do not use evil as the instrument of your resistance. If someone slaps you, you don't slap him back.

Instead, if somebody slaps you on your right cheek, offer him the other one too. And if anybody wants to drag you into court and take away your shirt, let him have your undershirt. If somebody makes you go a mile for him, go two miles. Give to him who asks of you, and don't turn your back on anyone who wants a loan.

Another thing you've always heard is, "Love your own group and hate the hostile outsider." But I'm telling you, love the outsiders and pray for those who try to do you in, so that you might be sons of your spiritual Father. For he lets his sun rise on both sinners and saints, and he sends rain on both good people and bad. Listen here, if you love only those who love you, what is your advantage? Don't even scalawags do that much? And if you speak to no one but your friends, how are you any different? Do not the non-Christians do as much? Now you, you-all must be mature, as your spiritual Father is mature.

Beyond all doubt, man's most vexing problem, from prehistoric times to the present, has been learning how to respond maturely to those who oppose him.

We have learned how to respond to our friends, but to respond to our enemies—that is the problem. How can we be mature? How can we make a grown-up response to people who want to do us in, to hound us, to beat us, to persecute us? We would expect our Lord to be quite clear in his teachings on this subject, and he is. He begins by going deep back into history and digging up various responses that men have made, and I think all of us will respond in one of the four ways with which our Lord dealt.

One is the method of unlimited retaliation. Somebody knocks out your eye, you knock both of his out. Somebody knocks out your tooth, you knock all his out if you can get to him. If somebody kills your dog, you kill his cow. If he kills your cow, you kill his mule. If he kills your mule, you kill him! No limit to the amount of retaliation. Unbridled anger. Unbridled vengeance. Now, mankind seems early to have outgrown this idea, but had lapsed back into it with the invention of the atom bomb. This seems to be the principle which dominates the State Departments of most so-called civilized nations. You bomb us, we'll obliterate you. You bomb a little city, we will annihilate a whole nation. Unlimited, massive retaliation.

Now this is so childish, so barbaric, so beastly that it never occurred to our Lord that anyone within his hearing would ever resort to it. He picked it up there, and said,

"But now wait. If somebody knocks out your eye, don't knock both his eyes out. Moses said, 'One eye for an eye. One tooth for a tooth.' If he knocks out your eye, don't knock them both out, just knock out one eye. If he knocks out your tooth, don't knock out all of his teeth, just knock out one tooth." This was the first effort at restraint on the strong. Now, he says, "Moses gave you that idea, but it is not enough. Let us move on up to another one." The old prophets came along and said, "Love your neighbor, and hate your enemy." This was the first glimmering of limited love. If your neighbor knocks out your tooth, forgive him. But if he's a person of another race or another nation, give him the works. In other words, limit your love to your own little group, your own nation, your own race. This is the rule of limited love. This concept enables men to live together as nations, limiting their love to their own nation, but it does not enable them to live together as a world family.

This seems to be the place that most of us really are at today. We love America, and limit our love to the shores and the boundaries of the United States. I think most of us reflect the idea that's inscribed on an old tombstone down in Mississippi. It says, "Here lies J.H.S. In his lifetime, he killed 99 Indians, and lived in the blessed hope of making it 100, until he fell asleep in the arms of Jesus." Now, Indians don't count. Ninety-nine of them, and you can live in "the blessed hope" of getting just one more to round it out at an even hundred and still fall asleep in the arms of Jesus. But if you have killed just one white man, you'd fall asleep in a noose. You see, it's all right to kill Indians because we don't care about Indians, but you better not kill a white man. So, a nation can drop an atom bomb on brown people, yellow people, and annihilate two whole cities of people and we give him the Congressional medal. If he kills one man in the United States, we give him the electric chair. . . .

Jesus said it is not enough to limit your love to your own nation, to your own race, to your own group. You must respond with love even to those outside of it, respond with love to those who hate you. This concept enables men to live together not as a nation, but as the human race. We are now at the stage in history where we will either take this step or perish. For we have learned with consummate skill to destroy mankind. We have learned how to efficiently annihilate the human race. But, somehow or other, we shrink with horror from the prospect not of annihilation, but of reconciliation. We will either be reconciled—we shall love one another—or we shall perish. . . .

GOD AGAINST THE RICH

Clarence Jordan

. . .JESUS INTRODUCES ANOTHER PARABLE which tells us what it is that wealth demands when it cries out for our souls. The "soul" is a general term that refers to the force that drives us, that motivates and consumes our lives. What is the effect of this force within us? What are the results when our riches start giving us orders, as they inevitably do? Jesus gives us a picture of what happens. . . .

Jesus said, "There was a certain rich man and he was dressed up in a tuxedo and a white shirt and pitched a big party every day, complete with mint juleps and magnolia blossoms. He had it made! There was also a beggar by the name of Lazarus sitting at his gate, full of sores. And he would have been happy to eat the scraps from the table of the rich man. More than that, the dogs came and licked his sores."

This parable contains a play on words in the original text. The word for "beggar" is related to the word for "spit" in Greek. Lazarus was a "spit-upon one," held in contempt by the rich man.

In Jesus' day one of the most contemptible things you could do to a man was to spit in his face. Still isn't too polite. It was out of contempt Jesus was playing on this spittle word. This old rich man, dressed up in his tuxedo, holding a conference, inviting all of his wealthy friends, putting on a big banquet. And poor old Lazarus, lying out there with the sores. And the rich man spit on him. But what did the dogs do? How did they use their spit? They licked his sores. Spittle was thought not only to show contempt, but to have healing properties. . . In other words, the dogs were acting in a more human way than a human was.

Most people in Jesus' day would catch the symbolism of these dogs. The dogs—the unsaved people, the unchurched people, the Gentiles, the outcast—they were using their spittle to heal a man. Who was the rich man? He was the person of God's inheritance. He had the law, the prophets, and the writings. He was rich in the sense of his religious heritage. He thought he had an edge on all of God's goodness.

It so happened that the spit-on man died, and he was carried away by angels to the bosom of Abraham. Jesus had to shift scenery to get over there on the other side of the grave so He could finish His story. Otherwise, His hearers would have been so immediately threatened by truth that they'd have lynched Him on the spot. Jesus will bring the parable back on this side of the grave as soon as He gets to a point where it's safe to do so. In the meantime, everyone has relaxed into thinking that Jesus doesn't have any more to say about the here and now.

The beggar was carried away into the bosom of Abraham. This was Jesus' way of saying that history has a habit of reversing itself. The first shall be last and the last shall be first. The poor beggar was turned upside down. He used to be on the bottom getting scraps from the table. Now he's sitting at the table with the Daddy of the Hebrew race. Lazarus is sitting right next to Abraham. That was a high honor for any Jew, especially one that was full of sores.

Where is the rich man? He is in torment. And he sees Abraham from afar and Lazarus at his bosom. He shouts out, "Oh, Father Abraham, send me my water boy. Water boy! Quick! I'm just about to perish down here. I need a drink of water." That old rich guy had always hollered for his water boy: "Boy, bring me water! Boy, bring me this! Boy, bring me that! Get away, boy! Come here, boy!"

But Abraham throws it right back in his teeth. Abraham says to him, "Boy!" Ain't that somethin'?" Abraham slings it back to him for the first time and says, "Boy, you remember that you got the good things while you were alive and Lazarus got what was left. You got the good schools. Lazarus got what was left. You got the good sections of town and paved streets. Lazarus got what was left. You got the good churches. Lazarus got what was left. You remember that, don't you? Don't you remember that? Back there when you were alive, before you died? You got the good things. Lazarus got the crumbs that had fallen from your table. Don't you remember that?"

"Hmmm. Seems like I do have a few memories."

"You betcha. Now Lazarus is the guest of honor and you are in great pain. And, more than that, there is between us and you a yawning chasm so that those who want to go between can't make it."

This is really the cutting edge of the parable, this yawning chasm. It's broken up traffic. The bridge is blasted. Big chasm between 'em. We can't get to you. You can't get to us. Who dug that ditch? Who dug that chasm? Where did it come from? That rich man knows who dug it. HE DUG IT! And why did he dig it? He dug it to break up traffic. He dug it to keep guys with sores out. He didn't want the value of his property to go down when sore people moved into his neighborhood. You know, you'd better be careful how you dig ditches to keep people out; you might want to cross them yourself some day. Be careful when you blow up bridges. You might want to cross that bridge some day. This rich man is caught in his own trap.

Then he says, "Well, sir, Father, I beg you to send him to my family, for I have five brothers. Let him testify to them, lest they come to the same place of torment that I have come to. I've got five brothers thinking just like I am. They're digging ditches, they're breaking up traffic, they're erecting barriers around themselves. Oh, Father Abraham, I know what a horrible thing this is now. Please let this Lazarus go back and tell my brothers what an awful thing it is to dig chasms."

And ol' Father Abraham says, "They got Moses and the prophets. Let them listen to them." In other words, he's saying, "They got the Bible and the preachers. What's the matter with those guys? Can't they read? Can't they hear? They got preachers all over everywhere who have skill in the interpretation of the Scriptures. Let them listen to what the Scriptures are saying."

"Oh, Father Abraham, they don't listen to those preachers. I know, I sat under preachers for thirty years and never paid attention to a single thing they said. But you just let Lazarus go down there—let him just ooze through the room a few times. I think you'll get some results. But they ain't goin' to listen to the preachers. And they ain't goin' to listen to the Bible."

Abraham said, "Oh, no, if they won't listen to the Bible and the preachers, they won't be persuaded if someone goes to them from the dead. If you can't get results by appealing to their minds and hearts, you're not going to get results by scaring them into the kingdom. You can't populate heaven with refugees from hell."

So this parable is a beautiful dramatization of the fact that the last shall be first and the first shall be last. And any time you break up traffic, you're blowing the bridges that some day you might want to travel.

We are all accustomed to living with gulfs that keep us from each other; the gulf of wealth, the gulf of pride, the gulf of race, the gulf of sex. Perhaps we would not admit we dug these ditches to keep certain people out. We just worked hard and got wealthy, and it's not our fault if poor people can't afford to live in our neighborhood, belong to our clubs, or join our church. The point of this parable which really condemns us is not that we dug the ditch. To a certain extent, if you were born white, if you were born American, and if your family could afford to "civilize" and educate you, then maybe fate did have a hand in digging the ditch. The question is: What are you and I doing, while we still have time, to fill in that ditch and to overcome the boundaries that shut other people in or out of our fellowships?

Building bridges must become our priority. We can no longer get by with the claim that we are open to anyone who *comes to us. We've got to go to them.* We can't salve our consciences by inviting and "helping" people to become rich along with us. We've got to become poor along with them. The burden of action—of bridge-building—is upon us. We must find ways to dispossess ourselves of whatever separates us from the least of our international brothers and sisters. . . .

The United States represents 6 percent of the world's population and 60 percent of the world's wealth. To say that God can't be God of the rich is, therefore, the same as to say that God can't be God of middle-class America. Our wealth/poverty is not measured by the amount of money we owe on cars, appliances, and homes compared to the amount of money we have in the bank. Practically all of us could plead poverty if that were the standard. It is measured, instead, by the outward comfort of our lives compared to the misery of the masses who are ill-fed, ill-clothed, and ill-housed. And by this standard all of us must confess wealth. *The gulf between ourselves and the poor is the gulf between ourselves and God.*

From: "OF HOLY DISOBEDIENCE" (1952)

A. J. Muste

T HE FOLLOWING EXCERPT IS from the conclusion of Muste's essay, Of Holy Disobedience, first published by Pendle Hill pamphlets in 1952. This pacifist classic appeared at a time when the postwar red scare gripped the country, the first peacetime draft in the country's history had been instituted, and the Cold War was heating up in Korea. *Of Holy Disobedience* identifies conscription as a taproot of war and attempts to persuade the peace movement to adopt a thoroughgoing commitment to draft resistance as well as to the young men of service age who would bear the heaviest burden of military refusal.

NON-CONFORMITY, HOLY DISOBEDIENCE, BECOMES a virtue, indeed a necessary and indispensable measure of spiritual self-preservation, in a day when the impulse to conform, to acquiesce, to go along, is used as an instrument to subject men to totalitarian rule and involve them in permanent war. To create the impression of at least outward unanimity, the impression that there is no "real" opposition, is something for which all dictators and military leaders strive. The more it seems that there is no opposition, the less worthwhile it seems to an ever larger number of people to cherish even the thought of opposition.

Surely, in such a situation, it is important not to place the pinch of incense before Caesar's image, not to make the gesture of conformity which is required, let us say, by registering under a military conscription law. . . . It is surely neither right nor wise to wait until the "system" has driven us into a corner where we cannot retain a vestige of self-respect unless we say NO. It does not seem wise or right to wait until this evil catches up with us, but rather to go out and meet it—to *resist*—before it has gone any further. . . .

Thus to embrace Holy Disobedience is not to substitute resistance for reconciliation. In so far as we help to build up or smooth the way for American militarism and the regimentation which accompanies it, we certainly are not practicing reconciliation toward the millions of people against whom American war preparations, including conscription, are directed. Nor are we practicing reconciliation toward the hundreds of millions in Asia and Africa whom we condemn to poverty and drive into the arms of Communism by our addiction to military "defense." Nor are we practicing love toward our own fellow-citizens, including the multitude of youths in the armed services, if, against our deepest insight, we help to fasten the chains of conscription and war upon them. . . .

The gospel of reconciliation will be preached with a new freedom and power when the preachers have broken decisively with American militarism. . . When we have gotten off the back of what someone has called the "wild elephant" of militarism and conscription on to the solid ground of freedom, and only then, we will be able to live and work constructively. Like Abraham, we shall have to depart from the city-which-is in order that we may help to build the city-which-is-to-be, whose true builder and maker is God. . . .

Finally it is of crucial importance that we should understand that for the individual to pit himself in Holy Disobedience against the war-making and conscripting state, wherever it or he be located, is not an act of despair or defeatism. Rather, I think we may say that precisely this individual refusal to "go along" is now the beginning and the core of any realistic and practical movement against war and for a more peaceful and brotherly world. For it becomes daily clearer that political and military leaders pay virtually no attention to protests against current foreign policy and pleas for peace since they know quite well that, when it comes to a showdown, all but a handful of the millions of protesters will "go along" with the war to which the policy leads. . . .

The failure of the policymakers to change their course does not, save perhaps in very rare instances, mean that they are evil men who want war. They feel, as indeed they so often declare in crucial moments, that the issues are so complicated, the forces arrayed against them so strong, that they "have no choice" but to add another score of billions to the military budget, and so on and on. Why should they think there is any reality, hope or salvation in "peace advocates" who, when the moment of decision comes, also act on the assumption that they "have no choice" but to conform?

Precisely on that day when the individual appears to be utterly hopeless, to "have no choice . . . ," there is absolutely no hope save in going back to the beginning. The human being, the child of God, must assert his humanity and his sonship again. He must exercise the choice which no longer is accorded him by society, which, "naked, weaponless, armourless, without shield or spear, but only with naked hands and open eyes," he must create again. He must understand that this naked human being is the one real thing in the face of the machines and the mechanized institutions of our age. He, by the grace of God, is the seed of all the human life there will be on earth, though he may have to die to make that harvest possible.

BAPTISM BY FIRE
THE STORY OF FANNIE
LOU HAMER
Susan Kling

*I*F YOU HAVE HEARD *the sentiment, "I'm sick and tired of being sick and tired,"* you have heard the words of Fannie Lou Hamer (1917-1977). In 1964 Fannie Lou travelled from the Missisippi Delta to Atlantic City, and sent tremors through the Democratic National Convention and the Johnson Administration. Hamer and the Mississippi Freedom Democratic Party (MFDP) attempted to unseat the fraudulently elected all-white delegation from Mississippi. A surprised and frightened President Johnson called upon Hubert Humphrey, Walter Mondale, J. Edgar Hoover, and Walter Reuther to block the MFDP challenge. Mondale gained his first national distinction at this convention by defeating Hamer and the MFDP: In a closed meeting which excluded Hamer, Mondale developed the infamous "two-seat" compromise, which he later deceitfully told the convention the MFDP had accepted. The "two-seat" scheme refused to replace the white Mississippians with the MFPD delegates. It allowed the MFDP to have just two "at-large" delegates who were to be selected by President Johnson in order to guarantee that the black delegates would not choose their own leaders—in particular, Hamer herself. "I used to say when I was working so hard in the (cotton) fields," noted Hamer, "if I could go to Washington—to the Justice Department—to the FBI—get close enough to let them know what was going on in Mississippi, I was sure that things would change in a week. Now that I have travelled across America, been to the Congress, to the Justice Department, to the FBI, I am faced with things I'm not too sure I wanted to find out. The sickness in Mississippi is not a Mississippi sickness. This is America's sickness." Hamer questioned things many of us are still unaware of. But hatred of her enemies she resisted. "I feel sorry," she said, "for anybody that could let hate wrap them up. Ain't no such thing as I can hate anybody and hope to see God's face."

The following piece, which originally appeared in *Reweaving the Web of Life: Feminism and Nonviolence* (1982: New Society Publishers), offers a glimpse into the spirit and soul of a remarkable woman.

THEN CAME THE SUMMER of '62, when the magic word "Freedom!" swept like a wild wind through the South. In late August, James Bevel of the Southern Christian Leadership Conference came down to Ruleville, Mississippi, and together with James Forman of the Student Nonviolent Coordinating Committee (SNCC) and other Black and white activists in the boiling civil rights movement, called a mass meeting at a church there.

Fannie Lou attended—and her life suddenly changed. "I had never heard the freedom songs before!" she said in wonder. And of the people she listened to: "They really wanted to change the world I knew—they wanted Blacks to register to vote!" They wanted Blacks to be able to have some small say about their destiny.

Fannie Lou felt that she was called, that this was the chance she had waited for, it seemed, all of her life. She and seventeen others in the church signed up to go to Sunflower County Courthouse the next Friday, to register to vote. Without any vote or special arrangement, Fannie Lou became the leader of the group. On the following Friday, August 31, she and the seventeen other Blacks, fearful but determined, boarded a bus owned by a friendly Black man, and rode to the courthouse in Indianola.

Police and other whites began to mill around the bus when it stopped. But the eighteen, with Fannie Lou in front, marched bravely into the courthouse. There they were promptly told to go outside and come in two at a time.

Fannie Lou was asked twenty-one questions, including one that required her to copy and interpret a part of the constitution of Mississippi. "I could copy it," she said later, "but I sure couldn't interpret it—because up to that time, I hadn't even known Mississippi *had* a constitution." She failed the registration test, as did all the others. But she made up her mind that she would come back, no matter how many times, until she did pass.

In the late afternoon, after all the others with her had gone through the same frustrating, threatening day, with rifle-carrying whites strolling in and out of the courthouse past them, they boarded the bus and started for home. They had gone only a few miles when they were stopped by a policeman and ordered to return to Indianola. There the driver was fined $100 for driving a bus "with the wrong color."

The severe backlash against Fannie Lou began with that first effort to register to vote. But for her, that day was also the beginning of a new level of struggle against racism, which lasted for the rest of her life.

Here is the story of what happened when she tried to register, as taken from a hearing before the Select Panel on Mississippi and Civil Rights, held at the National Theater, Washington, D.C., on Monday, June 8, 1964, and reprinted in the Congressional Record of June 16, 1964:

". . . I will begin from the first beginning, August 31, in 1962. I travelled twenty-six miles to the county courthouse to try to register to become a first class citizen. I was fired the 31st of August in 1962 from a plantation where I had worked as a timekeeper and a sharecropper for eighteen years. My husband had worked there thirty years.

"I was met by my children when I returned from the courthouse, and my girl (her eldest daughter) and my husband's cousin told me that this man my husband worked for was raising a lot of Cain. I went on in the house, and it wasn't long before my husband came and said this plantation owner said I would have to leave if I didn't go down and withdraw.

". . . (The plantation owner) said, 'Fannie Lou, you have been to the courthouse to try and register,' and he said, 'We are not ready for this in Mississippi.' I said, 'I didn't register for you, I tried to register for myself.' He said, 'We are not going to have this in Mississippi, and you will have to withdraw. I am looking for your answer yea or nay.'

"I just looked. He said, 'I will give you until tomorrow morning.'

"So I just left the same night."

She told the panel her husband was not allowed to leave the plantation until after harvest time, but in spite of this restriction, he took his wife to the home of a friend in Ruleville. She also said that the plantation owner had warned her husband, Pap, that if he decided to go with Fannie Lou their furniture would be confiscated and Pap would lose his job. Thus, because of the need for the family to have housing and some means of her husband earning a livelihood, Fannie Lou was forced to separate from her husband.

Her report to the panel continued, "On the 10th of September, they fired into the home of Mr. and Mrs. Robert Cuker sixteen times, for me. That same night, two girls were shot at Mr. Herman Sissel's; also, they shot into Mr. Joe Maglon's house. I was fired at that day, and haven't had a job since . . . ."

Her husband was fired anyway and the furniture confiscated by the plantation owner, who took their car as well, saying they owed him $300 on it.

Fannie Lou became a virtual fugitive, staying here and there with friends or distant relatives. At last the family found a bare house into which they moved. But even here, they were not left in peace. Cars full of white men armed with rifles would ride up and back in front of the house, shouting obscenities and threatening to shoot.

If any of the family left the house, for whatever reason, cars followed, with white men leaning out of the windows, shouting, cursing and threatening.

But these reprisals, as well as the abusive letters that she kept receiving, only stiffened her resolve and made her more determined to keep to the path on which she had set her feet. And her family, to their everlasting credit, stood solidly with her.

At last, word of what was happening to her reached the ears of the Student

Non-violent Co-ordinating Committee. Robert Moses, a leader in the Mississippi grassroots civil rights movement, came down to Ruleville and invited Fannie Lou to attend a SNCC conference at Fisk University in Nashville, Tennessee, in the fall of 1962. That conference instilled in her an even more total commitment, and she went to work for SNCC, "even when they didn't have any money." This work provided her with a kind of security, for after that she never felt alone in the ideals she had laid out for herself.

She not only worked for SNCC as a Field Secretary, but was tireless in half a dozen other avenues as well. She circulated a petition to get food and clothing from the government for needy families. She helped in getting welfare programs started, she got clothes from people who didn't need them to people who did, and she cooked for the many volunteer workers who continually came to help. In addition to all of this work, she was employed for a time at a Ruleville cotton gin, until she was fired for attempting to register Blacks to vote. She had to leave her house again.

When she returned to the Sunflower County Courthouse on December 4th to take the registration test a second time, as she explained later, "There was nothing they could do to me. They couldn't fire me, because I didn't have a job. They couldn't put me out of my house, because I didn't have one. There was nothing they could take from me any longer." She told them, "You'll see me every thirty days, until I pass." And on January 10, 1963, she passed—and became one of the first of Sunflower County's 30,000 Blacks to register to vote.

But on June 3, 1963, she paid heavily for that right and for the work she was doing to get Blacks to register.

"I had gone to a voter education workshop in Charleston, South Carolina," she told the Congressional Panel. "We left Mississippi June 3, 1963. We finished the workshop June 8th. We left on the 8th by Continental Trailways bus, returning back to Mississippi.

"We arrived in Winona, Mississippi, between 10:30 and 11 a.m., June 9th. Four of our group got off the bus to get food in the bus terminal. Two got off to use the washroom. I was still on the bus. I saw six people rush out, and I got off to see what was happening.

"Miss Ann Ponder told me the chief of police and a state highway patrolman had ordered them out. I said, 'Well this is Mississippi for you.' I went and got back on the bus.

"I looked out of the window and they were putting the Negroes in a car. I was holding Miss Ponder's iron. I got off to ask her what to do with it. My friends shouted, 'Get back on the bus!'

"A white officer said to me, 'You are under arrest. Get in the car.' As I went to get in, he kicked me. In the car, they would ask me questions. When I started to answer, they would curse and tell me to hush, and call me awful names.

"They carried me to the (Montgomery) County jail. Later I heard Miss Ponder's voice and the sound of licks. She was screaming awfully.

"Then three white men came to my room. A state highway policeman (he had the marking on his sleeve) asked me where I was from. I said, 'Ruleville.' He said, 'We're goin' to check that.' They left out. They came back and he said, 'You're damn right!'

"They said they were going to make me wish I was dead. They had me lay down on my face, and they ordered two Negro prisoners to beat me with a blackjack. That was unbearable. It was leather, loaded with something.

"The first prisoner beat me until he was exhausted. Then the second Negro began to beat. I have a limp. I had polio when I was about six years old. I was holding my hands behind me to protect my weak side. I began to work (move) my feet. The state highway patrolman ordered the other Negro to sit on my feet.

"My dress pulled up and I tried to smooth it down. One of the policeman walked over and raised my dress as high as he could. They beat me until my body was hard, 'til I couldn't bend my fingers or get up when they told me to. That's how I got this blood clot in my left eye—the sight's nearly gone, now. And my kidney was injured from the blows they gave me in the back."

She was left in the cell, bleeding and battered, listening to the screams of Ann Ponder, who was being beaten in another cell, and hearing the white men talk of "plotting to kill us, maybe to throw our bodies in the Big Black River, where nobody would ever find us."

At last, word of the beatings and detention at Winona reached the ears of Dr. Martin Luther King, Jr., who sent members of his staff to the jail, with the demand that Fannie Lou and the others be released at once. Andrew Young and James Bevel came to the jail, helped carry her out, half conscious, and took her to a doctor in Greenwood, Mississippi, where the blood was washed off her, and her wounds stitched and bandaged. Then they took her to Atlanta to some friends of the civil rights movement, where she remained for a month, convalescing. During this month, she refused to allow her husband to come to see how terrible she looked, until some of the scars were less livid and the swelling had gone down.

While she had been in the Winona jail, she told friends, "Medger Evers was killed, and they offered to let us go one night, but I knew it was just so they could kill us, and say we was trying to escape. I told 'em they'd have to kill me in my cell."[1]

The effects of the beatings plagued Fannie Lou for the rest of her life, until sometimes she would say caustically, "I'm sick and tired of being sick and tired!"

This brutal experience only served to make her more determined than ever to continue to get Blacks to register. As soon as she was able, even limping and almost nauseated with pain, she was out in the cotton fields at sun up, lining up prospective voters, and telling them how almighty powerful it would be to be able to vote. Evenings she spent going around to the many little churches in the countryside, talking about voter registration, and singing in that powerful voice that moved all who heard her sing the freedom songs she had learned. But her base was always Ruleville, where she had been born and raised.

Neither the beating nor the constant hate letters and abusive telephone calls she received detered her from her work, and she refused to move away. "I ain't goin' no place," she insisted. "I have a right to stay here. With all that my parents and grandparents gave to Mississippi, I have a right to stay here and fight for what they didn't get." And after her experience in the Winona jail, she added, "I don't want equal rights no more. I don't want to be equal to men that beat us. I want human rights!"[2]

Susan Kling is a long-time civil rights activist, writer and poet. She has written "slice of life" stories for newspapers in England, Hungary, Poland, and Czechoslovakia, based on her experiences in Chicago where she lives. She was awarded a prize for her articles in the Russian magazine *Soviet Woman*. When Fannie Lou Hamer died in 1977, Susan wrote her eulogy in the national newsletter of *Women for Racial and Economic Equality (WREE)*.

---

[1] George Sewell, *The Black Collegian*, May/June, 1978.

[2] Phyl Garland, "Builders of a New South," *Ebony Magazine*, August 1966.

THE PERSONALIST NONVIOLENCE OF THOMAS MERTON
Pat Coy

THOMAS MERTON (1915-1968), TRAPPIST MONK and prolific author, exerted a tremendous influence on the religious peace movement of the 1960's and beyond. While the day-to-day organizing so important to the struggle for peace was left to others more suited and available for the task, Merton supplied the peace movement with a sound theological basis for peacemaking and nonviolence.

Through a series of essays, poems, articles and personal letters, which sometimes seemed to flow out of the monastery at Gethsemani, Kentucky like a mighty stream, Merton inspired, cajoled, admonished, and supported the religious peace movement — and the idle churches — to become part of the solution to the pressing issue of peace in the nuclear age. As he put it in an essay in *The Catholic Worker* in 1961:

"The duty of the Christian in this crisis is to...work for the total abolition of war. . . . It is a problem of terrifying complexity and magnitude, for which the Church itself is not able to see clear and decisive solutions. Yet she must lead the way on the road to nonviolent settlement of difficulties and toward the gradual abolition of war as the way of settling international or civil disputes. . . . Peace is to be preached, non-violence is to be explained as a practical method, and not left to be mocked as an outlet for crackpots who want to make a show of themselves. Prayer and sacrifice must be used as the most effective spiritual weapons in the war against war, and like all weapons, they must be used with deliberate aim: not just with a vague aspiration for peace and security, but against violence and war. This implies that we are also willing to sacrifice and restrain our own instinct for violence and aggressiveness in our relations with other people. We may never succeed in this campaign, but whether we succeed or not, the duty is evident. It is the great Christian task of our time. Everything else is secondary, for the survival of the human race

159

itself depends upon it. We must at least face this responsibility and do something about it. And the first job of all is to understand the psychological factors at work in ourselves and in society."

In 1948, seven years after entering the austere Cistercian order of monks, Merton published his spiritual autobiography, *The Seven Storey Mountain.* It became an immediate best seller of colossal proportions. When Merton followed it with a series of other books exploring the spiritual life, he easily became the most popular religious writer in the Catholic world. His influence moved far beyond this, however, as he reached out through his critical and incisive writings on the cold war, racial injustice, technology, and the environment.

Perhaps Thomas Merton's most important contribution was his talent for slicing sharply to the core of a social issue. Partly due to the intense personal soul-searching that was a constitutive dimension of his life as a Trappist monk, sequestered on the margins of society, Merton could peel away the outer layers of social issues, those layers that appear immediately and which tend to distract most of us, and obfuscate the real, more deeply hidden issues. Merton saw, for instance, that the great problems facing humanity in the twentieth century were merely a reflection of our own individual lives.

When he began to write on the race issue he set the white religious world reeling with his simple yet revolutionary proposition that the race problem was essentially a WHITE problem. It existed in the heart and soul of individual people. Consequently it could only be solved by whites—liberals, conservatives and radicals alike—coming to terms with the fear and latent racism that lurked so menacingly in the dark corners of their own hearts. He took a similar approach to the issue of war and peace.

Merton insisted that the planners in the Pentagon and the Kremlin were not to be faulted for the volatile ingredients which made up the cold war. Each individual citizen contributed to the deadly recipe through the fear and alienation which kept people not only from knowing and trusting the foreigner or enemy, but from knowing themselves as well. The roots of war, Merton relentlessly preached, lie in the fearful heart of each individual, and too rare was the person who was willing to admit and work through this fear of self and others. He minced no words; he cut to the core in an impassioned search for true and lasting solutions to the scourge of war.

Merton served the peace movement by never letting it lose sight of the fact that the atomic age did not exist outside of its members. As with Gandhi, the starting point for Merton's nonviolence was self-knowledge. He consistently reminded both the cold war warriors and the peace activists who sat next to each other in church each Sunday of the capability and culpability, that each had to pull the trigger, to thrust the bayonet, and ultimately to push the button. He understood, and steadfastly refused to let the churches forget, that each citizen participates in the arms race, acquiescing to it, bit by bit, tax dollar by tax dollar, silent moment by silent moment. He was not so much bothered by the fear that some madman or woman would gain access to the button and bring down the nuclear curtain. He taught that each and every person was capable of that evil, a moral evil he once described as second only to the crucifixion.

In *Chant to be used in Processions Around a Site with Furnaces,* his powerful Holocaust prose poem reprinted here, the camp executioner closes the poem by declaring to the reader: "You smile at my career, but you would do as I do if you knew yourself and dared. . . . Do not think yourself better because you burn up friends and enemies with long range missiles without ever seeing what you have done."

This emphasis on personal responsibility for the fear which fuels the fire of war is why Merton believed nonviolence to be "per se and ideally the only really effective resistance to injustice," because the revolution it depends upon is the revolution of the individual, the conversion of the heart in the search for one's true self. In Merton's worldview, the nuclear reality was not isolated and apart from the common ordinary people who make up the world. As he starkly stated it in *Mysticism For The Nuclear Age,* "If you are looking for the Atomic Age, look inside yourself: because you are it. And so alas am I."

In his *Letter To A Young Activist,* Merton counsels a young Jim Forest, later to become Executive Secretary of the International Fellowship of Reconciliation in The Hague, in the ways of nonviolent peacemaking. His warnings on not getting caught up in the political results of one's peacework reflect his emphasis on the internal, personal dimension of nonviolence. Merton continually exhorted the peace movement "to concentrate not on the results but on the value, the rightness, the truth of the work itself." Reminiscent of Gandhi's insistence that nonviolent actionists must be detached from the results of their work and witness, Merton tried to free the religious peace movement from the Western world's slavish attention to effectiveness on its own terms. Nonviolent witness to an objective moral value was enough in Merton's view, as it not only set loose in the world the power of truthful action, but it set the nonviolent actionist free as well. Merton taught that the tremendous spiritual power present in nonviolence could only be fully unleashed when one was willing to be faithful to the truth of the action, trusting that results—both seen and unseen—would follow in their own time.

While Merton always reserved the recourse to violent revolution for those immersed in hopelessly oppressive situations, and while he refused to label himself an absolute pacifist, he was nevertheless a conscientious objector in World War II. Although his life was cut tragically short through accidental electrocution in Thailand during a 1968 pilgrimage to the East he so passionately loved, Merton still managed to do more to develop a coherent and comprehensive theology of nonviolence than any other U.S. writer either before or after him. Together with Dorothy Day, he is seen as a key figure in moving the U.S. Catholic Church toward greater involvement in issues of peace and nonviolence.

Beyond his own copious writings on war and nonviolence, Merton was also an astute student of Gandhi. In 1965 he provided the burgeoning nonviolent movement in the United States with an invaluable service by editing a book of topically arranged Gandhi quotations on various aspects of nonviolence. Gandhi's seminal experiments with nonviolence, and his reflections upon them, thereby became much more accessible to a whole generation of peace activists coming to maturity in the midst of the civil rights movement and the U.S. war on Indochina.

In the final analysis, it was the monk's own spirituality which led him to nonviolence, and which impelled him to write so deeply and broadly on it. The dynamics which fueled Merton's own intense spiritual life—the unrelenting search for his "true self"—and the dynamics of nonviolence are of a piece; they are cut from the same bolt of cloth. For nonviolence is less a contest against the other—the adversary—and more a struggle with oneself.

Merton recognized that at its deepest level, nonviolence involves the inner search to know and to root out the violence in one's own heart. That is why he insists in his essay, *Blessed Are The Meek: The Christian Roots of Nonviolence* (reprinted here, and originally written to more widely disseminate the Catholic Church's teaching on war through its issuance as a pamphlet of the Catholic Peace Fellowship), that a test of one's sincerity in the practice of nonviolence is whether one is "willing to *learn something from the adversary.* If a *new truth* is made known to us by or through the adversary, will we accept it?" (Emphasis in original.) Merton consistently counselled that this sort of humility is a vital prerequisite to the practice of Christian nonviolence: "The mission of Christian humility in social life is not merely to edify, but to *keep minds open to many alternatives*" (emphasis in original).

Thomas Merton was eminently successful in his own mission of Christian humility. His writings and prophetic witness from his hermitage on the backlot of a Trappist monastery helped keep minds open throughout the church to many alternatives, including the powerful but all too little understood alternative of nonviolence.

Patrick G. Coy is a member of the St. Louis Catholic Worker Community and is the Executive Director of the Lentz Peace Research Lab. He is a contributor to, and the editor of, *A Revolution Of The Heart: Essays on the Catholic Worker,* Temple University Press, 1988. His essays, poetry, and reviews have appeared widely, including in *Sojourners, Theology Today, Fellowship, Christian Century, National Catholic Reporter, Spirituality Today, and Journal of Religion and Intellectual Life.* He is the Vice Chair of the National Council of the Fellowship Of Reconciliation.

CHANT TO BE USED IN PROCESSIONS AROUND A SITE WITH FURNACES (1961)

Thomas Merton

How WE MADE THEM sleep and purified them

How we perfectly cleaned up the people and worked a big heater

I was the commander I made improvements and installed a guaranteed system taking account of human weakness I purified and I remained decent

How I commanded

I made cleaning appointments and then I made the travellers sleep and after that I made soap

I was born into a Catholic family but as these people were not going to need a priest I did not become a priest I installed a perfectly good machine it gave satisfaction to many

When trains arrived the soiled passengers received appointments for fun in the bathroom they did not guess

It was a very big bathroom for two thousand people it awaited arrival and they arrived safely

There would be an orchestra of merry widows not all the time much
art

If they arrived at all they would be given a greeting card to send home taken
care of with good jobs wishing you could come to our joke

Another improvement I made was I built the chambers for two thousand
invitations at a time the naked votaries were disinfected with ZykionB

Children of tender age were always invited by reason of their youth they were
unable to work they were marked out for play

They were washed like the others and more than the others

Very frequently women would hide their children in the piles of clothing but
of course when we came to find them we would send the children into the
chamber to be bathed

How I often commanded and made improvements and sealed the door on top
there were flowers the men came with crystals I guaranteed
always the crystal parlor

I guaranteed the chamber and it was sealed you could see through portholes

They waited for the shower it was not hot water that came through vents though
efficient winds gave full satisfaction portholes showed this

The satisfied all ran together to the doors awaiting arrival it
was guaranteed they made ends meet

How could I tell by screaming that love came to a full stop I
found the ones I had made clean after about a half hour

Jewish male inmates then worked up nice they had rubber boots
in return for adequate food I could not guess their appetite

Those at the door were taken apart out of a fully stopped love
for rubber male inmates strategic hair and teeth being used later
for defence

Then the males took off all clean rings and made away with
happy gold

A big new firm promoted steel forks operating on a cylinder they
got the contract and with faultless workmanship delivered very fast
goods

How I commanded and made soap 12 lbs fat 10 quarts water 8 oz to
a lb of caustic soda but it was hard to find any fat

"For transporting the customers we suggest using light carts on
wheels a drawing is submitted"

'We acknowledge four steady furnaces and an emergency guarantee"

"I am a big new commander operating on a cylinder I elevate the
purified materials boil for 2 to 3 hours and then cool"

For putting them into a test fragrance I suggested an express
elevator operated by the latest cylinder it was guaranteed

Their love was fully stopped by our perfected ovens but the love
rings were salvaged

Thanks to the satisfaction of male inmates operating the heaters
without need of compensation our guests were warmed

All the while I obeyed perfectly

So I was hanged in a commanding position with a full view of
the site plant and grounds

You smile at my career but you would do as I did if you know
yourself and dared

In my day we worked hard we saw what we did our self-sacrifice was
conscientious and complete our work was faultless and detailed

Do not think yourself better because you burn up friends and enemies with long
range missiles without ever seeing what you have done.

COMMUNISM AND ANTI-COMMUNISM (1961)

Statement of the Mennonite General Conference

*D*URING THE FIRST MENNONITE *Conference held in America, in 1725,* colonial Mennonites accepted the confession of faith, known as "The Eighteen Articles," adopted in Dortrecht, Holland in 1632. Article XIV of the confession forbids defense by force, stating, ". . . the Lord Jesus has forbidden his disciples and followers all revenge and resistance. . . ." The Mennonites offer us the best example of the nonresistance branch of nonviolence. Their opposition to war, oaths and capital punishment tends to take the form of withdrawal of support and cooperation from the offending rule or institution. Now established along with the Quakers as one of the strongest peace churches, their anti-war, pro-conscientious objection positions are well known. Less well known is the application of their nonresistant faith to other areas of conflict.

Written during the cold war, not long after the blacklists and red-baiting of the McCarthy era, *Communism and Anti-Communism* reflects the courage with which the Mennonite Church in the United States carried out its nonviolent witness. The statement reminded a country blinded by irrational fear that hate in the form of "holy wars" and ideological crusades creates an atmosphere conducive to the very immorality it fears in atheistic communism. In the face of the near hysteria accompanying anticommunist sentiment, the Mennonites acknowledged the problem present in communism but firmly rejected the anticommunist crusade mentality and its accompanying behavior. They offered instead a diffent view of how Christians can better cope with conflicting ideologies.

IN VIEW OF THE advance of communism in the world at large, the current strong anticommunist agitation which the cold-war climate has brought into our nation, and the challenge presented to our nonresistant position by these developments, we the representatives of the Mennonite Church, assembled in General Conference at Johnstown, Pennsylvania, August 23, 1961, reaffirm our commitment to our Biblical and historic nonresistant faith, calling special attention to the following points of emphasis in our General Conference pronouncements of 1937 and 1951.

1. Our love and ministry must go out to all, whether friend or foe.

2. While rejecting any ideology which opposes the Gospel or seeks to destroy the Christian faith, we cannot take any attitude or commit any act contrary to Christian love against those who hold or promote such views, but must seek to overcome their evil and win them through the Gospel.

3. If our country becomes involved in war, we shall endeavor to continue to live a quiet and peaceable life in all godliness and honesty and avoid joining in any wartime hysteria of hatred, revenge, and retaliation.

For the present situation specifically, we take this to mean, positively:

1. That we inform ourselves thoroughly and intelligently on the evils of all atheistic ideologies and practices and all materialistic philosophies, of whatever character.

2. That we must be faithful and effective in our witness against these ideologies and philosophies: (a) through the truth of the Gospel and (b) through works of mercy which demonstrate the way of love which the Gospel proclaims, even the feeding of our reputed enemies.

3. That we accept our obligation and privilege to bring in love the saving Gospel to communists everywhere, as well as to all men and to win them for Christ.

4. That our hand of love, encouragement, and help, and our prayers, must go out to Christians in all lands, especially to those who suffer for Christ behind the Iron Curtain.

5. That we must courageously proclaim all the implications of the Gospel in human life even at the risk, if need be, of being misunderstood and falsely accused.

6. That we urge upon governments such a positive course of action as may help to remove the conditions which contribute to the rise of communism and which tend to make people vulnerable to communist influence.

Negatively, we understand our commitment to mean:

1. That we recognize the incompatibility of Christianity and atheistic communism and the challenge to the cause of Christ which the latter represents.

2. That we recognize that atheistic communism can ultimately be overcome only by the witness of Christian truth in idea and life and not by force or violence.

3. That the nonresistant Christian witness in this matter must be clearly and

unequivocally divorced from any and all advocacy of force and violence, either physical or intellectual.

4. That we cannot equate Christianity with any particular economic or political system, or with Americanism. Accordingly, we cannot accept the view that to be anticommunist is therefore necessarily to be Christian, or that to exercise Christian love toward communist persons is therefore necessarily to be procommunist.

5. That although we teach and warn against atheistic communism we cannot be involved in any anticommunist crusade which takes the form of a "holy war" and employs distortion of facts, unfounded charges against persons and organizations (particularly against fellow Christians), promotes blind fear, and creates an atmosphere which can lead to a very dangerous type of totalitarian philosophy.

6. That our word of warning must go out particularly against the current use of the pulpit, radio, and the religious press, in the name of Christianity, for this purpose.

Believing that world communism today has been permitted by God as a judgement upon an unfaithful Christendom, we confess our own past failure to proclaim as we ought the whole truth of the Gospel by word and deed. We urge the brotherhood to be more concerned to live out the Gospel fully in all areas of life, and to give itself to prayer to the end that the providence of God may overrule in the affairs of nations that peace may prevail. And we pray for the direction of the Spirit that we may faithfully perform our mission as effective witnesses for Christ in a world replete with economic greed, hate, and warfare, and struggling with competing ideologies, remembering that we are pilgrims here whose citizenship is heaven, and who are looking for the consummation of all things in the return of our ascended Lord and in His ultimate eternal kingdom.

LETTER FROM A BIRMINGHAM JAIL (1963)

Dr. Martin Luther King, Jr.

*N*OTHING IN THE COLLECTIVE *literature of Christian nonviolence is* more incisive than the letter which Dr. Martin Luther King, Jr., (1929-1968) wrote on paper scraps and newspaper margins while sitting in the Birmingham City Jail in 1963. He was responding to a public statement in the April 12th issue of the *Birmingham News.* Eight Alabama clergy had called for law, order and patience in the face of the racial tensions in the city and had accused the demonstrating "negroes" of fomenting violence. In King's response we learn how common virtues can become a cover for injustice; and we learn of King's profound understanding of the dynamics of nonviolent struggle. He communicates a respect for the clergy even while rejecting their position. Rather than addressing the symptoms they present, he brings the underlying issues to the surface. Even in written form, he creates the tension which promotes change.

King also understood that self-sacrifice was required if the conscience of the city was to be reached. It was on Sunday, May 5th, not too long after this writing, that 3,000 children marched up to police barricades where firemen stood with hoses ready. The scene had been repeated over the previous weeks only to end in bloody chaos as Police Commissioner Bull Connor gave the command to "turn on the hoses." As before, Connor yelled his command. The firemen did not respond. Again Connor screamed, "Turn on the hoses." The firemen stood still and the marchers passed by. The marchers, and their families, had been willing to suffer in order to create the context for conversion, and had succeeded in disarming the hearts of "Bull Connor's men." King knew that only nonviolence could eventually redeem the soul of racist America.

My DEAR FELLOW CLERGYMEN,

While confined here in the Birmingham City Jail, I came across your recent statement calling our present activities "unwise and untimely." Seldom, if ever, do I pause to answer criticism of my work and ideas. If I sought to answer all of the criticisms that cross my desk, my secretaries would be engaged in little else in the course of the day, and I would have no time for constructive work. But since I feel that you are men of genuine goodwill and your criticisms are sincerely set forth, I would like to answer your statement in what I hope will be patient and reasonable terms.

I think I should give the reason for my being in Birmingham, since you have been influenced by the argument of "outsiders coming in." I have the honor of serving as president of the Southern Christian Leadership Conference, an organization operating in every Southern state, with headquarters in Atlanta, Georgia. We have some eighty-five affiliate organizations all across the South—one being the Alabama Christian Movement for Human Rights. Whenever necessary and possible we share staff, educational and financial resources with our affiliates. Several months ago our local affiliate here in Birmingham invited us to be on call to engage in a nonviolent direct action program if such were deemed necessary. We readily consented and when the hour came we lived up to our promises. So I am here, along with several members of my staff, because we were invited here. I am here because I have basic organizational ties here.

Beyond this, I am in Birmingham because injustice is here. Just as the eighth century prophets left their little villages and carried their "thus saith the Lord" far beyond the boundaries of their hometowns, and just as the Apostle Paul left his little village of Tarsus and carried the gospel of Jesus Christ to practically every hamlet and city of the Graeco-Roman world, I too am compelled to carry the gospel of freedom beyond my particular home town. Like Paul, I must constantly respond to the Macedonian call for aid.

Moreover, I am cognizant of the interrelatedness of all communities and states. I cannot sit idly by in Atlanta and not be concerned about what happens in Birmingham. Injustice anywhere is a threat to justice everywhere. We are caught in an inescapable network of mutuality, tied in a single garment of destiny. Whatever affects one directly affects all indirectly. Never again can we afford to live with the narrow, provincial "outside agitator" idea. Anyone who lives inside the United States can never be considered an outsider anywhere in this country.

You deplore the demonstrations that are presently taking place in Birmingham. But I am sorry that your statement did not express a similar concern for the conditions that brought the demonstrations into being. I am sure that each of you would want to go beyond the superficial social analyst who looks merely at effects, and does not grapple with underlying causes. I would not hesitate to say that it is unfortunate that so-called demonstrations are taking place in Birmingham at this time, but I would say in more emphatic terms that it is even more unfortunate that the white power structure of this city left the Negro community with no other alternative.

In any nonviolent campaign there are four basic steps: 1) Collection of the facts to determine whether injustices are alive 2) Negotiation 3) Self-purification and 4) Direct Action. We have gone through all of these steps in Birmingham. There can be no gainsaying of the fact that racial injustice engulfs this community.

Birmingham is probably the most thoroughly segregated city in the United States. Its ugly record of police brutality is known in every section of this country. Its unjust treatment of Negroes in the courts is a notorious reality. There have been more unsolved bombings of Negro homes and churches in Birmingham than any city in this nation. These are the hard, brutal and unbelievable facts. On the basis of these conditions Negro leaders sought to negotiate with the city fathers. But the political leaders consistently refused to engage in good faith negotiation.

Then came the opportunity last September to talk with some of the leaders of the economic community. In these negotiating sessions certain promises were made by the merchants—such as the promise to remove the humiliating racial signs from the stores. On the basis of these promises Rev. Shuttlesworth and the leaders of the Alabama Christian Movement for Human Rights agreed to call a moratorium on any type of demonstrations. As the weeks and months unfolded we realized that we were the victims of a broken promise. The signs remained. Like so many experiences of the past we were confronted with blasted hopes, and the dark shadow of a deep disappointment settled upon us. So we had no alternative except that of preparing for direct action, whereby we would present our very bodies as a means of laying our case before the conscience of the local and national community. We were not unmindful of the difficulties involved. So we decided to go through a process of self-purification. We started having workshops on nonviolence and repeatedly asked ourselves the questions, "Are you able to accept blows without retaliating?" "Are you able to endure the ordeals of jail?" We decided to set our direct action program around the Easter season, realizing that with the exception of Christmas, this was the largest shopping period of the year. Knowing that a strong economic withdrawal program would be the by-product of direct action, we felt that this was the best time to bring pressure on the merchants for the needed changes. Then it occurred to us that the March election was ahead and so we speedily decided to postpone action until after election day. When we discovered that Mr. Connor was in the run-off, we decided again to postpone action so that the demonstrations could not be used to cloud the issues. At this time we agreed to begin our nonviolent witness the day after the run-off.

This reveals that we did not move irresponsibly into direct action. We too wanted to see Mr. Connor defeated; so we went through postponement after postponement to aid in this community need. After this we felt that direct action could be delayed no longer.

Creative Tension

You may well ask, "Why direct action? Why sit-ins, marches, etc.? Isn't negotiation a better path?" You are exactly right in your call for negotiation. Indeed, this is the purpose of direct action. Nonviolent direct action seeks to create such a crisis and establish such creative tension that a community that has constantly refused to negotiate is forced to confront the issue. It seeks so to dramatize the issue that it can no longer be ignored. I just referred to the creation of tension as a part of the work of the nonviolent resister. This may sound rather shocking. But I must confess that I am not afraid of the word tension. I have earnestly worked and preached against violent tension, but there is a type of constructive nonviolent tension that is necessary for growth. Just as Socrates felt that it was necessary to create a tension in the mind so that individuals could rise from the bondage of myths and half-truths to the unfettered realm of creative analysis and objective appraisal, we must see the need of having nonviolent gadflies to create the kind of tension in society that will help men to rise from the dark depths of prejudice and racism to the majestic heights of understanding and brotherhood. So the purpose of the direct action is to create a situation so crisis-packed that it will inevitably open the door to negotiation. We, therefore, concur with you in your call for negotiation. Too long has our beloved Southland been bogged down in the tragic attempt to live in monologue rather than dialogue.

One of the basic points in your statement is that our acts are untimely. Some have asked, "Why didn't you give the new administration time to act?" The only answer that I can give to this inquiry is that the new administration must be prodded about as much as the outgoing one before it acts. We will be sadly mistaken if we feel that the election of Mr. Boutwell will bring the millennium to Birmingham. While Mr. Boutwell is much more articulate and gentle than Mr. Connor, they are both segregationists, dedicated to the task of maintaining the status quo. The hope I see in Mr. Boutwell is that he will be reasonable enough to see the futility of massive resistance to desegregation. But he will not see this without pressure from the devotees of civil rights. My friends, I must say to you that we have not made a single gain in civil rights without determined legal and nonviolent pressure. History is the long and tragic story of the fact that privileged groups seldom give up their privileges voluntarily. Individuals may see the moral light and voluntarily give up their unjust posture; but as Reinhold Niebuhr has reminded us, groups are more immoral than individuals.

We know through painful experience that freedom is never voluntarily given by the oppressor; it must be demanded by the oppressed. Frankly, I have never yet engaged in a direct action movement that was "well timed," according to the timetable of those who have not suffered unduly from the disease of segregation. For years now I have heard the word "Wait!" It rings in the ear of every Negro with a piercing familiarity. This "Wait" has almost always meant "Never." It has been a tranquilizing thalidomide, relieving the emotional stress for a moment, only to give birth to an ill-formed infant of frustration. We must come to see with the distinguished jurist of yesterday that "justice too long delayed is justice denied." We have waited for more than three hundred and forty years for our constitutional and God-given rights. The nations of Asia and Africa are moving with jet-like speed toward the goal of political independence, and we still creep at horse and buggy pace toward the gaining of a cup of coffee at a lunch counter. I guess it is easy for those who have never felt the stinging darts of segregation to say, "Wait." But when you have seen vicious mobs lynch your mothers and fathers at will and drown your sisters and brothers at whim; when you have seen hate-filled policemen curse, kick, brutalize and even kill your black brothers and sisters with impunity; when you see the vast majority of your twenty million Negro brothers smothering in an airtight cage of poverty in the midst of an affluent society; when you suddenly find your tongue twisted and your speech stammering as you seek to explain to your six-year-old daughter why she can't go to the public amusement park that has just been advertised on television, and see tears welling up in her little eyes when she is told that Funtown is closed to colored children, and see the depressing clouds of inferiority begin to form in her little mental sky, and see her begin to distort her little personality by unconsciously developing a bitterness toward white people; when you have to concoct an answer for a five-year-old son asking in agonizing pathos: "Daddy, why do white people treat colored people so mean?"; when you take a cross country drive and find it necessary to sleep night after night in the uncomfortable corners of your automobile because no motel will accept you; when you are humiliated day in and day out by nagging signs reading "white" and "colored"; when your first name becomes "nigger" and your middle name becomes "boy" (however old you are) and your last name becomes "John," and when your wife and mother are never given the respected title "Mrs."; when you are harried by day and haunted at night by the fact that you are a Negro, living constantly at tip-toe stance never quite knowing what to expect next, and plagued with inner fears and outer resentments; when you are forever fighting a degenerating sense of "nobodiness"; then you will understand why we find it difficult to wait. There comes a time when the cup of endurance runs over, and men are no longer willing to be plunged into an abyss of injustice where they experience the blackness of corroding despair. I hope, sirs, you can understand our legitimate and unavoidable impatience.

Breaking the Law

You express a great deal of anxiety over our willingness to break laws. This is certainly a legitimate concern. Since we so diligently urge people to obey the

Supreme Court's decision of 1954 outlawing segregation in the public schools, it is rather strange and paradoxical to find us consciously breaking laws. One may well ask, "How can you advocate breaking some laws and obeying others?" The answer is found in the fact that there are two types of laws: There are *just* and there are *unjust* laws. I would agree with Saint Augustine that "An unjust law is no law at all."

Now what is the difference between the two? How does one determine when a law is just or unjust? A just law is a man-made code that squares with the moral law or the law of God. An unjust law is a code that is out of harmony with the moral law. To put it in the terms of Saint Thomas Aquinas, an unjust law is a human law that is not rooted in eternal and natural law. Any law that uplifts human personality is just. Any law that degrades human personality is unjust. All segregation statutes are unjust because segregation distorts the soul and damages the personality. It gives the segregator a false sense of superiority, and the segregated a false sense of inferiority. To use the words of Martin Buber, the great Jewish philosopher, segregation substitutes an "I-it" relationship for the "I-thou" relationship, and ends up relegating persons to the status of things. So segregation is not only politically, economically and sociologically unsound, but it is morally wrong and sinful. Paul Tillich has said that sin is separation. Isn't segregation an existential expression of man's tragic separation, an expression of his awful estrangement, his terrible sinfulness? So I can urge men to disobey segregation ordinances because they are morally wrong.

Let us turn to a more concrete example of just and unjust laws. An unjust law is a code that a majority inflicts on a minority that is not binding on itself. This is difference made legal. On the other hand a just law is a code that a majority compels a minority to follow that it is willing to follow itself. This is sameness made legal.

Let me give another explanation. An unjust law is a code inflicted upon a minority which that minority had no part in enacting or creating because they did not have the unhampered right to vote. Who can say that the legislature of Alabama which set up the segregation laws was democratically elected? Throughout the state of Alabama all types of conniving methods are used to prevent Negroes from becoming registered voters and there are some counties without a single Negro registered to vote despite the fact that the Negro constitutes a majority of the population. Can any law set up in such a state be considered democratically structured?

These are just a few examples of unjust and just laws. There are some instances when a law is just on its face and unjust in its application. For instance, I was arrested Friday on a charge of parading without a permit. Now there is nothing wrong with an ordinance which requires a permit for a parade, but when the ordinance is used to preserve segregation and to deny citizens the First Amendment privilege of peaceful assembly and peaceful protest, then it becomes unjust.

I hope you can see the distinction I am trying to point out. In no sense do I advocate evading or defying the law as the rabid segregationist would do. This would lead to anarchy. One who breaks an unjust law must do it *openly, lovingly* (not hatefully as the white mothers did in New Orleans when they were seen on television screaming "nigger, nigger, nigger"), and with a willingness to accept the penalty. I submit that an individual who breaks a law that conscience tells him is unjust, and willingly accepts the penalty by staying in jail to arouse the conscience of the community over its injustice, is in reality expressing the very highest respect for law.

Of course, there is nothing new about this kind of civil disobedience. It was seen sublimely in the refusal of Shadrach, Meshach and Abednego to obey the laws of Nebuchadnezzar because a higher moral law was involved. It was practiced superbly by the early Christians who were willing to face hungry lions and the excruciating pain of chopping blocks, before submitting to certain unjust laws of the Roman empire. To a degree academic freedom is a reality today because Socrates practiced civil disobedience.

The White Moderate

We can never forget that everything Hitler did in Germany was "legal" and everything the Hungarian freedom fighters did in Hungary was "illegal." It was "illegal" to aid and comfort a Jew in Hitler's Germany. But I am sure that if I had lived in Germany during that time I would have aided and comforted my Jewish brothers even though it was illegal. If I lived in a Communist country today where certain principles dear to the Christian faith are suppressed, I believe I would openly advocate disobeying these anti-religious laws. I must make two honest confessions to you, my Christian and Jewish brothers. First, I must confess that over the last few years I have been gravely disappointed with the white moderate. I have almost reached the regrettable conclusion that the Negro's great stumbling block in the stride toward freedom is not the White Citizen's Counciler or the Ku Klux Klanner, but the white moderate who is more devoted to "order" than to justice; who prefers a negative peace which is the absence of tension to a positive peace which is the presence of justice; who constantly says "I agree with you in the goal you seek, but I can't agree with your methods of direct action"; who paternalistically feels that he can set the timetable for another man's freedom; who lives by the myth of time and who constantly advised the Negro to wait until a "more convenient season." Shallow understanding from people of goodwill is more frustrating than absolute misunderstanding from people of ill will. Lukewarm acceptance is much more bewildering than outright rejection.

I had hoped that the white moderate would understand that law and order exist for the purpose of establishing justice, and that when they fail to do this they become dangerously structured dams that block the flow of social progress. I had hoped that the white moderate would understand that the present tension in the South is merely a necessary phase of the transition from an obnoxious negative peace, where the Negro passively accepted his unjust plight, to a substance-filled positive peace, where all men will respect the dignity and worth of human personality. Actually, we who engage in nonviolent direct action are not the creators of tension. We merely bring to the surface the hidden tension that is already alive. We bring it out in the open where it can be seen and dealt with. Like a boil that can never be cured as long as it is covered up but must be opened with all its pus-flowing ugliness to the natural medicines of air and light, injustice must likewise be exposed, with all of the tension its exposing creates, to the light of human conscience and the air of national opinion before it can be cured.

In your statement you asserted that our actions, even though peaceful, must be condemned because they precipitate violence. But can this assertion be logically made? Isn't this like condemning the robbed man because his possession of money precipitated the evil act of robbery? Isn't this like condemning Socrates because his unswerving commitment to truth and his philosophical delvings precipitated the misguided popular mind to make him drink the hemlock? Isn't this like condemning Jesus because His unique God-Consciousness and never-ceasing devotion to His will precipitated the evil act of crucifixion? We must come to see, as federal courts have consistently affirmed, that it is immoral to urge an individual to withdraw his efforts to gain his basic constitutional rights because the quest precipitates violence. Society must protect the robbed and punish the robber.

I had also hoped that the white moderate would reject the myth of time. I received a letter this morning from a white brother in Texas which said: "All Christians know that the colored people will receive equal rights eventually, but it is possible that you are in too great of a religious hurry. It has taken Christianity almost 2000 years to accomplish what it has. The teachings of Christ take time to come to earth." All that is said here grows out of a tragic misconception of time. It is the strangely irrational notion that there is something in the very flow of time that will inevitably cure all ills. Actually time is neutral. It can be used either destructively or constructively. I am coming to feel that the people of ill will have used time much more effectively than the people of good will. We will have to repent in this generation not merely for the vitriolic words and actions of the bad people, but for the appalling silence of the good people. We must come to see that human progress never rolls in on wheels of inevitability. It comes through the tireless efforts and persistent work of men willing to be co-workers with God, and without this hard work time itself becomes an ally of the forces of social stagnation. We must use time creatively, and forever realize that the time is always ripe to do right. Now is the time to make real the promise of democracy, and transform our pending national elegy into a creative psalm of brotherhood. Now is the time to lift our national policy from the quicksand of racial injustice to the solid rock of human dignity.

You spoke of our activity in Birmingham as extreme. At first I was rather disappointed that fellow clergymen would see my nonviolent efforts as those of the extremist. I started thinking about the fact that I stand in the middle of two opposing forces in the Negro community. One is a force of complacency made up of Negroes who, as a result of long years of oppression, have been so completely drained of self-respect and a sense of "somebodiness" that they have adjusted to segregation, and, of a few Negroes in the middle class who, because of a degree of academic and economic security, and because at points they profit by segregation, have unconsciously become insensitive to the problems of the masses. The other force is one of bitterness and hatred, and comes perilously close to advocating violence. It is expressed in the various black nationalist groups that are springing up over the nation, the largest and best known being Elijah Muhammad's Muslim movement. This movement is nourished by the contemporary frustration over the continued existence of racial discrimination. It is made up of people who have lost faith in America, who have absolutely repudiated Christianity, and who have concluded that the white man is an incurable "devil." I have tried to stand between these two forces saying that we need not follow the "do-nothingism" of the complacent or the hatred and despair of the black nationalist. There is the more excellent way of love and nonviolent protest. I'm grateful to God that, through the Negro church, the dimension of nonviolence entered our struggle. If this philosophy had not emerged, I am convinced that by now many streets of the South would be flowing with floods of blood. And I am further convinced that if our white brothers dismiss as "rabble rousers" and "outside agitators" those of us who are working through the channels of nonviolent direct action and refuse to support our nonviolent efforts, millions of Negroes, out of frustration and despair, will seek solace and security in black nationist ideologies, a development that will lead inevitably to a frightening racial nightmare.

Oppressed people cannot remain oppressed forever. The urge for freedom will eventually come. This is what happened to the American Negro. Something within has reminded him of his birthright of freedom; something without has reminded him that he can gain it. Consciously and unconsciously, he has been swept in by what the Germans call the *Zeitgeist*, and with his black brothers of Africa, and his brown and yellow brothers of Asia, South America and the Caribbean, he is moving with a sense of cosmic urgency toward the promised land of racial justice. Recognizing this vital urge that has engulfed the Negro community, one should readily understand public demonstrations. The Negro has many pent-up resentments and latent frustrations. He has to get them out. So let him march sometime; let him have his prayer pilgrimages to the city hall; understand why he must have sit-ins and freedom rides. If his repressed emotions do not come out in these nonviolent ways, they will come out in ominous expressions of violence. This is not a threat; it is a fact of history. So I have not said to my people "get rid of your discontent." But I have tried to say that this normal and healthy discontent can be channelized through the creative outlet of nonviolent direct action. Now this approach is being dismissed as extremist. I must admit that I was initially disappointed in being so categorized.

Extremists for Love

But as I continued to think about the matter I gradually gained a bit of satisfaction from being considered an extremist. Was not Jesus an extremist in love—"Love your enemies, bless them that curse you, pray for them that despitefully use you." Was not Amos an extremist for justice—"Let justice roll down like waters and righteousness like a mighty stream." Was not Paul an extremist for the gospel of Jesus Christ—"I bear in my body the marks of the Lord Jesus." Was not Martin Luther an extremist—"Here I stand; I can do none other so help me God." Was not John Bunyan an extremist—"I will stay in jail to the end of my days before I make a butchery of my conscience." Was not Abraham Lincoln an extremist—"This nation cannot survive half slave and half free." Was not Thomas Jefferson an extremist—"We hold these truths to be self-evident, that all men are created equal." So the question is not whether we will be extremist but what kind of extremist will we be. Will we be extremists for hate or will we be extremists for love? Will we be extremists for the preservation of injustice—or will we be extremists for the cause of justice? In that dramatic scene on Calvary's hill, three men were crucified. We must not forget that all three were crucified for the same crime—the crime of extremism. Two were extremists for immorality, and thusly fell below their environment. The other, Jesus Christ, was an extremist for love, truth, and goodness, and thereby rose above his environment. So, after all, maybe the South, the nation and the world are in dire need of creative extremists.

I had hoped that the white moderate would see this. Maybe I was too optimistic. Maybe I expected too much. I guess I should have realized that few members of a race that has oppressed another race can understand or appreciate the deep groans and passionate yearnings of those that have been oppressed and still fewer have the vision to see that injustice must be rooted out by strong, persistent and determined action. I am thankful, however, that some of our white brothers have grasped the meaning of this social revolution and committed themselves to it. They are still all too small in quantity, but they are big in quality. Some like Ralph McGill, Lillian Smith, Harry Golden and James Dabbs have written about our struggle in eloquent, prophetic and understanding terms. Others have marched with us down nameless streets of the South. They have languished in filthy roach-infested jails, suffering the abuse and brutality of angry policemen who see them as "dirty nigger lovers." They, unlike so many of their moderate brothers and sisters, have recognized the urgency of the moment and sensed the need for powerful "action" antidotes to combat the disease of segregation.

The White Church

Let me rush on to mention my other disappointment. I have been so greatly disappointed with the white church and its leadership. Of course, there are some notable exceptions. I am not unmindful of the fact that each of you has taken some significant stands on this issue. I commend you, Rev. Stallings, for your Christian stand on this past Sunday, in welcoming Negroes to your worship service on a non-segregated basis. I commend the Catholic leaders of this state for integrating Springhill College several years ago.

But despite these notable exceptions I must honestly reiterate that I have been disappointed with the church. I do not say that as one of the negative critics who can always find something wrong with the church. I say it as a minister of the gospel, who loves the church; who was nurtured in its bosom; who has been sustained by its spiritual blessings and who will remain true to it as long as the cord of life shall lengthen.

I had the strange feeling when I was suddenly catapulted into the leadership of the bus protest in Montgomery several years ago that we would have the support of the white church. I felt that the white ministers, priests and rabbis of the South would be some of our strongest allies. Instead, some have been outright opponents, refusing to understand the freedom movement and misrepresenting its leaders; all too many others have been more cautious than courageous and have remained silent behind the anesthetizing security of the stained-glass windows.

In spite of my shattered dreams of the past, I came to Birmingham with the hope that the white religious leadership of this community would see the justice of our cause, and with deep moral concern, serve as the channel through which our just grievances would get to the power structure. I had hoped that each of you would understand. But again I have been disappointed. I have heard numerous religious leaders of the South call upon their worshippers to comply with a desegregation decision because it is the *law*, but I have longed to hear white ministers say, "Follow this decree because integration is morally *right* and the Negro is your brother." In the midst of blatant injustices inflicted upon the Negro, I have watched white churches stand on the sideline and merely mouth pious irrelevancies and sanctimonious trivialities. In the midst of a mighty struggle to rid our nation of racial and economic injustice, I have heard so many ministers say, "Those are social issues with which the gospel has no real concern," and I have watched so many churches commit themselves to a completely other-worldly religion which made a strange distinction between body and soul, the sacred and the secular.

So here we are moving toward the exit of the twentieth century with a religious community largely adjusted to the status quo, standing as a tail-light behind other community agencies rather than a headlight leading men to higher levels of justice.

Disturbers of the Peace

. . . But the judgment of God is upon the church as never before. If the church of today does not recapture the sacrificial spirit of the early church, it will lose its authentic ring, forfeit the loyalty of millions, and be dismissed as an irrelevant social club with no meaning for the twentieth century. I am meeting young people every day whose disappointment with the church has risen to outright disgust.

Maybe again, I have been too optimistic. Is organized religion too inextricably bound to the status-quo to save our nation and the world? Maybe I must turn my faith to the inner spiritual church, the church within the church, as the true *ecclesia* and the hope of the world. But again I am thankful to God that some noble souls from the ranks of organized religion have broken loose from the paralyzing chains of conformity and joined us as active partners in the struggle for freedom. They have left their secure congregations and walked the streets of Albany, Georgia, with us. They have gone through the highways of the South on tortuous rides for freedom. Yes, they have gone to jail with us. Some have been kicked out of their churches, and lost support of their bishops and fellow ministers. But they have gone with the faith that right defeated is stronger than evil triumphant. These men have been the leaven in the lump of the race. Their witness has been the spiritual salt that has preserved the true meaning of the Gospel in these troubled times. They have carved a tunnel of hope through the dark mountain of disappointment.

I hope the church as a whole will meet the challenge of this decisive hour. But even if the church does not come to the aid of justice, I have no despair about the future. I have no fear about the outcome of our struggle in Birmingham, even if our motives are presently misunderstood. We will reach the goal of freedom in Birmingham and all over the nation, because the goal of America is freedom. Abused and scorned though we may be, our destiny is tied up with the destiny of America. Before the pilgrims landed at Plymouth we were here. Before the pen of Jefferson etched across the pages of history the majestic words of the Declaration of Independence, we were here. For more than two centuries our fore-parents labored in this country without wages; they made cotton king; and they built the homes of their masters in the midst of brutal injustice and shameful humiliation—and yet out of a bottomless vitality they continued to thrive and develop. If the inexpressible cruelties of slavery could not stop us, the opposition we now face will surely fail. We will win our freedom because the sacred heritage of our nation and the eternal will of God are embodied in our echoing demands.

Bull Connor's Police

I must close now. But before closing I am impelled to mention one other point in your statement that troubled me profoundly. You warmly commended the Birmingham police force for keeping "order" and "preventing violence." I don't believe you would have so warmly commended the police force if you had seen its angry violent dogs literally biting six unarmed, nonviolent Negroes. I don't believe you would so quickly commend the policemen if you would observe their ugly and inhuman treatment of Negroes here in the city jail; if you would watch them push and curse old Negro women and young Negro girls; if you would see them slap and kick old Negro men and young boys; if you will observe them, as they did on two occasions, refuse to give us food because we wanted to sing our grace together. I'm sorry that I can't join you in praise for the police department.

It is true that they have been rather disciplined in their public handling of the demonstrators. In this sense they have been rather publicly "nonviolent." But for what purpose? To preserve the evil system of segregation. Over the last few years I have consistently preached that nonviolence demands that the means we use must be as pure as the ends we seek. So I have tried to make it clear that it is wrong to use immoral means to attain moral ends. But now I must affirm that it is just as wrong, or even more so, to use moral means to preserve immoral ends. Maybe Mr. Connor and his policemen have been rather publicly nonviolent, as Chief Pritchett was in Albany, Georgia, but they have used the moral means of nonviolence to maintain the immoral end of flagrant racial injustice. T. S. Eliot has said that there is no greater treason then to do the right deed for the wrong reason.

I wish you had commended the Negro sit-inners and demonstrators of Birmingham for their sublime courage, their willingness to suffer and their amazing discipline in the midst of the most inhuman provocation. One day the South will recognize its real heroes. They will be the James Merediths, courageously and with a majestic sense of purpose, facing jeering and hostile mobs and the agonizing loneliness that characterizes the life of the pioneer. They will be old oppressed, battered Negro women, symbolized in the seventy-two-year-old woman of Montgomery, Alabama, who rose up with a sense of dignity and with her people decided not to ride the segregated buses, and responded to one who inquired about her tiredness with ungrammatical profundity; "My feet is tired, but my soul is rested." They will be the young high school and college students, young ministers of the Gospel and a host of their elders courageously and nonviolently sitting-in at lunch counters and willingly going to jail for conscience's sake. One day the South will know that when these disinherited children of God sat down at lunch counters they were in reality standing up for the best in the American dream and the most sacred values in our Judeo-Christian heritage, and thusly, carrying our whole nation back to those great wells of democracy which were dug deep by the founding fathers in the formulation of the Constitution and the Declaration of Independence.

Never before have I written a letter this long (or should I say a book?). I'm afraid that it is much too long to take your precious time. I can assure you that it would have been much shorter if I had been writing from a comfortable desk, but what else is there to do when you are alone for days in the dull monotony of a narrow jail cell other than write long letters, think strange thoughts, and pray long prayers?

If I have said anything in this letter that is an overstatement of the truth and is indicative of an unreasonable impatience, I beg you to forgive me. If I have said anything in this letter that is an understatement of the truth and is indicative of my having a patience that makes me patient with anything less than brotherhood, I beg God to forgive me.

I hope this letter finds you strong in the faith. I also hope that circumstances will soon make it possible for me to meet each of you, not as an integrationist or a civil rights leader, but as a fellow clergyman and a Christian brother. Let us all hope that the dark clouds of racial prejudice will soon pass away and the deep fog of misunderstanding will be lifted from our fear-drenched communities and in some not too distant tomorrow the radiant stars of love and brotherhood will shine over our great nation with all of their scintillating beauty.

  Yours for the cause of Peace and Brotherhood,
  Martin Luther King, Jr.

TEN "HOW TO'S" IN NONVIOLENCE
The Fellowship of Reconciliation

THESE GUIDELINES WERE FIRST developed during the civil rights struggles by the Fellowship of Reconciliation (FOR) at the request of Dr. Martin Luther King, Jr. They were later revised for international use, focusing on the problem of nuclear weapons. The principles and strategies presented here have become a kind of primer for those beginning their involvement in nonviolent campaigns, as well as a set of criteria for long-time activists.

The Fellowship of Reconciliation, a working fellowship of pacifists from Christian, Jewish and Buddhist traditions, began its participation in the civil rights struggle with the first interracial sit-ins in 1943. Later, in the spring of 1947, FOR and the Congress on Racial Equality (CORE) co-sponsored the first freedom rides. They organized interracial groups which rode Greyhound and Trailways buses through the upper South to test the implementation of the 1946 Supreme Court decision outlawing segregation on interstate travel. Three of the freedom riders, Bayard Rustin, Joe Felmet and Igal Roodenko were arrested and served thirty-day sentences on segregated North Carolina chaingangs for sitting together in the front of the bus.

Four Basic Principles

1. **D**EFINE YOUR OBJECTIVES. Injustice and violence are everywhere around us. A single campaign or action will not remove it all. One must begin by focusing on a specific injustice; it should be possible to discuss in fairly simple and clear-cut terms. Decision-making and negotiation during a campaign will be helped immensely if you have defined clearly your short-range objectives.

2. **Be honest and listen well.** Part of your goal is to win your opponents' respect. Conduct yourself in a way which encourages that respect by showing

185

your scrupulous care for truth and justice. A crucial part of nonviolent direct action is the understanding that no one knows the complete truth about the issue at hand. Listening with openness to what your opponents have to say about your campaign is very important in your pursuit of the real truth. Similarly, listening carefully to those who are struggling at your side helps ensure that the oppression which you are fighting is not replaced by another kind of oppression.

3. Love your enemies. No matter how deeply involved in unjust and violent systems some people are, your goal is to break down those systems, not to punish others for wrongdoing. Real justice is established when people refuse to maintain oppressive systems, not when the people in those systems are destroyed. History has taught us over and over again that to focus on a small group as a basic source of injustice tends to promote disrespect for human life and even can mean avoiding recognition of the systemic foundations of injustice. Nonviolence requires a steadfast and conscious willingness to mentally separate respect for all people from disrespect for what some people are doing in a given situation.

4. Give your opponents a way out. By using nonviolence you are showing a kind of strength that overcomes injustice. Avoid self-righteousness with opponents. Recognize their weakness, embarrassment and fear. In a specific confrontation, and in the larger campaign, find a way to let them participate in finding a solution. Give them options to respond to, not non-negotiable demands. Make it as easy as possible for them to compromise to your position without having to concede defeat.

Six Strategic Steps

1. Investigate. Get the facts. Clear up any possible misunderstanding right at the start. If an injustice clearly has been done, be equally certain exactly who or what is to blame for it. The complexity of society today requires patient investigation to accurately determine responsibility for a particular injustice. The ability to explain with facts rather than just rhetoric will win support and prevent misunderstandings.

2. Negotiate. Meet with opponents and put the case to them. A solution may be worked out at this point. It is possible that your opponents have a grievance which you didn't know about. Now is the time to find out. If no solution is possible, let your opponents know that you intend to stand firm to establish justice. Let them know, however, that you are always ready to negotiate further.

3. Educate. Keep campaign participants and supporters well-informed of the issues, and spread the word to the public. This may involve issuing simple but carefully prepared leaflets. It may also call for street theater, informal street speaking, door-to-door personal visits, phone calls, and press releases. Talk to the editor of the local newspaper and explain your position. Organize others to send letters to newspapers and government officials. Always stick to the facts, avoid exaggeration, be brief and show good will. Remember that the attitudes of local people about your campaign can have an important effect on its outcome.

4. Demonstrate. Picketing, vigiling, mass rallies, and the handing out of leaflets on the street are the next step. All of these make more impact on your opponent, the public, the press, and law enforcement officials when conducted in a well-organized manner. Those demonstrating should be well-informed, cool-headed, able to endure possible heckling and to withstand possible violence without panic and without resorting to violence in return. It is most important to maintain discipline at this stage and to "keep cool under fire."

5. Resist. Nonviolent resistance is the final step, to be added to the first four as a last resort. This may mean a boycott, a fast, a strike, tax resistance, nonviolent blockade or other forms of civil disobedience. Planning must be carefully done and nonviolent training is essential. Discipline must be firm to avoid making your resistance vulnerable to violent provocation. Every provocation must be answered calmly and without retaliation. The general public as well as the direct action participants themselves can be moved most favorably by a well-organized, orderly expression of resistance. A crucial part of nonviolent resistance is the willingness to suffer the consequences. You are saying in effect, "I am so determined to right this injustice that I am willing to suffer to bring about change," instead of the more common and less effective reasoning, "I am so determined to right this injustice that I'm going to make my opponent suffer for it." The willingness to accept and absorb violence and suffering can often be the cutting edge for change. If your actions are directly against weapons of mass-destruction, for example, remember that your resistance is not directed simply against the weapons themselves, but also, and more importantly, against the popular support for those weapons which allows them to exist, and the fears they represent. When properly carried out, actions of resistance build a position of moral clarity which will strengthen your own courage and create widespread respect for your campaign.

6. Be patient. Meaningful change cannot be accomplished overnight. Like the building of a cathedral, it requires years of work. To deepen one's analysis of injustice and oppression means to become aware of how deeply entrenched are the structures which produce them. These structures can be eliminated, but this requires a long-term commitment and strategy. Individual actions are much more effective if they are integrated in a nonviolent campaign which may have to continue not only for months, but for years. Along the way, there will be many experiences of failure and temptations to give up. Your work may not only seem to fail but to have results opposite to those being sought. "Concentrate not on the results," Thomas Merton advised, "but on the value, the rightness, the truth of the work itself." To survive defeats and to carry on, we need one another's support, forgiveness, humor and occasions for celebration so that our struggle remains a labor of love.

Some Practical Details

1. Be creative. Nonviolent direct action does not mean avoiding engagement or failing to act. You must act creatively in all stages of your campaign.

2. Train your participants. Detailed preparation especially for demonstrations and resistance actions, will contribute to a sense of purposeful community and get everyone at ease with a clearer sense of what is going to happen. It will also help you cope more effectively with possible emergencies, and will point out unnoticed details which need further attention.

3. Communicate. Those who engage in direct action strategies often neglect one of the most important aspects of a nonviolent campaign: communicating with the opponent. Nonviolence holds open the possibility of converting, or being reconciled with, one's opponents. Education and negotiation therefore must continue, even in the intensity and excitement of a demonstration or a resistance action.

4. Control incidents. The success of demonstrations is always enhanced if disruptive incidents are handled in a quiet, effective and caring way. Hecklers can be talked with; violent incidents can be isolated from the demonstration; and persons unexpectedly arrested can be given support and assistance, all without diverting attention from the overall demonstration.

THE FUTURE OF NONVIOLENCE (1965)

David Dellinger

*D*AVID DELLINGER (1915-   ) CAME TO *public attention on October 16,* 1940, the first day of registration under the new WWII draft law. In the first act of resistance to the war, Dellinger and seven other students from Union Theological Seminary in New York, all eligible for ministerial deferments, announced their refusal to register for the draft. As with many other conscientious objectors to the war, Dellinger's prison term was a training ground for nonviolent direct action, especially against racial segregation. Both before and after his prison experience Dellinger was involved in the Gandhian movement which had recently come to the attention of peacemakers in the United States. The movement emphasized nonviolence as a lifestyle rather than merely as a social change strategy.

In 1939 he founded the Newark Commune, a community based on Gandhian and Christian principles including voluntary poverty and communal decision-making. Located in the center of the Newark ghetto, it became a cultural center for both black and white children. Its members also organized a cooperative buying program for the neighborhood. Later, the community helped found Liberation Press, a workers' cooperative which published *Liberation* magazine. As an editor of *Liberation*, Dellinger worked with A. J. Muste to present the radical pacifist perspective to the public and helped catalyze wider disarmament, civil rights, and anti-war actions. Dellinger was indicted in 1968 for his role in organizing demonstrations at the Democratic National Convention in Chicago, and as a member of the Chicago Eight, was tried and convicted in a widely publicized "conspiracy" trial, the conviction later being overturned. In this article, originally written for *Studies on the Left*, Dellinger explores the relationship of revolution and nonviolence and the limits of defending the interests of the United States through nonviolent defense.

189

I

THE THEORY AND PRACTICE of active nonviolence are roughly at the stage of development today as those of electricity in the early days of Marconi and Edison. A new source of power has been discovered and crudely utilized in certain specialized situations, but our experience is so limited and our knowledge so primitive that there is legitimate dispute about its applicability to a wide range of complicated and critical tasks. One often hears it said that nonviolent resistance was powerful enough to drive the British out of India but would have been suicidal against the Nazis. Or that Negroes can desegregate a restaurant or bus by nonviolence but can hardly solve the problem of jobs or getting rid of the Northern ghettos, since both of these attempts require major assaults on the very structure of society and run head on into the opposition of entrenched interests in the fields of business, finance, and public information. Finally, most of those who urge nonviolent methods on the Negro hesitate to claim that the United States should do away with its entire military force and prepare to defend itself in the jungle of international politics by nonviolent methods.

There is no doubt in my mind that nonviolence is currently incapable of resolving some of the problems that must be solved if the human race is to survive—let alone create a society in which all persons have a realistic opportunity to achieve material fulfillment and personal dignity. Those who are convinced that nonviolence can be used in all conflict situations have a responsibility to devise concrete methods by which it can be made effective. For example, can we urge the Negroes of Harlem or the obreros and campesinos (workers and peasants) of Latin America to refrain from violence if we offer them no positive method of breaking out of the slums, poverty, and cultural privation that blight their lives and condemn their children to a similar fate? It is contrary to the best tradition of nonviolence to do so. Gandhi often made the point that it is better to resist injustice by violent methods than not to resist at all. He staked his own life on his theory that nonviolent resistance was the superior method, but he never counselled appeasement or passive nonresistance.

The major advances in nonviolence have not come from people who have approached nonviolence as an end in itself, but from persons who were passionately striving to free themselves from social injustice. . . .

In 1956 the Negroes of Montgomery, Alabama catapulted nonviolence into the limelight in the United States, not out of conversion to pacifism or love for their oppressors, but because they had reached a point where they could no longer tolerate certain racial injustices. Martin Luther King, who later became a pacifist, employed an armed defense guard to protect his home and family during one stage of the Montgomery conflict. In 1963, one of the leaders of the mass demonstrations in Birmingham said to me: "You might as well say that we never heard of Gandhi or nonviolence, but we were determined to get our freedom, and in the course of the struggle for it we came upon nonviolence like gold in the ground."

There is not much point in preaching the virtues of nonviolence to a Negro in Harlem or Mississippi except as a method for winning his freedom. For one thing, the built-in institutional violence imposed on him every day of his life looms too large. He can rightly say that he wants no part of a nonviolence that condemns his spasmodic rock-throwing or desperate and often knowingly unrealistic talk of armed self-defense, but mounts no alternative campaign. It is all too easy for those with jobs, adequate educational opportunities, and decent housing to insist that Negroes remain nonviolent—to rally to the defense of "law and order." "Law and order is the Negro's best friend," Mayor Robert Wagner announced in the midst of the 1964 riots in Harlem. But nonviolence and a repressive law and order have nothing in common. The most destructive violence in Harlem is not the bottle-throwing, looting, or muggings of frustrated and demoralized Negroes. Nor is it the frequent shootings of juvenile delinquents and suspected criminals by white policemen, who often reflect both the racial prejudices of society and the personal propensity to violence that led them to choose a job whose tools are the club and the revolver. The basic violence in Harlem is the vast, impersonal violation of bodies and souls by an unemployment rate four times that of white New Yorkers, a median family income between half and two-thirds that of white families, an infant mortality rate of 45.3 per thousand compared to 26.3 for New York as a whole, and inhuman crowding into subhuman housing.

Commitment to nonviolence must not be based on patient acquiescence in intolerable conditions. Rather, it stems from a deeper knowledge of the self-defeating, self-corrupting effect of lapses into violence. On the one hand, Gandhi did not ally himself with those who profit from injustice and conveniently condemn others who violently fight oppression. On the other hand, he temporarily suspended several of his own nonviolent campaigns because some of his followers had succumbed to the temptations of violent reprisal. In perfecting methods of nonviolence, he gradually crystallized certain attitudes toward the nature of man (even oppressive, exploitative, foreign-invader man), which he formulated in the terminology of his native religion and which he considered indispensable for true nonviolence.

The key attitudes stem from a feeling for the solidarity of all human beings, even those who find themselves in deep conflict. George Meredith once said that a truly cultivated man is one who realizes that the things which seem to separate him from his fellows are as nothing compared with those which unite him with all humanity. Nonviolence may start, as it did with the young Gandhi and has with many an American Negro, as a technique for wresting gains from an unloved and unlovely oppressor. But somewhere along the line, if a nonviolent movement is to cope with deep-seated fears and privileges, its strategy must flow from a sense of the underlying unity of all human beings. So must the crucial, semi-spontaneous, inventive actions that emerge in the midst of crisis.

This does not mean that Negroes, for example, must "love" in a sentimental or emotional way those who are imprisoning, shooting, beating, or impoverishing them. Nor need they feel personal affection for complacent white liberals. But it is not enough to abandon the use of fists, clubs, Molotov cocktails, and guns. Real nonviolence requires an awareness that white oppressors and black victims are mutually entrapped in a set of relationships that violate the submerged better instincts of everyone. A way has to be found to release the trap and free both sets of victims. Appeals to reason or decency have little effect (except in isolated instances) unless they are accompanied by tangible pressures—on the pocketbook, for example—or the inconveniences associated with sit-ins, move-ins, strikes, boycotts or nonviolent obstructionism. But for any lasting gain to take place the struggle must appeal to the whole man, including his encrusted sense of decency and solidarity, his yearnings to recapture the lost innocence when human beings were persons to be loved, not objects to rule, obey, or exploit. . . .

This reaching out to the oppressor has nothing to do with tokenism, which tends to creep into any movement, including a nonviolent one. In fact, tokenism is a double violation of the attitude of solidarity, because it permits the oppressor to make, and the oppressed to accept, a gesture which leaves intact the institutional barriers that separate them. One can gain a token victory or make a political deal without needing to have any invigorating personal contact with the "enemy," certainly without bothering to imagine oneself in his place so as to understand his needs, fears and aspirations. But the more revolutionary a movement's demands, the more imperative it is to understand what is necessary for the legitimate fulfillment of the persons who make up the opposition.

"We're going to win our freedom," a Negro leader said at a mass meeting in Birmingham last year, "and as we do it we're going to set our white brothers free." A short while later, when the Negroes faced a barricade of police dogs, clubs and fire hoses, they "became spiritually intoxicated," as another leader described it. "This was sensed by the police and firemen and it began to have an effect on them. . . I don't know what happened to me. I got up from my knees and said to the cops: 'We're not turning back. We haven't done anything wrong. All we want is our freedom. How do you feel doing these things?'" The Negroes started advancing and Bull Connor shouted: "Turn on the water!" But the firemen did not respond. Again he gave the order and nothing happened. Some observers claim they saw firemen crying. Whatever happened, the Negroes went through the lines.

Vinoba Bhave[1] indicates something of the same sort on the level of international conflict when he says: "Russia says America has dangerous ideas so she has to increase her armaments. America says exactly the same thing about Russia . . . The image in the mirror is your own image; the sword in its hand is your own sword. And when we grasp our own sword in fear of what we see, the image in the mirror does the same. What we see in front of us is nothing but a reflection of ourselves. If India could find courage to reduce her army to the minimum, it would demonstrate to the world her moral strength. But we are cowards and cowards have no imagination."

II

The potential uses of nonviolent power are tremendous and as yet virtually unrealized. But it is important to understand that nonviolence can never be "developed" in such a way as to carry out some of the tasks assigned to it by its more naive converts. It would be impossible, for instance, to defend the United States of America, as we know it, nonviolently. This is not because of any inherent defect in the nonviolent method but because of a very important strength: nonviolence cannot be used successfully to protect special privileges that have been won by violence. The British could not have continued to rule India by taking a leaf out of Gandhi's book and becoming "nonviolent." Nor would the United States be able to maintain its dominant position in Latin America if it got rid of its armies, navies, "special forces," C.I.A.-guerrillas, etc. Does anyone think that a majority of the natives work for a few cents a day, live in rural or urban slums, and allow forty-four percent of their children to die before the age of five because they love us? Or that they are content to have American business drain away five hundred million dollars a year in interest and dividends, on the theory that the shareholders of United Fruit Company or the Chase Manhattan Bank are more needy or deserving than themselves?

It follows that advocates of nonviolence are overly optimistic when they argue from the unthinkability of nuclear war and the partially proven power of nonviolence to the position that simple common sense will lead the United States (the richest, most powerful nation in the world, on whose business investments and armed forces the sun never sets) to substitute nonviolent for violent national defense. In recent years a number of well-intentioned peace groups have tried to convince the government and members of the power elite that the Pentagon should sponsor studies with this end in view. But nonviolent defense requires not only the willingness to risk one's life (as any good soldier, rich or poor, will do). It requires renunciation of all claims to special privileges and power at the expense of other people. In our society most people find it more difficult to face economic loss while alive than death itself. Surrender of special privilege is certainly foreign to the psychology of those who supply, command, and rely on the military. Nonviolence is supremely the weapon of the dispossessed, the underprivileged, and the egalitarian, not of those who are still addicted to private profit, commercial values, and great wealth.

Nonviolence simply cannot defend property rights over human rights. The primacy of human rights would have to be established within the United States and in all of its dealings with other peoples before nonviolence could defend this country successfully. Nonviolence could defend what is worth defending in the United States, but a badly needed social revolution would have to take place in the process. Guerrilla warfare cannot be carried on successfully without the active support and cooperation of the surrounding population, which must identify justice (or at least its own welfare) with the triumph of the guerrillas. Nonviolence must rely even more heavily than guerrilla warfare on the justice of its cause. It has no chance of succeeding unless it can win supporters from previously hostile or neutral sections of the populace. It must do this by the fairness of its goals. Its objectives and methods are intimately interrelated and must be equally nonviolent.

Perhaps we can paraphrase Von Clausewitz's well known observation that war is but the continuation of the politics of peace by other means, and say that the social attitudes of nonviolent defense must be the continuation of the social attitudes of the society it is defending. . . .

On the crudest level, as long as we are willing to condemn two out of five children in Latin America to early death, in order to increase our material comforts and prosperity, by what newly found awareness of human brotherhood will we be able to resist the temptation to wipe out two out of five, three out of five, or even five out of five of the children of China in overt warfare if it is dinned into us that this is necessary to preserve our freedom, or the lives of ourselves and our own children? If we cannot respect our neighbors more than to keep large numbers of them penned up in rat-infested slum ghettos, how will we develop the sense of human solidarity with our opponents, without which nonviolence becomes an empty technicality and loses its power to undermine and sap enemy hostility and aggressiveness? How will we reach across the propaganda-induced barriers of hate, fear, and self-righteousness (belief in the superiority of one's country, race or system) to disarm ourselves and our enemies?

---

[1]Vinoba Bhave (1895-1982), direct spiritual successor to Mahatma Gandhi after Indian independence, for almost two decades led and inspired major campaigns for the nonviolent redistribution of land to the poor, resulting in the gift and/or voluntary collectivization of some 5 1/2 million acres. He is generally considered father of the modern "land-trust" movement.

BLESSED ARE THE MEEK: THE ROOTS OF CHRISTIAN NONVIOLENCE (1967)

Thomas Merton

It WOULD BE A SERIOUS mistake to regard Christian nonviolence simply as a novel tactic which is at once efficacious and even edifying, and which enables the sensitive man to participate in the struggles of the world without being dirtied with blood. Nonviolence is not simply a way of proving one's point and getting what one wants without being involved in behavior that one considers ugly and evil. Nor is it, for that matter, a means which anyone legitimately can make use of according to his fancy for any purpose whatever. To practice nonviolence for a purely selfish or arbitrary end would in fact discredit and distort the truth of nonviolent resistance.

Nonviolence is perhaps the most exacting of all forms of struggle, not only because it demands first of all that one be ready to suffer evil and even face the threat of death without violent retaliation, but because it excludes mere transient self-interest from its considerations. In a very real sense, he who practices nonviolent resistance must commit himself not to the defense of his own interests or even those of a particular group: he must commit himself to the defense of objective truth and right and above all of *man*. His aim is then not simply to 'prevail' or to prove that he is right and the adversary wrong, or to make the adversary give in and yield what is demanded of him.

Nor should the nonviolent resister be content to prove *to himself* that *he* is virtuous and right, that *his* hands and heart are pure even though the adversary's may be evil and defiled. Still less should he seek for himself the psychological gratification of upsetting the adversary's conscience and perhaps driving him to an act of bad faith and refusal of the truth. We know that our unconscious motives may, at times, make our nonviolence a form of

195

moral aggression and even a subtle provocation designed (without our awareness) to bring out the evil we hope to find in the adversary, and thus to justify ourselves in our own eyes and in the eyes of 'decent people.' Wherever there is a high moral ideal there is an attendant risk of pharisaism and nonviolence is no exception. The basis of pharisaism is division: on one hand this morally or socially privileged self and the elite to which it belongs. On the other hand, the "others," the wicked, the unenlightened, whoever they may be, communists, capitalists, colonialists, traitors, international Jewry, racists etc.

Christian nonviolence is not built on a presupposed division, but on the basic unity of man. It is not out for the conversion of the wicked to the ideas of the good, but for the healing and reconciliation of man with himself, man the person and man the human family.

The nonviolent resister is not fighting simply for "his" truth or for "his" pure conscience, or for the right that is on "his side." On the contrary, both his strength and his weakness come from the fact that he is fighting for *the* truth, common to him and to the adversary, *the* right which is objective and universal. He is fighting for *everybody*.

For this very reason, as Gandhi saw, the fully consistent practice of nonviolence demands a solid metaphysical and religious basis both in being and in God. This comes *before* subjective good intentions and sincerity. For the Hindu this metaphysical basis was provided by the Vedantist doctrine of the Atman, the true transcendent Self which alone is absolutely real, and before which the empirical self of the individual must be effaced in the faithful practice of *dharma*. For the Christian the basis of nonviolence is the Gospel message of salvation for all and of the Kingdom of God to which *all* are summoned. The disciple of Christ, who has heard the good news, the announcement of the Lord's coming and of victory, and is aware of the definitive establishment of the Kingdom, proves his faith by the gift of his whole self to the Lord in order that *all* may enter the Kingdom.

The great historical event, the coming of the Kingdom, is made clear and is "realized" in proportion as Christians themselves live the life of the Kingdom in the circumstances of their own place and time. The saving grace of God in the Lord Jesus is proclaimed to man existentially in the love, the openness, the simplicity, the humility and the self-sacrifice of Christians. By their example of a truly Christian understanding of the world, expressed in a living and active application of the Christian faith to the human problems of their own time, Christians manifest the love of Christ for men (John 13:35, 17:21), and by that fact make him visibly present in the world. The religious basis of Christian nonviolence is then faith in Christ the Redeemer and obedience to his demand to love and manifest himself in us by a certain manner of acting in the world and in relation to other men. This obedience enables us to live as true citizens of the Kingdom, in which the divine mercy, the grace, favor and redeeming love of God are active in our lives. Then the Holy Spirit will indeed "rest upon us" and act in us, not for our own good alone but for God and his Kingdom.

And if the Spirit dwells in us and works in us, our lives will be a continuous and progressive conversion and transformation in which we also, in some measure, help to transform others and allow ourselves to be transformed by and with others, in Christ.

The chief place in which this new mode of life is set forth in detail is the Sermon on the Mount. At the very beginning of this great inaugural discourse, the Lord numbers the beatitudes, which are the theological foundation of Christian nonviolence: Blessed are the poor in spirit . . . blessed are the meek (Matthew 5:3-4).

This does not mean "blessed are they who are endowed with a tranquil natural temperament, who are not easily moved to anger, who are always quiet and obedient, who do not naturally resist." Still less does it mean "blessed are they who passively submit to unjust oppression." On the contrary, we know that the "poor in spirit" are those of whom the prophets spoke, those who in the last days will be the "humble of the earth," that is to say the oppressed who have no human weapons to rely on and who nevertheless are true to the commandments of Yahweh, and who hear the voice that tells them: "Seek justice, seek humility, perhaps you will find shelter on the day of the Lord's wrath." (Sophia 2:3). In other words they seek justice in the power of truth and of God, not by the power of man. Note that Christian meekness, which is essential to true nonviolence, has this eschatological quality about it. It refrains from self-assertion and from violent aggression because it sees all things in the light of the great judgment. Hence it does not struggle and fight merely for this or that ephemeral gain. It struggles for the truth and the right which alone will stand in that day when all is to be tried by fire (I Corinthians 3:10-15).

Furthermore, Christian nonviolence and meekness imply a particular understanding of the power of human poverty and powerlessness when they are united with the invisible strength of Christ. The beatitudes indeed convey a profound existential understanding of the dynamic of the Kingdom of God—a dynamic made clear in the parables of the mustard seed and of the yeast. This is a dynamism of patient and secret growth, in belief that out of the smallest, weakest, and most insignificant seed the greatest tree will come. This is not merely a matter of blind and arbitrary faith. The early history of the Church, the record of the apostles and martyrs remains to testify to this inherent and mysterious dynamism of the ecclesial 'event' in the world of history and time. Christian nonviolence is rooted in this consciousness and this faith.

This aspect of Christian nonviolence is extremely important and it gives us the key to a proper understanding of the meekness which accepts being 'without strength' (*gewaltlos*) not out of masochism, quietism, defeatism or false passitivity, but trusting in the strength of the Lord of truth. Indeed, we repeat, Christian nonviolence is nothing if not first of all a formal profession of faith in the Gospel message that the *Kingdom has been established* and that the Lord of truth is indeed risen and reigning over his Kingdom.

Faith of course tells us that we live in a time of eschatological struggle, facing a fierce combat which marshals all the forces of evil and darkness against the still invisible truth, yet this combat is already decided by the victory of Christ over death and over sin. The Christian can renounce the protection of violence and risk being humble, therefore *vulnerable,* not because he trusts in the supposed efficacy of a gentle and persuasive tactic that will disarm hatred and tame cruelty, but because he believes that the hidden power of the Gospel is demanding to be manifested in and through his own poor person. Hence in perfect obedience to the Gospel, he effaces himself and his own interests and even risks his life in order to testify not simply to 'the truth' in a sweeping, idealistic and purely platonic sense, but to the truth that is incarnate in a concrete human situation, involving living persons whose rights are denied or whose lives are threatened.

Here it must be remarked that a holy zeal for the cause of humanity in the abstract may sometimes be mere lovelessness and indifference for concrete and living human beings. When we appeal to the highest and most noble ideals, we are more easily tempted to hate and condemn those who, so we believe, are standing in the way of their realization.

Christian nonviolence does not encourage or excuse hatred of a special class, nation or social group. It is not merely *anti-* this or that. In other words, the evangelical realism which is demanded of the Christian should make it impossible for him to generalize about "the wicked" against whom he takes up moral arms in a struggle for righteousness. He will not let himself be persuaded that the adversary is totally wicked and can therefore never be reasonable or well-intentioned, and hence need never be listened to. This attitude, which defeats the very purpose of nonviolence—openness, communication, dialogue —often accounts for the fact that some acts of civil disobedience merely antagonize the adversary without making him willing to communicate in any way whatever, except with bullets or missiles. Thomas a Becket, in Eliot's play *Murder in the Cathedral,* debated with himself, fearing that he might be seeking martyrdom merely in order to demonstrate his own righteousness and the King's injustice: "This is the greatest treason, to do the right thing for the wrong reason."

Now all these principles are fine and they accord with our Christian faith. But once we view the principles in the light of current facts, a practical difficulty confronts us. If the Gospel is preached to the poor, if the Christian message is essentially a message of hope and redemption for the poor, the oppressed, the underprivileged and those who have no power humanly speaking, how are we to reconcile ourselves to the fact that Christians belong for the most part to the rich and powerful nations of the earth? Seventeen percent of the world's population control eighty percent of the world's wealth, and most of these seventeen percent are supposedly Christian. Admittedly those Christians who are interested in nonviolence are not ordinarily wealthy ones. Nevertheless, like it or not, they share in the power and privilege of the most wealthy and mighty society the world has ever known. Even with the best subjective intentions in the world, how can they avoid a certain ambiguity in preaching nonviolence? Is this not a mystification?

We must remember Marx's accusation that, "The social principles of Christianity encourage dullness, lack of self-respect, submissiveness, self-abasement, in short all the characteristics of the proletariat." We must frankly face the possibility that the nonviolence of the European or American preaching Christian meekness may conceivably be adulterated by bourgeois feelings and by an unconscious desire to preserve the status quo against violent upheaval.

Let us however seriously consider at least the *conditions* for relative honesty in the practice of Christian nonviolence.

1) Nonviolence must be aimed above all at the transformation of the present state of the world, and it must therefore be free from all occult, unconscious connivance with an unjust use of power. This poses enormous problems—for if nonviolence is too political it becomes drawn into the power struggle and identified with one side or another in that struggle, while if it is totally apolitical it runs the risk of being ineffective or at best merely symbolic.

2) The nonviolent resistance of the Christian who belongs to one of the powerful nations and who is himself in some sense a privileged member of world society will have to be clearly not *for himself* but *for others*, that is for the poor and underprivileged. (Obviously in the case of Negroes in the United States, though they may be citizens of a privileged nation, their case is different. They are clearly entitled to wage a nonviolent struggle for their rights, but even for them this struggle should be primarily for *truth itself*—this being the source of their power.)

3) In the case of nonviolent struggle for peace—the threat of nuclear war abolishes all privileges. Under the bomb there is not much distinction between rich and poor. In fact the richest nations are usually the most threatened. Nonviolence must simply avoid the ambiguity of an unclear and *confusing protest* that hardens the warmakers in their self-righteous blindness. This means in fact that *in this case above all nonviolence must avoid a facile and fanatical self-righteousness*, and refrain from being satisfied with dramatic self-justifying gestures.

4) Perhaps the most insidious temptation to be avoided is one which is characteristic of the power structure itself: this fetishism of immediate visible results. Modern society understands "possibilities" and "results" in terms of a superficial and quantitative idea of efficacy. One of the missions of Christian nonviolence is to restore a different standard of practical judgment in social conflicts. This means that the Christian humility of nonviolent action must establish itself in the minds and memories of modern man not only as *conceivable* and possible, but as a *desirable alternative* to what he now considers the only realistic possibility: namely political technique backed by

force. Here the human dignity of nonviolence must manifest itself clearly in terms of a freedom and a nobility which are able to resist political manipulation and brute force and show them up as arbitrary, barbarous and irrational. This will not be easy. The temptation to get publicity and quick results by spectacular tricks or by forms of protest that are merely odd and provocative but whose human meaning is not clear, may defeat this purpose. The realism of nonviolence must be made evident by humility and self-restraint which clearly show frankness and open-mindedness and invite the adversary to serious and reasonable discussion.

Instead of trying to use the adversary as leverage for one's own effort to realize an ideal, nonviolence seeks only to enter into a dialogue with him in order to attain, together with him, the common good of *man*. Nonviolence must be realistic and concrete. Like ordinary political action, it is no more than the 'art of the possible.' But precisely the advantage of nonviolence is that it has a *more Christian and more humane notion of what is possible.* Where the powerful believe that only power is efficacious, the nonviolent resister is persuaded of the superior efficacy of love, openness, peaceful negotiation and above all of truth. For power can guarantee the interests of *some men* but it can never foster the good of *man*. Power always protects the good of some at the expense of all the others. Only love can attain and preserve the good of all. Any claim to build the security of *all* on force is a manifest imposture.

It is here that genuine humility is of the greatest importance. Such humility, united with true Christian courage (because it is based on trust in God and not in one's own ingenuity and tenacity), is itself a way of communicating the message that one is interested only in truth and in the genuine rights of others. Conversely, our authentic interest in the common good above all will help us to be humble, and to distrust our own hidden drive to self-assertion.

5) Christian nonviolence, therefore, is convinced that the manner in which the conflict for truth is waged will itself manifest or obscure the truth. To fight for truth by dishonest, violent, inhuman, or unreasonable means would simply betray the truth one is trying to vindicate. The absolute refusal of evil or suspect means is a necessary element in the witness of nonviolence.

As Pope Paul said before the United Nations Assembly in 1965, "Men cannot be brothers if they are not humble. No matter how justified it may appear, pride provokes tensions and struggles for prestige, domination, colonialism and egoism. In a word *pride shatters brotherhood.*" He went on to say that the attempts to establish peace on the basis of violence were in fact a manifestation of human pride. "If you wish to be brothers, let the weapons fall from your hands. You cannot love with offensive weapons in your hands."

6) A test of our sincerity in the practice of nonviolence is this: are we willing to *learn something from the adversary?* If a *new truth* is made known to us by him or through him, will we accept it? Are we willing to admit that he is not totally inhuman, wrong, unreasonable, cruel, etc.? This is important. If he sees that we are completely incapable of listening to him with an open mind, our

nonviolence will have nothing to say to him except that we distrust him and seek to outwit him. Our readiness to see some good in him and to agree with some of his ideas (though tactically this might look like a weakness on our part), actually gives us power: the power of sincerity and of truth. On the other hand, if we are obviously unwilling to accept any truth that we have not first discovered and declared ourselves, we show by that very fact that we are interested not in the truth so much as in "being right." Since the adversary is presumably interested in being right also, and in proving himself right by what he considers the superior argument of force, we end up where we started. Nonviolence has great power, provided that it really witnesses to truth and not just to self-righteousness.

The dread of being open to the ideas of others generally comes from our hidden insecurity about our own convictions. We fear that we may be 'converted'—or perverted—by a pernicious doctrine. On the other hand, if we are mature and objective in our open-mindedness, we may find that viewing things from a basically different perspective—that of our adversary—we discover our own truth in a new light and are able to understand our own ideal more realistically.

Our willingness to take *an alternative approach* to a problem will perhaps relax the obsessive fixation of the adversary on his view, which he believes is the only reasonable possibility and which he is determined to impose on everyone else by coercion.

It is the refusal of alternatives—a compulsive state of mind which one might call the 'ultimatum complex'—which makes wars in order to force the unconditional acceptance of one over-simplified interpretation of reality. The mission of Christian humility in social life is not merely to edify, but to *keep minds open to many alternatives*. The rigidity of a certain type of Christian thought has seriously impaired this capacity, which nonviolence must recover.

Needless to say, Christian humility must not be confused with a mere desire to win approval and to find reassurance by conciliating others superficially.

7) Christian hope and Christian humility are inseparable. The quality of nonviolence is decided largely by the purity of the Christian hope behind it. In its insistence on certain human values, the Second Vatican Council, following *Pacem in Terris,* displayed a basically optimistic trust *in man himself.* Not that there is not wickedness in the world, but today trust in God cannot be completely divorced from a certain trust in man. The Christian knows that there are radically sound possibilities in every man, and he believes that love and grace always have the power to bring out those possibilities at the most unexpected moments. Therefore if he has hopes that God will grant peace to the world it is because he also trusts that man, God's creature, is not basically evil: that there is in man a potentiality for peace and order which can be realized provided the right conditions are there. The Christian will do his part in creating these conditions by preferring love and trust to hate and suspiciousness. Obviously, once again, this "hope in man" must not be naive.

But experience itself has shown, in the last few years, how much an attitude of simplicity and openness can do to break down barriers of suspicion that had divided men for centuries.

In resume, the meekness and humility which Christ extolled in the Sermon on the Mount and which are the basis of true Christian nonviolence, are inseparable from an eschatological Christian hope which is completely open to the presence of God in the world and therefore to the presence of our brother who is always seen, no matter who he may be, in the perspectives of the Kingdom. Despair is not permitted to the meek, the humble, the afflicted, the ones famished for justice, the merciful, the clean of heart and the peacemakers. All the beatitudes 'hope against hope,' "bear everything, believe everything, hope for everything, endure everything" (I Corinthians 13:7). The beatitudes are simply aspects of love. They refuse to despair of the world and abandon it to a supposedly evil fate which it has brought upon itself. Instead, like Christ himself, the Christian takes upon his own shoulders the yoke of the Savior, meek and humble of heart. This yoke is the burden of the world's sin with all its confusions and all its problems. These sins, confusions and problems are our very own. We do not disown them.

NONVIOLENT NAPALM IN CATONSVILLE (1968)
Tom Cornell

Religious activists in the Vietnam era antiwar movement were faced with many challenges to their understanding and implementation of nonviolence, but the issues of property destruction and self-immolation were two of the most difficult to address. The following article by Tom Cornell (1934-   ), who had burned his own draft card in a public action on November 6, 1965, proved to be a significant contribution to the debate over the destruction of property as a method of nonviolent resistance to war.

The Catholic Left was promoting a new perspective within the antiwar coalition that advocated the destruction of war-related property far beyond the traditional burning of draft cards. In 1968, Philip Berrigan invited his brother Daniel to join him and several friends in an act of ultraresistance: a raid on the Selective Service Local Board No. 3, in Catonsville, Maryland. Cornell, then editor of the *Catholic Worker*, a primary vehicle for debate within Catholic and other antiwar coalitions, decided to write an analysis of the Catonsville raid. In *Nonviolent Napalm in Catonsville* he explores the challenge which the raid presented to traditional Christian and Gandhian teachings on nonviolence. Conscious of the fact that advocates of nonviolent resistance had lost control of the anti-Vietnam war coalition, he feared that growing frustration and anger could turn the movement into a caldron of destructive passions. He argued against those who believed that the force owned by the state justified the use of violence to overcome it and asserted that fascism rather than revolution would be the outcome. At the same time Cornell also rejected the position of those who would support the violence of the status quo while condemning as violent any attempt to protect those adversely affected by it. Cornell writes from a belief that human rights take moral precedence over property rights in life-or-death matters. He agreed with the argument echoed later during the trial of the Catonsville Nine that immoral property, which destroys human life, does not enjoy an absolute guarantee of protection. Only human life, created in God's image, is dignified by that right.

On October 4, 1967, Fr. Philip Berrigan, S.S.J., Thomas Lewis, Rev. Jambes Mengel and David Eberhardt of the Baltimore Interfaith Peace Mission entered the office of Selective Service Local Board No. 3 in Baltimore, opened file cabinets containing the draft records of men registered with that board and poured several cups of their own—and animal—blood into them. On May 24, 1968, they stood for sentencing, having been convicted of the criminal charges growing out of that incident.

One week before they were to be sentenced, on May 17, Fr. Philip Berrigan and Tom Lewis were joined by seven others, Fr. Daniel Berrigan, S.J., John Hogan, Brother David Darst, Mr. and Mrs. Thomas Melville, Miss Mary Moylan and George Mische at Selective Service Local Board No. 33, in Catonsville, Maryland, where they seized the files of six hundred registrants and destroyed them with home-made napalm in a parking lot adjacent to the local board's office.

Fr. Phil Berrigan and Tom Lewis were sentenced to six years in federal prison, David Eberhardt to three years, and Rev. Mengel's sentence was deferred pending psychiatric consultation. The lawyer for the group, Fred Weisgal, filed an appeal immediately. The trial judge, Edward Northrop, however, refused to allow Fr. Phil and Tom to be released on bail pending their appeal. They were a "menace to the community," and were returned to Baltimore County Jail in Towson, Maryland, where they and the seven others face charges brought against them by the county for the Catonsville action: theft, assault, arson and sabotage. . . .

The Catonsville board was selected because it was logistically well situated and relatively vulnerable. There was a parking lot outside where records could be burned with no danger to any person or any other property. The Special Forces Handbook supplied the formula for napalm, the jellied gasoline which has killed, crippled and disfigured so many innocent Vietnamese people, especially children. The protestors carried the ten-pound package of napalm with them, past two workmen plastering up a recruiting poster outside Local Board No. 33, and placed it under the stairway leading up to the office.

Tom Lewis, Mary Moylan and Marjorie Melville entered first. Three women workers were at their desks. Lewis began to speak, to try to explain what they were about. He was ignored. The Fathers Berrigan, Mische, Melville, and the others entered brusquely carrying large wire trash baskets, proceeded immediately to the file cabinets where registrants' records are kept and emptied their contents into the baskets. Mrs. Murphy, the clerk of the board, became upset. "My files," she shouted, "Get away from my files!" Fr. Dan went after the 1-A's first, then the 2-A's, and then the 1-Y's,[1] stuffing them furiously into the baskets. George Mische warned him not to pack them too tight, lest they fail to burn through. One of the local board assistants darted to the telephone to summon the police. Mary Moylan put her hand on the phone, telling the young woman to wait till they were through. As soon as the files were safely basketed Mary gave the woman the phone, saying, "Now you can call whoever you want." The young woman then threw the phone out the closed window, to attract the attention of those on the street below. Mrs. Murphy, the clerk, lunged toward George Mische, still screaming, "MY FILES! Get away from MY FILES!," and grabbed George by the seat of his pants. They gave at the seams. With a basket in one hand and his dignity upheld with the other, George made it to the parking lot outside. Mrs. Murphy's finger was scratched when she attempted to wrest George's basket from him: hence the charge of assault. One of the billboard plasterers, still at work as the team passed, remarked to his fellow worker, "I think they need us upstairs." One of the men retrieved the napalm from under the stairway and brought it to the parking lot. Newsmen, alerted beforehand, were emerging as if from nowhere. The napalm was thrown upon the files, and, too volatile to be safely ignited by a match, was set off with a cigarette thrown upon the mass. The fire burned fiercely for perhaps ten minutes, devouring the files of six hundred Catonsville registrants. The team gathered around the pyre to recite the Lord's prayer and to sing hymns. Thus they were found by a local policeman who asked, "Who is responsible for this?"

The sentencing of the first team, the "Baltimore Four," took place on Friday, May 24, before Judge Northrop. The courtroom was large, with three rows of benches six deep in the spectators' section. There were about one hundred and eighty persons in attendance, many wearing religious garb, and perhaps fifteen or twenty crowded outside the entrance to the court. . . . Berrigan and Lewis were sentenced to six years in federal prison. Dave Eberhardt declared that he was not contrite either and was sentenced to three years.

The prisoners were led away, with Judge Northrop still sitting upon his bench. Slowly, an ovation rose from the spectators, swelling to thunder as everyone rose to pay homage to these brave men. Judge Northrop was at a loss to control the situation or reclaim his courtroom. Authority no longer sat on the bench behind the "bar of justice," but had devolved upon those who deserved it. With his few words of sentencing, severe, unfeeling and unseeing, Judge Northrop might as well have proclaimed the commencement of the revolution, or so many of us felt at that moment, and we might just be proven right.

But is this truly nonviolence? When an individual takes his own draft cards and burns them then he makes a decision for himself: I will no longer be a part of the war system. He does not make a decision for anybody else. This is the kind of nonviolence we have grown used to (though just two years ago it shocked many of our natural allies). But did the men whose files these were decide to have them there? And if they had, does that give this property the right to exist? In their statement of purpose that Catonsville team wrote, "Some property has no right to exist. Hitler's gas ovens, Stalin's concentration camps, atomic-biological-chemical weaponry, files of conscription and slum properties are examples. . . ."

The burning of the Catonsville files signals a shift in tactics, from nonviolent protest to resistance to revolution. It is debatable whether revolutionary tactics are appropriate in a modern highly-organized industrial and complex society such as our own. It is certainly true that the establishment, the white power structure, the power elite, have an effective monopoly on conventional force. They have the guns, the tanks, the prisons and the McCarran Act detention camps, and they could scoop all the New Left, Old Left, Black Power activists and underground newspaper editors into their camps overnight with hardly a ripple from the liberals, just as in World War II the Japanese-Americans disappeared with almost no protest in their behalf. Compare the War Department budget with that of the Movement. We bring a quarter of a million people to Central Park for an afternoon and the Pentagon sends half a million to Vietnam for the duration. No, violent revolutionary tactics are not very hopeful . . . . The only revolution they are likely to effect in the U.S. is one of the Right. Moreover as pacifists we know that violence will not bring about what we desire. The means inevitably determine the ends.

The word revolution has been cheapened by overuse; still it retains meaning, in calling for a restructuring of power in American society, a rechanneling of wealth and resources, and a devolution of political decision-making power so that everyone might have a voice in those decisions which most seriously affect his life. The scholars tell us that we are sufficiently advanced in technology to make it possible for us to offer a decent life to all Americans without scratching affluence from the backs of other Americans, or of Latin Americans, Africans and Asians. It would be pleasant and reassuring to believe that this kind of restructuring could come about as a result of protest, of the presentation of petitions for redress of grievances, through mass demonstrations and parades and the conventional electoral system. We will keep these actions up where appropriate. Nevertheless, there is not one shred of evidence that any substantial change in the distribution of wealth or decision-making power has been effected by such means so far. The best that can be said is that nonviolence has succeeded through its own kinds of protest and resistance activities in generating greater pressures for change and proving that ways other than those of conventional politics are more effective in generating the kinds of pressures needed for change out of the established patterns. Now it remains to develop yet more vigorous forms of nonviolent intervention against the processes of murder and exploitation, and the Berrigans have given an example, an ingenious act of nonviolent revolution.

There are draft boards, induction centers, offices and properties which administer racism and war and which are amazingly vulnerable to those of their victims with the integrity, courage and imagination to dismantle them out of deep respect and love for life and the living. If nothing short of such revolutionary acts will accomplish the goal of the overthrow of the institutions of death and oppression then let it be! George Washington was far less justified in his revolutionary aspirations to make the North Atlantic free for Yankee merchants and slave traders. And he used violence, impressment of soldiers, confiscation of property, the harassment and even murder of Tories. His soldiers looted and burned and they brought down upon the heads of the majority of the colonists (who did not side with the Revolution) the wrath of the British Army, which burned and pillaged its way until called elsewhere. Still we have Fourth of July parades, and George Washington's portrait hangs on so many grammar school classroom walls that it is impossible to count the number of maiden-lady teachers who have come to look like him.

Moreover, for those who have not rejected violence in the maintenance of the status quo, who believe in the use of violent force to suppress the realization of the legitimate aspirations of the great majority of emerging peoples, for those who echo Mr. Johnson in regard to ghetto riots, that violence never accomplishes anything, while he increases the tonnage of bombs dropped daily on Vietnam, to fault the Berrigans, Tom Lewis, the Melvilles and the others for escalating nonviolence to this vigorous and daring level in the light of all this is, at best, blind hypocrisy.

If the movement is to turn to revolutionary strategy we must ask what kind of revolution we are looking for. Violent revolution is impossible for those of us who are convinced that violence is fundamentally counterrevolutionary and corrupting beyond tolerance, an outmoded method of expression in today's world though it has always been antithetical to The Good. It is truly Providential that in our time we have at least the beginnings of a theory and a technique of nonviolent action, forged by Gandhi, Martin Luther King and A. J. Muste and their followers with which to build a nonviolent revolution.

The Catonsville Action may prove to be a powerful model for the next phase of the nonviolent revolution in America. Its power cuts through the fanciful rhetoric of the New Left to the core of frustration and longing for the Beloved Community that motivates those involved in the antiwar, student and black movements. The action was small, carefully planned by people who knew and trusted each other, and easily controlled. It was designed so that no one would be in danger of physical harm nor otherwise violated. It was aimed at things, at property that is violating young men and causing immense grief, suffering and death around the world, property that has no right to exist, but which current folklore invests with a certain mystical inviolability. The participants in the action made no effort to conceal their identities. They know what penalties they face and do not shrink from paying the price, which is an important part of the action itself, essential in the generating of the moral energies necessary for the kind of change they seek.

The price is high. Fr. Phil and Tom Lewis, with six year sentences, will stand trial twice more. They speak all the louder for this. They did not dissimulate or try to extricate themselves from the processes of retribution by invoking legal technicalities. On the other hand they are right to appeal and fight their conviction on moral and constitutional grounds, since by doing so they may widen liberty under law for those who follow.

Some of our friends were shocked by the Catonsville Action, primarily, I suspect, because of the terrible price that is likely to be exacted. Do they think that revolutions come for the asking, or that its victims are always anonymous? Even a nonviolent revolution, or rather, especially a nonviolent revolution will demand blood, our blood, not theirs, and that's the difference. It sounded stirring to us white men a few years ago to hear our Negro fellow demonstrators answer Dr. King's call to let the blood of his own followers flow in the streets before one of us should touch a hair on the head of one white man. To come to believe in the literal truth of the necessity of this for the only kind of revolution that can mean anything in today's America is harder in the cold light of day, away from the singing and the shouting of an Alabama camp meeting. It is nonetheless indispensable.

---

[1] The codes refer to draft status: 1-A indicated the registrant was available for military service. 2-A was a deferment for men in approved trade, business, or vocational school or junior college. 1-Y was a medical deferment.

LETTER FROM DELANO (1969)
Cesar Chavez

*C*ESAR CHAVEZ (1927-   ) BEGAN BUILDING the United Farmworkers Union in 1962 with $1,200, the hope of his Catholic faith, and simple grassroots organizing methods. It was to be a union of, by, and for the migrant farmworkers—an unheard of phenomenon at that time. Using strikes and national boycotts, marches and fasts, Chavez and the UFW succeeded in focusing nationwide attention on the farmworkers' struggle for basic human rights. That attention became a source of national pressure on growers to negotiate contracts with the United Farmworkers' Union. "We're not nonviolent because we want to save our souls," said Chavez, "we're nonviolent because we want to get some social justice for the workers." But the farmworkers' rights had to be won again and again as agribusiness struggled to keep its costs low and profits high. In the late 1980's the union continues to struggle, this time to stop growers from spraying toxic pesticides over the fields where they labor. These pesticides are known to cause disease, death, and a growing rate of malformed children born to farmworker families.

Letter From Delano was first issued in the form of an open letter published simultaneously in *The National Catholic Reporter* and *The Christian Century*. It not only offers insight into Chavez' understanding of nonviolence; it is, in itself, an act of nonviolence. It is the act of reaching toward the "enemy"; of involving the other in resolving the conflict. Chavez presents his case, then boldly invites his opponent to meet him on the only common ground possible at that historical moment—the desire to keep violence at bay.

GOOD FRIDAY 1969

E.L. Barr, Jr., President
California Grape and Tree Fruit League
717 Market St.
San Francisco, California

Dear Mr. Barr:

I am sad to hear about your accusations in the press that our union movement and table grape boycott have been successful because we have used violence and terror tactics. If what you say is true, I have been a failure and should withdraw from the struggle; but you are left with the awesome moral responsibility, before God and Man, to come forward with whatever information you have so that corrective action can begin at once. If for any reason you fail to come forth to substantiate your charges, then you must be held responsible for committing violence against us, albeit of the tongue. I am convinced that you as a human being did not mean what you said but rather acted hastily under pressure from the public relations firm that has been hired to try to counteract the tremendous moral force of our movement. How many times we ourselves have felt the need to lash out in anger and bitterness.

Today on Good Friday, 1969, we remember the life and the sacrifice of Martin Luther King, Jr., who gave himself totally to the nonviolent struggle for peace and justice. In his *Letter From a Birmingham Jail* Dr. King describes better than I could our hopes for the strike and boycott: "Injustice must be exposed, with all the tensions its exposure creates, to the light of human conscience and the air of national opinion before it can be cured." For our part I admit that we have seized upon every tactic and strategy consistent with the morality of our cause to expose that injustice and thus to heighten the sensitivity of the American conscience so that farmworkers will have, without bloodshed, their own union and the dignity of bargaining with their agribusiness employers. By lying about the nature of our movement, Mr. Barr, you are working against nonviolent social change. Unwittingly perhaps, you may unleash that other force which our union by discipline and deed, censure and education has sought to avoid, that panacean shortcut: that senseless violence which honors no color, class, or neighborhood.

You must understand—I must make you understand—that our membership and the hopes and aspirations of the hundreds of thousands of the poor and dispossessed that have been raised on our account are, above all, human beings, no better and no worse than any other cross-section of human society; we are not saints because we are poor, but by the same measure neither are we immoral. We are men and women who have suffered and endured much, and not only because of our abject poverty but because we have been kept poor.

The colors of our skins, the languages of our cultural and native origins, the lack of formal education, the exclusion from the democratic process, the numbers of our men slain in recent wars—all these burdens generation after generation have sought to demoralize us, to break our human spirit. But God knows that we are not beasts of burden, agricultural implements or rented slaves; we are men. And mark this well Mr. Barr, we are men locked in a death struggle against man's inhumanity to man in the industry that you represent. And this struggle itself gives meaning to our life and ennobles our dying.

As your industry has experienced, our strikers here in Delano and those who represent us throughout the world are well trained for this struggle. They have been under the gun, they have been kicked and beaten and herded by dogs, they have been cursed and ridiculed, they have been stripped and chained and jailed, they have been sprayed with the poisons used in the vineyards; but they have been taught not to lie down and die nor to flee in shame, but to resist with every ounce of human endurance and spirit. To resist not with retaliation in kind but to overcome with love and compassion, with ingenuity and creativity, with hard work and longer hours, with stamina and patient tenacity, with truth and public appeal, with friends and allies, with mobility and discipline, with politics and law, and with prayer and fasting. They were not trained in a month or even a year; after all, this new harvest season will mark our fourth full year of strike and even now we continue to plan and prepare for the years to come. Time accomplishes for the poor what money does for the rich.

This is not to pretend that we have everywhere been successful enough or that we have not made mistakes. And while we do not belittle or underestimate our adversaries—for they are the rich and the powerful and they possess the land—we are not afraid nor do we cringe from the confrontation. We welcome it! We have planned for it. We know that our cause is just, that history is a story of social revolution, and that the poor shall inherit the land.

Once again, I appeal to you as the representative of your industry and as a man. I ask you to recognize and bargain with our union before the economic pressure of the boycott and strike takes an irrevocable toll; but if not, I ask you to at least sit down with us to discuss the safeguards necessary to keep our historical struggle free of violence. I make this appeal because as one of the leaders of our nonviolent movement, I know and accept my responsibility for preventing, if possible, the destruction of human life and property. For these reasons, and knowing of Gandhi's admonition that fasting is the last resort in place of the sword, during a most critical time in our movement last February 1968 I undertook a 25-day fast. I repeat to you the principle enunciated to the membership at the start of the fast: if to build our union required the deliberate taking of life, either the life of a grower or his child, or the life of a farmworker or his child, then I choose not to see the union built.

Mr. Barr, let me be painfully honest with you. You must understand these things. We advocate militant nonviolence as our means for social revolution and to achieve justice for our people, but we are not blind or deaf to the desperate and moody winds of human frustration, impatience and rage that blow among us.   Gandhi himself admitted that if his only choice were cowardice or violence, he would choose violence.   Men are not angels, and time and tide wait for no man.   Precisely because of these powerful human emotions, we have tried to involve masses of people in their own struggle. Participation and self-determination remain the best experience of freedom, and free men instinctively prefer democratic change and even protect the rights guaranteed to seek it.   Only the enslaved in despair have need of violent overthrow.

This letter does not express all that is in my heart, Mr. Barr.   But if it says nothing else it says that we do not hate you or rejoice to see your industry destroyed; we hate the agribusiness system that seeks to keep us enslaved and we shall overcome and change it not by retaliation or bloodshed but by a determined nonviolent struggle carried on by those masses of farm workers who intend to be free and human.

Sincerely yours,

Cesar E. Chavez

United Farm Workers Organizing Committee
A.F.L-C.I.O.
Delano, California

LETTER TO THE WEATHERMEN (1970)

Daniel Berrigan

FATHER DANIEL BERRIGAN (1921-   ) is known as a poet, a priest, a peacemaker and a felon. When understood in their most radical sense, each of these titles comes down to the same thing. Certainly they each shed light on Berrigan's understanding of the call to nonviolence in the Christian Gospels. For Berrigan, they are aspects of applying the Gospel of nonviolence in a society enslaved by possessiveness and willing to hold the world hostage to its greed.

The Weathermen, a group dedicated to violent revolutionary action, had formed in 1969 when Students for a Democratic Society (SDS) could no longer satisfy its increasingly polarized factions. In October of the same year the Weathermen held their "Days of Rage" in Chicago in an attempt to bring the realities of the Vietnam War—and the policies it represented—back home. Six hundred demonstrators participated and eluded two thousand police as the demonstrators rushed through the streets, smashing windows and dynamiting statues. A militia of about seventy women charged police lines. In December 1969, the organization decided to break into small groups and go underground believing it the best way to force revolution and protect itself from the security apparatus of the United States.

In *Letter To The Weathermen,* written when both Berrigan and the Weathermen were underground due to anti-war activities, he identifies with their view of the U.S. social problems embodied in the Vietnam War. At the same time, he explores the question of means and ends and the issue of tactics such as sabotage. The question of sabotage is of particular interest because, as we have seen in *Nonviolent Napalm at Catonsville,* Berrigan himself used, and would use again, tactics some considered to be sabotage.

We also include here two poems by Daniel Berrigan. *Children In The Shelter* is part of a twelve-poem comment written during his 1968 trip to Hanoi. *The Sermon On The Mount, And The War That Will Not End Forever,* is a synthesis of Berrigan's understanding of Christianity and the human condition.

D EAR BROTHERS AND SISTERS,

Let me express a deep sense of gratitude that the chance has come to speak to you across the underground. It's a great moment; I rejoice in the fact that we can start a dialogue that I hope will continue through the smoke signals, all with a view to enlarging the circle. Indeed the times demand not that we narrow our method of communication but that we enlarge it, if anything new or better is to emerge.

The cold war alliance between politics, labor, and the military finds many Americans at the big end of the cornucopia. What has not yet risen in them is the question of whose blood is paying for all this, what families elsewhere are being blasted, what separation and agony and death are at the narrow end of our abundance. These connections are hard to make, and very few come on them. Many can hardly imagine that all being right with America means that much must go wrong elsewhere. How do we get such a message across to others? It seems to me that this is one way of putting the very substance of our task. Trying to keep connections, or to create new ones. It's a most difficult job, and in hours of depression it seems all but impossible to speak to Americans across the military, diplomatic, and economic idiocies. Yet I think we have to carry our reflection further, realizing that the difficulty of our task is the other side of the judgement Americans are constantly making about persons like ourselves. This determination to keep talking with all who seek a rightful place in the world, or all who have not yet awakened to any sense at all of the real world—this, I think, is the revolution. And the United States perversely and negatively knows it, and this is why we are in trouble. And this is why we accept trouble, ostracism, and fear of jail and of death as the normal condition under which decent men and women are called upon to function today.

Undoubtedly the FBI comes with guns in pursuit of people like me because, beyond their personal chagrin and corporate machismo (a kind of debased esprit de corps; they always get their man), there was the threat that the Panthers and the Vietnamese have so valiantly offered. The threat is a very simple one; we are making connections, religious and moral connections, connections with prisoners and Cubans and Vietnamese, and these connections are forbidden under policies which J. Edgar Hoover is greatly skilled in enacting and enforcing. They know by now what we are about, they know we are serious. And they are serious about us. Just as with mortal fear, for the last five years they have known what the Vietnamese are about, and the Brazilians and Angolans and Guatemalans. We are guilty of making connections, we urge others to explore new ways of getting connected, of getting married, of educating children, of sharing goods and skills, of being religious, of being human, of resisting. We speak for prisoners and exiles and that silent, silent majority which is that of the dead and the unavenged as well as the unborn. And I am guilty of making connections with you.

By and large the public is petrified of you Weather People. There is a great mythology surrounding you—much more than around me. You come through in public as the embodiment of the public nightmare, menacing, sinister, senseless, and violent: a spin-off of the public dread of Panthers and Vietcong, of Latins and Africans, of the poor of our country, of all those expendable and cluttering, and clamorous lives, those who have refused to lie down and die on command, to perish at peace with their fate, or to drag out their lives in the world as suppliants and slaves.

But in a sense, of course, your case is more complicated because your rebellion is not the passionate consequence of the stigma of slavery. Yours is a choice. It's one of the few momentous choices in American history. Your no could have been a yes; society realizes this—you had everything going for you. Your lives could have been posh and secure; but you said no. And you said it by attacking the very properties you were supposed to have inherited and expanded—an amazing kind of turnabout.

Society, I think, was traumatized by your existence, which was the consequence of your choice. What to do with Vietcong or Panthers had never been a very complicated matter, after all. They were jailed or shot down or disposed of by the National Guard. But what to do with you—this indeed was one hell of a question. There was no blueprint. And yet this question too, was not long in finding its answer, as we learned at Kent State. That is to say, when the choice between property and human life comes up close, the metaphor is once more invariably military. It is lives that go up and down. And we know now that even if those lives are white and middle-class, they are going to lie in the same gun sights.

The mythology of fear that surrounds you is exactly what the society demands, as it demands more and more mythology, more and more unreality to live by. But it also offers a very special opportunity to break this myth that flourishes on silence and ignorance and has you stereotyped as mindless, indifferent to human life and death, determined to raise hell at any hour or place. We have to deal with this as we go along; but from what values, what mentality, what views of one another and ourselves? Not from a mimicry of insanity or useless rage, but with a new kind of anger which is both useful in communicating and imaginative and slow-burning, to fuel the long haul of our lives.

I'm trying to say that when people look about them for lives to run with and when hopeless people look to others, the gift we can offer is so simple a thing as hope. As they said about Che, as they say about Jesus, some people, even to this day; he gave us hope. So my hope is that you see your lives in somewhat this way, which is to say I hope your lives are about something more than sabotage. I'm certain they are. I hope the sabotage question is tactical and peripheral. I hope indeed that you are uneasy about its meaning and usefulness and that you realize that the burning of properties whether at Catonsville or Chase Manhattan or anywhere else, by no means guarantees a change of consciousness, the risk always being very great that sabotage will change people for the worse and harden them against enlightenment.

I hope you see yourselves as Che saw himself, that is to say as teachers of the people, sensitive as we must be to the vast range of human life that awaits liberation, education, consciousness. If I'm learning anything it is that nearly everyone is in need of these gifts—and therefore in need of us, whether or not they realize it. I think of all those we so easily dismiss, whose rage against us is an index of the blank pages of their lives, those to whom no meaning or value has ever been attached by politicians or generals or churches or universities or indeed anyone, those whose sons fight the wars, those who are constantly mortgaged and indebted to the consumer system; and I think also of those closer to ourselves, students who are still enchanted by careerism and selfishness, unaware that the human future must be created out of suffering and loss.

How shall we speak to our people, to the people everywhere? We must never refuse, in spite of their refusal of us, to call them our brothers. I must say to you as simply as I know how; if the people are not the main issue, there simply is no main issue and you and I are fooling ourselves, and American fear and dread of change has only transferred itself to a new setting.

Thus, I think a sensible, humane movement operates on several levels at once if it is to get anywhere. So it says communication yes, organizing yes, community yes, sabotage yes—as a tool. That is the conviction that took us where we went, to Catonsville. We reasoned that the purpose of our act could not be simply to impede the war, or much less to stop the war in its tracks. God help us; if that had been our intention, we were fools before the fact and doubly fools after it, for in fact the war went on. Still we undertook sabotage long before any of you. It might be worthwhile reflecting on our reasons why. We were trying first of all to say something about the pernicious effect of certain properties on the lives of those who guarded them or died in consequence of them. And we were determined to talk to as many people as possible and as long as possible afterward, to interpret, to write, and through our conduct, through our appeal, through questioning ourselves again and again to discuss where we were, where we were going, where people might follow.

My hope is that affection and compassion and nonviolence are now common resources once more and that we can proceed on one assumption, the assumption that the quality of life within our communities is exactly what we have to offer. I think a mistake in SDS's past was to kick out any evidence of this community sense as weakening, reactionary, counter-productive. Against this it must be said that the mark of inhuman treatment of humans is a mark that also hovers over us. And it is the mark of a beast, whether its insignia is the military or the movement.

No principle is worth the sacrifice of a single human being. That's a very hard statement. At various stages of the movement some have acted as if almost the opposite were true, as people got purer and purer. More and more people have been kicked out for less and less reason. At one remote period of the past, the result of such thinking was the religious wars, or wars of extinction. At another time it was Hitler; he wanted a tone of purity too. Still another is still with us in the war against the Panthers and the Vietnamese. I think I'm in the underground because I want part in none of this inhumanity, whatever name it goes by, whatever rhetoric it justifies itself with.

When madness is the acceptable public state of mind, we're all in danger, all in danger; for madness is an infection in the air. And I submit that we all breathe the infection and that the movement has at times been sickened by it too.

The madness has to do with the disposition of human conflict by forms of violence. In or out of the military, in or out of the movement, it seems to me that we had best call things by their name, and the name for this thing, it seems to me, is the death game, no matter where it appears. And as for myself, I would as soon be under the heel of former masters as under the heel of new ones.

Some of your actions are going to involve inciting and conflict and trashing, and these actions are very difficult for thoughtful people. But I came upon a rule of thumb somewhere which might be of some help to us: Do only that which one cannot not do. Maybe it isn't very helpful, and of course it's going to be applied differently by the Joint Chiefs of Staff and an underground group of sane men and women. In the former, hypocritical expressions of sympathy will always be sown along the path of the latest rampage. Such grief is like that of a mortician in a year of plague. But our realization is that a movement has historic meaning only insofar as it puts itself on the side of human dignity and the protection of life, even of the lives most unworthy of such respect. A revolution is interesting insofar as it avoids like the plague the plague it promised to heal. Ultimately if we want to define the plague as death (a good definition), a prohuman movement will neither put people to death nor fill the prisons nor inhibit freedoms nor brainwash nor torture enemies nor be mendacious nor exploit women, children, Blacks, the poor. It will have a certain respect for the power of the truth, a power which created the revolution in the first place.

We may take it, I think, as a simple rule of thumb that the revolution will be no better and no more truthful and no more populist and no more attractive than those who brought it into being. Which is to say we are not killers, as America would stigmatize us, and indeed *as America perversely longs for us to be*. We are something far different. We are teachers of the people who have come on a new vision of things. We struggle to embody that vision day after day, to make it a reality among those we live with, so that people are literally disarmed by knowing us; so that their fear of change, their dread of life are exorcised, and their dread of human differences slowly expunged.

Instead of thinking of the underground as temporary, exotic, abnormal, perhaps we should start thinking of its implication as an entirely self-sufficient, mobile, internal revival community; the underground as a definition of our future. What does it mean literally to have nowhere to go in America, to be kicked out of America? It must mean—let us go somewhere in America, let us stay here and play here and love here and build here, and in this way join not only those who like us are kicked out also, but those who have never been inside at all, the Blacks and the Puerto Ricans and the Chicanos.

Next, we are to strive to become such men and women as may, in a new world, be nonviolent. If there's any definition of the new man and woman, the man or woman of the future, it seems to me that they are persons who do violence unwillingly, by exceptions. They know that destruction of property is only a means; they keep the end as vivid and urgent and as alive as the means, so that the means are judged in every instance by their relation to the ends. Violence as legitimate means: I have a great fear of American violence, not only in the military and diplomacy, in economics, in industry and advertising; but also in here, in me, up close, among us. On the other hand, I must say, I have very little fear, from firsthand experience, of the violence of the Vietcong or Panthers (I hesitate to use the word violence), for their acts come from the proximate threat of extinction, from being invariably put on the line of self-defense. But the same cannot be said of us and our history. We stand outside the culture of these others, no matter what admiration or fraternity we feel with them; we are unlike them, we have other demons to battle.

But the history of the movement, in the last years, it seems to me, shows how constantly and easily we are seduced by violence, not only as a method but as an end in itself. Very little new politics, very little ethics, very little direction, and only a minimum moral sense, if any at all. Indeed one might conclude in despair: the movement is debased beyond recognition, I can't be a part of it. Far from giving birth to the new man, it has only proliferated the armed, bellicose, and inflated spirit of the army, the plantation, the corporation, the diplomat.

Yet it seems to me good, in public as well as in our own house, to turn the question of violence back on its true creators and purveyors, working as we must from a very different ethos and for very different ends. I remember being on a television program recently and having the question of violence thrown at me and responding—look, ask the question in the seats of power, don't ask it of me, don't ask me why I broke the law, ask Nixon why he breaks the law constantly, ask the Justice Department, ask the racists. Obviously, but for Johnson and Nixon and their fetching ways, Catonsville would never have taken place and you and I would not be where we are today; just as but for the same people SDS would never have grown into the Weather People or the Weather People have gone underground. In a decent society, functioning on behalf of its people, all of us would be doing things that decent people do for one another. That we are forbidden so to act, forced to meet so secretly and with so few, is a tragedy we must live with. We have been forbidden a future by the forms of power, which include death as the ordinary social method; we have rejected the future they drafted us into, having refused, on the other hand, to be kicked out of America, either by aping their methods or leaving the country.

The question now is what can we create. I feel at your side across the miles, and I hope that sometime, sometime in this mad world, in this mad time, it will be possible for us to sit down face to face, brother to brother, brother to sister, and find that our hopes and our sweat, and the hopes and sweat and death and tears and blood of our brothers and sisters throughout the world, have brought to birth that for which we began.

Shalom to you.

Children in the Shelter

Imagine; three of them.

As though survival
were a rat's word,
and a rat's death
waited there at the end

and I must have
in the century's boneyard
heft of flesh and bone in my arms

I picked up the littlest
a boy, his face
breaded with rice (his sister calmly feeding him
as we climbed down)

In my arms fathered
in a moment's grace, the messiah
of all my tears. I bore, reborn
a Hiroshima child from hell.

The Sermon on the Mount, and the War that Will not End Forever

Jesus came down from Crough Patrick
crazy with cold, starry with vision.
The sun undid what the moon did; unlocked him.

Light headed ecstasy; *love*
he commended, as tongue and teeth
fixed on it; *love* for meat after fast;

then *poverty*, &
mild and clean hearts stood commended.

Next spring, mounted Crough Patrick
and perished.
The word came down
comes down and down, comes what he said.

men say, gainsy, say nay.

Not easy for those who man
the mountain, forever ringed and fired.
And the children, the children
                            die

die like our last chance
                    day
                        after Christian day.

SPIRITUALITY AND POLITICAL COMMITMENT: Notes on a Liberation Theology of Nonviolence (1981)

Beldon C. Lane

*B*ELDON LANE (1943-) IS A *Presbyterian minister and Associate* Professor of Theological Studies and American Studies at St. Louis University in Missouri. This article grew out of his own efforts to discover the means of personal change and also from a course on Spirituality and Political Commitment which he has taught for several years. In it he explores options for action in conflict situations where ordinary ways of proceeding fail and an impasse is reached. While cultural wisdom usually counsels ever more aggressive responses to such situations, Lane suggests that reframing our perception of the problem and the people involved may be a far more direct road to liberation. A lover of stories and the art of storytelling, Dr. Lane has recently published *Landscapes of the Sacred*. This book explores different spiritual traditions in American history and shows how a faith community's experience of God is conditioned by their sense of place. Communities such as the Native American, the Shakers, and the Catholic Worker are explored.

İN HIS BOOK *Giving Up the Gun: Japan's Reversion to the Sword, 1543-1879*, Noel Perrin describes the decision of the Japanese under the Tokugawa shogunate not to use the firearms recently introduced to their nation by the Portuguese. They based their decision not simply upon a national abhorrence of bloodshed, but rather upon the values traditionally associated with the samurai warrior. The gun unfairly enabled any common soldier to overcome all the prowess, learning and piety that constituted samurai spirituality. Hence, for 250 years Tokugawa Japan enjoyed peace without guns. By the end of that period, only scholars were still familiar with the words used to describe such weapons. Furthermore, the nation escaped invasion during that period — at least in part by hanging canvas murals along the seacoasts to frighten away enemy ships. On the murals were painted large fortresses with threatening cannons atop their walls.

This delightful story from Asian history raises important questions about the interrelationship between nonviolent liberating action and the creative revisioning of the world that occurs through spiritual reflection. It lends itself to rethinking the classic tension between action and contemplation, especially as it relates to political decision making. In a post-Puebla, mid-SALT II era, the need for an imaginative and liberating theology of nonviolence is more prevalent than ever. And it can only be discovered as praxis and meditation are drawn inseparably together. Segundo Galilea has urged that "as well as a theology, we need a spirituality of liberation." Paradoxically, our lives require both the apatheia of which the desert fathers wrote (a spiritual distance from our own suffering) and a consciousness of the deepest pathos in the world around us (especially in the third world). Spirituality and political commitment can no longer be disjoined.

How, then, does one begin with Galilea the task of "transforming contemplatives into prophets and militants into mystics?" Where do the two poles of action and contemplation come together? This article will make an effort at proposing a model for relating the two through an analysis of impasse situations and their resolution. Making use of change theory, Laingian psychoanalysis and the Zen conception of the koan, it will suggest ways of rethinking the Sermon on the Mount as a theology of the unexpected, offering an appreciation of the power of the paradoxical in behavioral change. Drawing upon the experience of contemporary proponents of nonviolence, it seeks, in other words, to understand anew the words of Our Lord: "Blessed are the meek, for they shall inherit the earth."

Impasse Situations and Consciousness

Impasse situations are those intensely irritable frustrations that we invariably seek to avoid, but which sometimes—because of their very difficulty—result in breakthroughs of enormous creativity. They form a meeting place for the world of activity and the world of reflection, the Taoist yang and yin. On the one hand, in a genuine impasse every normal way of action is brought to a standstill. The left side of the brain, with its usual application of conventional thinking, is ground to a halt. The impasse forces us to start all over again, driving us to contemplation. On the other hand, the same impasse provides a challenge and concrete focus for contemplation, keeping it from evaporating into lofty speculations. It forces the right side of the brain into gear, seeking intuitive, unconventional answers so that action can be renewed with greater purpose.

The idea is nothing new. Impasse situations have long been viewed by visionaries as creative junctures. St. James told his readers to "count it all joy when you meet various trials" (James 1:2). But Christians have never taken that as seriously as they might have; nor have they applied it sufficiently to political realities. Ironically, we seldom are fully aware of the trials or impasses we actually face. Therefore, we carry on with the same hopeless activity and fail to reflect on new alternatives long after the need for change has become apparent. Particularly, we find ourselves amidst impasse situations formed by social and political forces, and we view them with a passive sense of inevitability. They contain no joy, offer no promise of paradox. Instead of letting them take form before us as thoroughgoing impasse, forcing to an end our habitual methods of acting, we simply carry on with conventional solutions. Nowhere is this more dangerous than in our attitudes toward violence and its structures.

Dom Helder Camara, Archbishop of Recife and Olinda in Brazil, speaks out of his third world experience of the deadly impasse formed by the "spiral of violence." This, he insists, is what most threatens our world today, primarily because we are unconscious of its operation. The spiral begins with what he calls violence number one, the injustice that is written into society and readily accepted by those in power. It is an institutionalized violence, often of the white-collar variety though seldom identified as such. But it breeds an angry frustration among the oppressed, which often breaks out into violence number two, the violence of despair. This, in turn, usually becomes an excuse for the reaction of those in power and the continuation of the spiral into violence number three, the violence of backlash or fascist violence, with its ersatz appeal to law and order. Hence the impasse is brought to completion, with all its seeming inescapability. Each stage is a conventional and predictable response to the one previous.

As a way out of this spiral, Dom Helder looks to those Abrahamic minorities in the world who possess tremendous energy in their "hope against hope." Daring to imagine the impossible, they respond out of the full consciousness of their own suffering within situations of violent impasse. Their consciousness then becomes the key to identifying and awakening the consciousness of all those involved directly or indirectly in the formation of such conditions. With Paulo Freire, he knows that only as people recognize the spiral of violence to be the impasse that it is can there be any hope of resolution. Consciousness must always precede change.

This focus of consciousness directly upon impasse situations is an extremely important concept. Robert Pirsig, in *Zen and the Art of Motorcycle Maintenance*, describes the same experience in terms of the concept of "stuckness." He describes sitting along the highway one afternoon confronted with a screw that sticks on the side cover assembly of his stalled motorcycle.

Experience in the past has told him to apply force to a stuck screw. So he clamps the vice grips onto his screwdriver, twists as hard as he can and suddenly tears the slot right out of the screw. Immediately he is caught in the kind of impasse we all have experienced. His first inclination is to push the whole machine over the embankment on the side of the road. But instead, he suggests that now is the time to roll a cigarette, to sit back and to let the right side of the brain begin to wander. He thinks about the screw not as an object to be moved, but as a set of functions of rigidness and adhesiveness. This may lead him to thoughts of solvents or the use of a torch or drill. In fact, if he stayed at it long enough, he might come up with a way of extracting screws never thought of before, something patentable and able to make him a millionaire. Such are the possibilities inherent in cases of "stuckness."

The Principle of Second Order Change

A genuine impasse situation is one where the more action one applies to escape it, the worse it gets. Ordinary ways of proceeding fail directly in proportion to the intensity with which they are tried. The only way to resolve the problem, therefore, is to completely reframe the situation in one's mind, looking again at the assumptions previously made about it and formulating altogether new plans for action (or inaction). Three Stanford psychiatrists have recently proposed a theory of behavioral change designed to enable their clients to work through problems not readily solved by ordinary psychotherapies. They offer a contrast between what they label as principles of first and second-order change; their conclusions speak directly to the questions of impasse situations and their resolution.

First-order change, they suggest, is our usual procedure for solving problems. When confronted with an obstacle, we generally resort to emphasizing its opposite, opposing force with force. We assume that when something is bad, then its opposite has to be good. When resolution is not immediately forthcoming, our response then is usually to double the intensity of our effort. Yet what often happens is that the opposite becomes simply more of the same. The more Jack urges Jill not to be frightened, the more anxious she becomes. Genuine change, therefore, only occurs through a second-order response, one which rethinks the solution previously tried and suggests something altogether unexpected. This quality of paradox is at the heart of second-order change. It requires a radical breaking out of the conceptual blocks that normally limit our thinking. Paul Watzalawick, John Weakland and Richard Fisch begin their book *Change: Principles of Problem Formation and Problem Resolution* with a compelling illustration of this:

> "When in 1334 the Duchess of Tyrol, Margareta Maultasch, encircled the castle of Hochosterwitz in the province of Carinthia, she knew only too well that the fortress, situated on an incredibly steep rock rising high above the valley floor, was impregnable to direct attack and would yield only to

a long siege. In due course, the situation of the defenders became critical: They were down to their last ox and had only two bags of barley left. Margareta's situation was becoming equally pressing, albeit for different reasons: Her troops were beginning to be unruly, there seemed to be no end to the siege in sight and she had similarly urgent military business elsewhere. At this point, the commandant of the castle decided on a desperate course of action which to his men must have seemed sheer folly. He had the last ox slaughtered, had its abdominal cavity filled with the remaining barley and ordered the carcass thrown down the steep cliff onto a meadow in front of the enemy camp. Upon receiving this scornful message from above, the discouraged duchess abandoned the siege and moved on."

Had the commandant persisted in an attempt at first-order change, he would have ordered a further cut in rations, hoping to outlast the enemy by countering their siege. But his second-order response was a stroke of genius, an absurd and wholly unexpected action that put the entire impasse into a new light. The duchess departed, fully persuaded that the castle had food to last for months.

In such a way, second-order change redefines one's conception of the impasse. Previous solutions are evaluated and attempts are made at doing less instead of more of the same. As a result, there is a lessening of the tension caused by opposite joined against opposite. In the case of Jack's efforts at easing Jill's fear, for example, he may have to choose a wholly different and unexpected approach. This happened by accident in our home recently. My wife expressed fear about a graduate course in which she was involved, and my initial response was to follow exactly the lines of the Laingian knot, assuring her that she had nothing to be afraid of. But on later reflection (as this obviously did nothing to help), I suggested that maybe she really did have reason to fear. Maybe the professor and other students in the class were secretly laughing together about how little she knew. Maybe they hid behind the door before she came in, waiting to see what ignorant thing she might do next. And, of course, the absurdity of it all made us both laugh. There is a refreshing quality about being able to imagine the worst in a situation, especially after one has been repeatedly told that she has no reason whatever to fear. The element of laughter, surprise, paradox is central here. The solution is so immediately welcomed because of its sudden release of pressure.

But the discovery of such solutions demands a consistent eye for the unexpected, a keen taste for paradox. As Heraclitus, that great student of change, understood, "If you do not expect it, you will not find the unexpected, for it is hard to find and difficult." G. K. Chesterton speaks of St. Francis of Assisi as God's jester or tumbler—one who stands on his head for the pleasure of God, a fool for Christ's sake. The image is an apt one for those who would understand second-order change. By standing on his head, Francis sees the world in a new way, "with all the trees and towers hanging head downwards." The result is a new perception of reality. "Instead of being merely proud of his strong city because it would not be moved, he would be thankful to God

Almighty that it had not been dropped." He would be struck by the dependence of all things upon God, the world for him would be reframed and with divine absurdity he would embrace poverty as his greatest joy.

One last illustration of this principle of second-order change, given by Watzalawick, Weakland and Fisch, will help to indicate its particular application to impasse situations charged with violence: "During one of the many 19th century riots in Paris, the commander of an army detachment received orders to clear a city square by firing at the *canaille* (rabble, mob, scum of the populace). He commanded his soldiers to take up firing positions, their rifles leveled at the crowd, and as a ghastly silence descended he drew his sword and shouted at the top of his lungs: 'Mesdames, m'sieurs, I have orders to fire at the canaille. But as I see a great number of honest, respectable citizens before me, I request that they leave so that I can safely shoot the canaille.' The square was empty in a few minutes."

In the face of a hostile, violent crowd, the commander refused to view the situation as it had been framed for him by his superiors. Instead of pitting himself and his men against the people, his redefinition of the impasse allowed him to identify with them and still accomplish his task.

The question, of course, is how one develops this facility for recognizing new possibilities in a world tragically lacking in second-order change. Is it possible to prepare in advance for discovering the unexpected? In a sense, that is precisely one of the byproducts of Christian spirituality. Taking time for reflection on the character of the Christian faith reveals the paradox that lies at its very heart. The whole scandal of the Gospel is that it is not what people expect. "God chose what is foolish in the world to shame the wise and . . . what is weak in the world to shame the strong" (I Corinthians 1:27). At its best, then, Christian contemplation leads to an appreciation of paradox. It is critical of action which has become conventional, customary and merely traditional, and it nurtures instead that action which provokes surprise, laughter, the joy of the unexpected. Here then is an action-contemplation synthesis which is rooted in a celebrative theology of the unexpected.

Its specific implications for political life, however, need to be drawn out more carefully. How do action and contemplation so conceived lend themselves to a liberating theology of nonviolence? Can the element of surprise or paradox be applied to sociopolitical impasses, for example, in a way similar to the philosophy and technique of judo? Instead of opposing the opponent's thrust with a counterthrust, is it possible to find ways of yielding to the initial force, disarming the opponent by one's nonresistance, and thus creating a new situation altogether? Such is the technique as applied by proponents of nonviolent resistance in this century. The model of the impasse situation and second-order change can readily be applied to their experience in order to suggest elements that will be common to any liberating theology of nonviolence, especially one that is Christian. Specifically, five axioms can be set forth, each put in the form of a paradox, each characterized by the unexpected.

Axioms for Nonviolent Liberating Action

1. *Liberating change will always begin with consciousness rather than action.*
Danilo Dolci, the Italian architect who became the "Gandhi of Sicily," went to the wretched village of Trappeto twenty-seven years ago to do nothing. He simply began asking questions, gradually urging the people to think about their plight through a process he liked to call "popular self-analysis." His imaginative "strike in reverse," the construction of the dam on the Lato River and his direct opposition to Mafia rule all came later. He knew that the raising of consciousness had to precede any liberating action.

After her first foray into labor organization among mine workers in southern France, while still a teacher in the girls' lycee (high school) at Le Puy, Simone Weil realized her utter lack of the consciousness that workers possessed. Therefore, she spent most of 1934-35 as a factory worker in Paris, driven to physical collapse by the pressure constantly to produce more pieces on the lathe or metal press. "Exhaustion ends by making me forget the real reasons for my working in the factory," she wrote. But in the process the workers' consciousness of grinding monotony became her own.

Liberating change can only emerge out of conscientization. As Paulo Freire so well insists, the initiative for such liberation always lies with the oppressed and their own struggle for consciousness. Those of us in the first world, therefore, find ourselves in many ways dependent upon others for our own liberation. The Gospel can only be heard by people who are caught in impasses, by those who are oppressed. Only to them does it ring as a liberating "good news."

Liberation, therefore, must begin not with action (especially not with the simple expenditure of large sums of money for the schooling of society, as Ivan Illich deplores), but with the raising of consciousness, with the awareness of suffering and repentance. The various impasses of poverty and oppression can never be moved by first-order change.

2. *Liberating change will involve respect for the opponent, not his repudiation.*
A second paradoxical axiom for liberating nonviolent action involves the reframing of one's perception of both oppressor and oppressed. The image of the intractable enemy is particularly called into question here. Gandhi's conception of satyagraha, or the force of truth, insisted on seeing both parties within a conflict as subject to truth and in need of its wholeness. Gustavo Gutierrez urges similarly that the liberating love of Christ has to be applied in two directions. The oppressed need to be liberated from their misery, and the oppressors need to be liberated from their sin. He writes: "One loves the oppressors by liberating them from their inhuman condition as oppressors, by

liberating them from themselves. . . . It is not a question of having no enemies, but rather of not excluding them from our love."

The conviction, therefore, is strong that full liberation occurs only when both oppressor and oppressed are set free. Instead of hardening the impasse by matching force against force, the two sides are now seen to be mutual parts of a larger whole. The satyagrahi acts toward his opponent not simply so as to get power from him, but so as to someday make him his neighbor. Gandhi's experience with Gen. Jan Christaan Smuts is a classic example. When the Indian leader left South Africa for the last time in 1914, he presented a pair of leather sandals he had made in prison to the very man responsible for placing him there. Twenty-five years later, Smuts returned them as a gesture of friendship, saying that while he had often worn them he had never felt worthy to stand in the shoes of such a man. The beauty of Gandhi's action was that he had not merely won a victory over his opponent; he had won his opponent over. In their conflict they had enhanced each other's stature, growing together into a mutual respect.

3. *Liberating change will require the appropriation of suffering rather than the escape from it.* For twenty-five years, Cesar Chavez has been rallying farm workers around the principle that their suffering is the only thing they can truly call their own. They are painfully familiar with it and good at it. Hence, all they need to learn is how to claim it as their own and use it as a persuasive tool. Ironically, as he knows, liberation is discovered not through the escape from one's suffering, but through one's own appropriation of it. Suffering exerts a far greater persuasive force than reason ever could alone. As Gandhi understood, "reason has to be strengthened by suffering and suffering opens the eyes of understanding." When it is made one's own, suffering can then become a powerful moral force. Mr. Chavez has known this since his earliest days in community organizing under Saul Alinsky. In fact, his life growing up reads like a page taken from Steinbeck's description of dustbowl migrants in the 1930's. Never has he escaped the anguished experience of struggling migrant workers.

His celebrated fast at Delano in 1968, therefore, came as a natural recourse to him. For twenty-five days he fasted, not to humiliate or threaten the growers who had refused negotiation, but rather to urge a commitment to nonviolence within the United Farm Workers movement itself. His self-assumed suffering was directed toward those who could most be moved by it.

4. *Liberating change will necessitate the initiation of tension, though without the usual recourse to violence.* Nonviolent liberating action can never be the choice of those who are by nature weak and submissive. Gandhi insisted that *ahimsa* (harmlessness) can be practiced only by those who know themselves to be strong. Hence, only the fearless are free to explore the energies of peace, whereas cowardice is necessarily the mother of violence.

Warriors of peace recognize the importance of initiating tensions in which impasse situations will become fully visible as such. Their hope will always be that the opponent will play into their hand by a relentless application of first-order change. If they can provoke a response of this kind, the situation suddenly becomes ripe for the introduction of a second-order solution.

Martin Luther King was similarly grateful for Bull Connor's crucial and ironic role in the success of the demonstrations in Birmingham in 1963. Using all the weapons of first-order change—from billy clubs and police dogs to fire hoses and mass arrests—the police commissioner made the impasse so complete as to virtually welcome the new solution King proposed. With singing children being loaded into patrol wagons and school buses to be carried away to jail, the nation recognized that the impasse had reached that absurd point at which it must break into something new. The tension had been carried to a glorious conclusion.

5. *Finally, liberating change will be made possible by a spiritual discipline, not simply a political ideology.*

In Gandhi's case, his commitment to truth (satya), as formed by his study of the Bhagavad-Gita (as well as the Sermon on the Mount), gave him an amazing lack of interest in the actual results of his action. Since he was never anxious to achieve the ends of ideological struggle, his life was marked rather by the quietness of a spiritual discipline. "Just as one must learn the art of killing in the training for violence," he wrote, "so one must learn the art of dying in the training for nonviolence." This dying, in Christian theology, is rooted in one's baptism, wherein one dies to sin and is raised anew to life in Christ. It means the conquering of the fear of death and the nurturing of a discipline that both pleases God and changes the world. Gilbert Murray's tribute to Gandhi indicates the power of such a discipline: "Be careful in dealing with a man who cares nothing for sensual pleasures, nothing for comfort or praise or promotion, but is simply determined to do what he believes to be right. He is a dangerous and uncomfortable enemy because his body, which you can always conquer, gives you so little purchase over his soul."

This was exactly what Martin Luther King sought to instill in the volunteers who satisfied his qualifications for service as demonstrators in the Birmingham struggle. All were required to pledge themselves to a strict discipline. It committed them to daily meditation on the teachings and life of Jesus, as well as prayer that all people might be free. It reminded them of the nonviolent movement's quest for justice and reconciliation rather than victory. It enjoined them to observe the ordinary rules of courtesy with both friend and foe and to repudiate all violence of fist, tongue or heart. It made extraordinary demands. But it was only by such discipline that Dr. King was able to commit his followers to practice of second-order change.

Rethinking the Politics of the Possible

These axioms help explain the effectiveness of nonviolent action within a situation where a violent response would most often be expected. They emphasize the paradoxical character of that behavior which evokes second-order change.

By contrast, our own culture remains extremely wary of nonviolent alternatives in general. Deeply suspicious of the quixotic, we pride ourselves on a hardheaded realism that deals with rugged certainties rather than imaginative possibilities. Hence, we find it difficult to entertain the ideas that make second-order change possible. A combination of American pragmatism, the frontier experience and our extraordinary confidence in technology makes us unusually susceptible to the logic of first-order change. We have always been persuaded that any impasse could be broken if only sufficient pressure were brought to bear upon it. Therefore, the massive expenditure of force, money or technical savvy has been our usual approach to problem solving. It may not often have worked in earlier circumstances, but it always had the advantage of appearing to be practical and tough-minded.

As a result, second-order change, with its appeal to the unexpected and unconventional, is generally hampered by the cultural blocks we throw up against it. One is taught not to waste time in fantasy and reflection, for example. Playfulness and humor may be acceptable in our dealings with children, but they have no role in the sober business of problem solving. Dreaming is similarly impugned with a vehemence like that reserved for idleness by the Puritans. Yet dreams, as we have seen, are the stuff of which liberating action is made. They carry us beyond the languish of impasse to the impossible possibility of change.

In 1947, Gandhi was assassinated by a tough-minded realist named N. V. Godse, one who ridiculed the idea that Hindus and Muslims could live together in peace. His words at his trial were an eloquent assault upon all that Gandhi had taught: "To imagine that the bulk of mankind is or can ever become capable of scrupulous adherence to these lofty principles in its normal life from day to day is a mere dream." The image of the dream is an appropriate one. It is echoed in the words inscribed on the stone over Martin Luther King's grave. Taken from the story of Joseph and his brothers, the inscription reads: "And they said one to another, Behold, the dreamer cometh. Come now therefore, and let us slay him . . . and we shall see what will become of his dreams" (Genesis 37:19-20).

Gandhi did have a dream, like Martin Luther King, a political dream that emerged out of the dreams which filled his spiritual life. Whether it was a mere dream is something yet to be judged by ourselves in the world we will make. With all of its absurdity, the dream of nonviolent liberation still lives today.

THEOLOGY OF SANCTUARY (1983)

Michael McConnell and Renny Golden

MICHAEL McCONNELL (1946-   ), AND RENNY GOLDEN (1937-   ), members of the Chicago Religious Task Force on Central America, have been "conductors" on the underground railroad since its inception. They are both poets and have published several articles on sanctuary and Central America in *Christianity and Crisis*, *The National Catholic Reporter*, *Sojourners*, and *USA Today*. Michael is a United Church of Christ (UCC) minister and a member of the Wellington Avenue UCC, one of the first public sanctuaries outside of a border state. Renny has taught at Harvard Divinity School's Women's Religious Studies Program. She is currently a professor at Northeastern Illinois University. In 1986 both co-authored *Sanctuary: The Underground Railroad*, which tells the story of the sanctuary movement and its unparalleled grassroots impact on the North American religious community.

The following article first appeared in *Sanctuary Nuts and Bolts*, an organizer's manual for Sanctuary workers. *Theology of Sanctuary* reminds North American Christians that what is legal is not always moral and conversely, what is illegal is not always immoral. It presents us with the choice of providing refuge for Central Americans fleeing the violence in their homelands—an illegal act in the eyes of the U. S. government—or obeying the law and shunning the refugee.

WHEN IT IS ILLEGAL to provide refuge for homeless people the struggle for justice has reached a new stage. At that historic moment the pastoral has merged with the political, service is prophetic, love is subversive, and remembering is a revolutionary act.

The theology of sanctuary has not been written in academia, it has been

231

written on the road. It has been articulated by "coyotes for the people" who have sat huddled in dark churches holding refugee children in their arms, waiting for the border guards to pass. It has passed from stopover to stopover along the new underground railroad as individuals risked imprisonment to give meals and rides to refugees.

Declarations of sanctuary were born from the failure of civil law to uphold moral justice. And so on March 24, 1982, Southside Presbyterian Church in Tucson, Arizona, the first U.S. church to declare itself a sanctuary, turned to religious tradition in an act of hope for thousands of Central American refugees and an act of defiance of U.S. immigration law.

The issue had become clear: The North American church must choose sides. Either it would stand with the United States government or with the refugees. As Quaker Jim Corbett, one of the "coyotes for the people," has said, " We can take our stand with the oppressed or we can take our stand with organized oppression, we can serve the Kingdom of Love or the Kingdom of Money, but not both. The presence of the undocumented refugees here among us makes the definitive nature of our choice particularly clear and concrete. When the government itself sponsors the torture of entire peoples and then makes it a felony to shelter those seeking refuge, law-abiding protest merely trains us to live with atrocity."

This is the historic moment when the North American church can stand in solidarity with its sisters and brothers in Central America by encountering some of the risk that the Latin American church has been laboring under for years. Clearly the risks are uneven. For the refugee it could mean deportation and death. For officials in the church, at the most, it could mean imprisonment and/or fines. And yet this is the beginning of authentic solidarity. Liberation theology has crossed the border, not in books to be read and discussed but in praxis. An insurgent faith is on the move, undertaken in hope and sustained in resistance. And the declaration of sanctuary is the pivotal act in this new religious solidarity movement.

The Exodus Event

The Judeo-Christian faith was born in the travail of escape. God was revealed as the One who liberated the Hebrew people from the bondage of Pharaoh's dictatorship. God was the force that acted in history on the side of those first refugees, to change their plight from slavery to freedom. In the centuries that followed God was remembered as "the One who brought us out of the bondage of Egypt" (Exodus 20:2). God's identity was rooted in action and proclaimed in the verbs of struggle—leading, delivering, freeing.

The proclamation of sanctuary draws its power from the centrality of the Exodus event. The elements of that story are being reinterpreted in the light of present realities. The Central American refugees, by their presence among us, are forcing the North American church to choose whether to embark on a new exodus or remain in bondage to the present power arrangements.

There are strong external and internal forces that keep us in bondage, like the loss of privilege and the fear of how our lives will of necessity change if true justice comes to pass. And yet there are powerful forces driving us out of bondage and into liberation—the stories of the victims of violence in Central America, the witness of the martyrs in El Salvador and Guatemala called by their faith to act on behalf of the outcast, the death and resurrection of a people who still hope in the midst of unimaginable atrocities, and the vision of a new order.

Because the refugees are here a new exodus has already begun. Those enforced exiles are being joined by North American religious people who are voluntarily exiling themselves from a civil law without justice. Undocumented refugees and outlawed Christians and Jews are together forming a new exodus community that takes seriously a God who acts in history.

Public sanctuary is an act that refuses to leave foreign policy to ambassadors and generals and compassion to the limits of law. The church is becoming the vehicle for the life-giving power of the Spirit shaping history rather than being shaped by it. The new exodus community is beginning to live a love that demands justice and acts with the power and authority that that love carries. It is an authority rooted deep in Judeo-Christian tradition and U.S. history itself.

The Biblical and Historical Tradition of Sanctuary

Yahweh was the first to proclaim sanctuary, commanding Moses to set aside cities and places of refuge in Canaan where people could seek asylum from the "blood avengers." The cities of refuge were for Israelites, "as well as for the stranger and sojourner among you" (Numbers 35:15). God acting through the faithful created a specific cultural-political structure to insure that God's justice would be done, even in the midst of human attempts at its distortion.

More importantly, God was seen as the ultimate refuge. "God is our refuge and strength, a very present help in trouble" (Psalm 46). But sanctuary was more than passive safety or a secure hiding place: "Defend me, take up my cause against the people who have no pity; from the treacherous and cunning man, rescue me God. It is you God who are my shelter" (Psalm 42).

"Defend me," "rescue me," "take up my cause against the people," are all words of advocacy and liberation. Sanctuary is not merely a safe place to hide in, but a prophetic platform from which to speak out. It is a plan of action, a strategy of struggle. It is the basic stipulation in the covenant relationship between God and the faithful, and among the faithful and their neighbors.

In the New Testament understanding, sanctuary is broadened to the whole idea of hospitality. Nowhere in the New Testament is the stranger spoken of in any other terms but welcome. The sojourner is to be taken in and cared for because "you were once sojourners in the land of Egypt." Sanctuary became such a strong element of religious tradition that it was incorporated into secular law.

We live in a culture that has encrusted over that religious tradition with civil law and then elevated those laws to sacred status. Too often today within the church the breaking of civil law remains an unquestioned taboo. This is a form of idolatry, elevating the provisional to the status of the ultimate. Jesus decries such behavior: "Alas for you scribes and pharisees, you hypocrites. You who pay your tithe of mint and dill and cumin, but have overlooked the weightier demands of the Law—justice, mercy and good faith. It is these you should have practiced without ignoring the rest. Blind guides. You strain off a midge and swallow a camel" (Matthew 23:23).

As Rev. David Chevrier so loudly proclaimed from the pulpit on July 24, 1982, the day that Wellington Ave. United Church of Christ in Chicago was declared a sanctuary, "This is the time and we are the people to reinvoke the ancient law of sanctuary, to say to the government, 'You shall go this far and no further.' This is the time and we are the people to provide sanctuary for those people fleeing the blood vengeance of the powers that be in Central America. We provide a safe place and cry, 'Basta! Enough!' The blood stops here at our doors.' This is the time to claim our sacred right to invoke the name of God in this place—to push back all the powers of violation and violence in the name of the spirit to whom we owe our ultimate allegiance. At this moment we are the people to tell Caesar, 'No trespassing, for the ground upon which you walk is holy.' "

THE POWER OF NONCOOPERATION (1983)

Shelley Douglass

*S*HELLEY DOUGLASS (1944-   ), AN ORDAINED *minister in the United* Church of Canada, is perhaps best known for her work at the Ground Zero Center for Nonviolent action. Since 1982, the Center has conducted public education and direct action campaigns focused on the White Train and Trident missile system. Shelley's first explorations of nonviolence began during the Civil Rights Movement, specifically through her involvement in the Selma-to-Montgomery march. It was during that experience that she began to feel "another kind of power, equal to the power I'd been afraid of in the (Cuban) missile crises. . . ." While she participated in the Vietnam-era anti-war activities, the sexism of the peace movement left her disillusioned and struggling to understand the oppression within the movement, where it came from, and how it could be changed.

Then, in 1973, Shelley and Jim Douglass were visited by Bob Aldridge, a designer of the Trident missile system. Bob had come to understand himself as a war criminal because he was designing first-strike capacity weapons. He was looking for advice on redirecting his life after sixteen years as a missile designer. After learning from him that the Trident system would be based in Seattle, Washington, the Douglasses and the Pacific Life Community founded the Trident Campaign as an expression of their commitment to nonviolence. During the process of building both the campaign and the community, the group realized that each "side" contributes to situations of injustice and thus must also contribute to the creation of justice. The Trident Campaign became a vehicle for applying these insights to their resistance to the arms race.

At the end of three years the group became aware that there was a violence in the process of coming from the outside and telling people they were doing wrong. The group didn't share in the problems, didn't know the workers, and

235

didn't understand their perspectives. In an attempt to build relationships with the armament workers while continuing to resist the armaments themselves, Shelley and Jim moved to a house one-half mile from the naval base's weapons storage facility and named it "Ground Zero." "Living there," commented Shelley, "we experienced the sterotypes from both sides. The Navy and local people looked at us like drug-crazed hippies left over from the sixties, ready to tear everything apart. We tended on our part to see them as right-wing militarists ready to blow up the world with pleasure. Of course what we discovered is that it wasn't really true on either side.... We were able to make contact with the people on the other side of the fence and find common ground."

Partially out of that insight the Ground Zero Center for Nonviolent Action was born. Shelley and others felt that if they were truly committed to nonviolence, they had to learn to be nonviolent with the people they saw as enemies. For them, it was not the Soviet Union that was the enemy, it was the people building the weapons. They began actions, such as weekly leafleting at the base, geared to creating communications between the workers and the resisters and breaking down the stereotypes that grow up in the space between enemies. It was only an extension of this perspective that brought Shelley and Jim Douglass to move again, this time to a house next to the train tracks fifty yards from the fence surrounding the Bangor base. There they continued their campaign of dialogue and resistance through the White Train Campaign. Along these tracks travel the trains carrying missile motors and nuclear warheads from an assembly plant in Amarillo, Texas, to Bangor and to Charleston, South Carolina. Although it had delivered warheads for years, the train did not become public knowledge until the Douglasses sent out the alarm.

As a result, a community of prayer and resistance has developed along the tracks across the entire United States. In *The Power of Noncooperation*, Shelley explores the Gandhian insight which parallels her own: part of the struggle for social change requires recognizing our cooperation with evil and withdrawing that cooperation while at the same time remaining in relationship with the individual people who make up the system. She asserts that "we must learn to love the people while we confront the system with our lives."

"*N*ONCOOPERATION WITH EVIL IS *as much a duty as cooperation with good.*"

M. K. Gandhi to the people of India, 1921

Gandhi used to tell his followers that *swaraj*, home-rule for India, would come only when every Indian exercised *swaraj*, self-rule, in his or her own life. The dependence of India upon the British, he said, was the sum of the dependence of each Indian upon British cloth, British thought, British custom, British government. British rule continued because Indians felt powerless to remove it, and because by their actions they in fact rendered themselves powerless. Gandhi was able to bring about a nonviolent freedom struggle insofar as people were able to see the truth in this insight of his: The imposition of British rule was made possible by Indian cooperation, and could be ended by noncooperation. Indians had to learn to respect themselves, to throw off the limitations of untouchability and of their own reverse racism; Indians had to learn to govern their own desires for wealth and property; Indians had to refuse to surrender to their centuries of conditioning to caste divisions so that they could work together for freedom.

For the Gandhian movement protest was not enough. One could not stand by shouting objections as a major miscarriage of justice occurred. Violence did not meet in case; violence did not recognize the responsibility of Indians for their own problems, and so would not change anything at the deepest level. What Gandhi called for and sometimes achieved was a struggle within each person's soul to take responsibility for the evil in which she or he was complicit, and having taken responsibility, to exercise self-control and begin to change. The Salt March to the sea and the magnificent control exhibited by demonstrating Indians grew slowly from humble roots: the scrubbing of latrines in the face of social taboo, the sharing of gold jewelry by the wealthy, living and eating together in defiance of caste regulations, wearing Indian *khadi* (homespun) to withdraw support from the British economic empire. These actions and many others were symbolic of the deep change brought about by the Gandhian movement, a change in which people acknowledged their own responsibility for the wrong they sought to change, and thus in changing themselves were able to change their situation.

When violence broke out during the freedom struggle and later during partition, it happened because that vital insight was lost for a time. People again located the source of evil outside of themselves and tried to eliminate it with force. Gandhi's fasts and teachings were then concentrated on taking responsibility for the violence he might have caused, and calling people to take steps to stop their own violence. He understood that in giving up our own responsibility for evil we also give up the possibility of changing it. Gandhi's refusal to see the British as solely responsible for the situation of India was the key to Indian independence.

I believe that Gandhi's insistence upon recognizing our cooperation with evil and withdrawing it, is essential to the struggle for social change and nuclear disarmament in which we are engaged today. So often people feel powerless to create change—the leaders of political parties, the generals, the multinational executives, and such groups and persons are held responsible for our situation, and they do not listen to the voices of the poor and the disenchanted. This is true, of course. Governments and corporations exist to hold power or make a profit, and they rarely listen to polite words of protest. If our hope for change rests upon the reasonableness of any government or economic system, then our hope is slim indeed.

The underlying fact that we tend to overlook is that while systems do not listen to people very well, they are made up of the very people to whom they do not listen. The existence of a given system depends upon the cooperation of all those who do not benefit from it and all who are hurt by it, as well as upon the smaller number of people who gain status or wealth from it. If those of us who protest the injustice of our system were instead to withdraw our support from the system, then change would begin.

There are some logical steps to be taken in recognizing our responsibility and withdrawing our complicity. First, we have to know what it is that is wrong enough to justify such a step; secondly, we need to know how we are involved in supporting it; third, how we can best withdraw our support; fourth, what do we do with the support withdrawn from the system?

Involvements with the nuclear system vary. Because Kitsap County, where we are living, is overwhelmingly military in its nature, the decision to noncooperate here is for many a decision to leave a job. For others it has been a decision to help distribute Ground Zero's disarmament leaflets despite military prohibitions, to criticize waste and dishonesty in the Navy itself, or simply to refuse to accept the stereotypes so prevalent now of who and what "protesters" are, and try instead to hear and share.

For people not so directly involved with the military, the most obvious connection with nuclear policy is often the payment of taxes. Refusing all or part of our taxes, or paying them under protest, is a direct way to withdraw our cooperation with the making of nuclear weapons. For some, refusal to pay taxes has meant a re-examination of their convictions and life-style. They have had to become more open to uncertainty and more reliant upon faith for security as they wait to see what action will be taken by the courts. For others, the decision to live below the taxable income level has helped them to become less dependent upon the consumer goods that we take for granted. In reducing their income level to avoid financing nuclear weapons they have also begun to move out of the consumer society that necessitates these weapons.

As people refuse to give their money to the state to finance weapons, they are able to take personal responsibility for the use of their money, channeling it to a soup kitchen, a child care center, a social change project that expresses their commitment to peace and justice. Sharing of one's substance for the good of all becomes more powerful when it is done with personal involvement.

Noncooperation may include marches, vigils and tax refusal, but it includes also an inner dimension: the refusal to allow our minds to be manipulated, our hearts to be controlled. Refusing to hate those who are identified as enemies is also noncooperation.

The discipline of nonviolence requires of us that we move into the various forms of noncooperation. We will probably move slowly, one step at a time. Each step will lead to another step; each step will be a withdrawal from support of what is wrong and at the same time a building of an alternative. Negativity is never enough. It is not enough to oppose the wrong without suggesting the right. Our religious roots can help us here, with their insistence on confronting the evil within ourselves and on our unity with all peoples.

The difficult thing about nonviolence is that it is a new kind of power to us, a new way of thinking. Even as we resist the structures in our society that separate us from others, we incorporate those structures in our own minds. Nonviolence becomes not only a process of resisting our own unloving impulses. Jesus' injunction to remove the beam from our own eye before presuming to treat our sisters' and brothers' eyes, and his direction to overcome evil with good can point our way. It is true that we resist what we understand to be evil. The system does evil. But the individual people who make up the system are people like you and me: combinations of good and evil, of strength and weakness. To hate people is to incorporate part of the evil that we resist. We must learn instead to love the people while we confront the system with our lives.

At the base of love for those caught within an evil system is the understanding that we are they: that we too are caught in the same system. Just as people in the peace movement have important insights and criticisms for people in the military, military folk have critical insights to share with us. No one person owns the truth—each one has a piece of it, as Gandhi said, and if we can put all our pieces together we may find a bigger truth. Recognizing our own complicity in an evil system means that we can take responsibility for it through noncooperation. It also means that we can confront our own failures, forgive ourselves, and from that process learn compassion. We can be honest enough to admit our own imperfections and our lack of certainty, and accept the same in other people.

Just as we do not have to hate Russian people or Chinese people, we do not have to hate those who stand against our beliefs within our own country. We can be friends. We can work together in ways acceptable to all of us: to feed the hungry, to help at a school, to plan a liturgy, to sponsor activities for our children, to encourage freedom and creativity. As we work together we can get to know each other, and when that happens we can begin to explore our feelings about disarmament with mutual acceptance. Even when we feel that the people who range themselves against us have become close-minded or unreasonable, we do not have to retaliate in kind. We can find the places in ourselves where we are close-minded and unreasonable, and understand the fear behind such feelings. We can forgive and refuse to be drawn into a cycle of hate and fear. It is possible to hold out the hope of community to all people, and to work at conflicts within our communities and neighborhoods in the same spirit that we would like to bring to international conflict.

The new power of nonviolence comes from taking responsibility: personal responsibility for our own lives, and our share of responsibility for the country and the systems in which we live. The power of nonviolence lies in facing ourselves with love and compassion while honestly confronting our own evil, and then in facing the evil of our country honestly, while confronting it with love and compassion. Nonviolence is an invitation to nurture the good, to confront the evil, and in doing so to build a new community which will bear in it the best of the old.

DEFENSE THROUGH DISARMAMENT: NONVIOLENCE AND PERSONAL ASSAULT (1983)

Angie O'Gorman

NEXT TO WAR, PERSONAL assault is one of the most terrifying human experiences we encounter. Still, the faith questions must be asked. What does it mean to live out my belief in Gospel-based nonviolence when there is a man standing in my bedroom? Does the Sermon on the Mount, the call to love of enemies, or the centrality of reconciliation in the Christian ethic mean anything as I stand face to face with a burglar? A rapist? A man who may be a murderer? Or, is it more accurate to say —as has been said for centuries in regard to war— that when the issue is defense from aggression, a different set of norms comes into play? The question takes on more urgency for those of us committed to disarmament between nations. If I believe that disarmament is possible on the international level, how do I handle my own defense when personally threatened? How do I image my own "preparedness?" Are there alternatives to our culture-bound perceptions which equate defense with violence, and peace with passivity?

When defense is the issue, westernized Christianity tends to define responsibility and right in terms of destroying whatever is experienced as threatening. In fact, in theological terms, we tend to see the destruction of evil as a necessary prelude to the coming of the Kingdom spoken of by Jesus. Therefore, If I kill the rapist, blind him, or render him sexually impaired, I have not only protected my safety, I have bettered society; I have furthered the coming of the reign of God. We may not say this quite so bluntly, but the logic is there. In this view destruction of evil is seen as the method for promoting the

241

good. Examples of this rationale are not hard to find. St. Augustine included in his Just War Theory the prohibiton against killing a "man" unless you loved him because the required motivation had to include the desire to save his soul. Interestingly enough, however, even Augustine did not permit killing in self-defense. In Augustine's view private citizens could not defend themselves by killing an aggressor because they could not do so without the loss of love. One could only kill in defense of the church or state. As this became the orthodox Catholic perspective it merged with other theological understandings of the church's role as the keeper of God's law in the midst of an imperfect society; a role that theologicaly legitimized killing in defense. In the Vietnam era we heard this same logic used when General Westmoreland told us, "We had to destroy the village in order to save it."

It is hard to find a basis for this logic in the Christian scriptures. Rather than destruction of enemies, the Christian ethic calls for their conversion and counts on enough love on my part to facilitate the process. Somehow the oppressed, the victim, has a role to play in the life of the person held by evil (whether the roots of that evil are economic, psychological, or the effects of our cultural racism and sexism). But what can this possibly mean for a person confronted by dangerous assaultive behavior? When there is no time for response in the interaction it doesn't mean much. With or without a gun, if you are clubbed on the head from behind, the possibility for any defense is nil. But when the time sequence in an assault allows for defense, it allows for more than violence.

Jesus offered a different method of defense. He called it *love of enemies* by which he meant wanting wholeness and well-being and life for those who may be broken and sick and deadly. It was meant to be the cornerstone of an entirely new process of disarming evil; one which would decrease evil instead of feeding it as violence does. In the context of assault, it means, among other things, to want safety for the assailant.

I agree, it sounds absurd, yet I have felt the power of that desire as a disarming force—not of an assailant, but of myself. I was awakened late one night several years ago by a man kicking open the door to my bedroom. The house was empty. The phone was downstairs. He was somewhat verbally abusive as he walked over to my bed. I could not find his eyes in the darkness but could see the outline of his form. As I lay there, feeling a fear and vulnerability I had never before experienced, several thoughts ran through my head—all in a matter of seconds. The first was the uselessness of screaming. The second was the fallacy of thinking safety depends on having a gun hidden under your pillow. Somehow I could not imagine this man standing patiently while I reached under my pillow for my gun. The third thought, I believe, saved my life. I realized with a certain clarity that either he and I made it through this situation safely—together—or we would both be damaged. Our safety was connected. If he raped me, I would be hurt both physically and emotionally. If he raped me he would be hurt as well. If he went to prison, the damage would be greater. That thought disarmed *me*. It freed me from my own desire to lash out and at the same time from my own paralysis. It did not free me from feelings of fear but from fear's control over my ability to respond. I found myself acting out of a concern for both our safety which caused me to react with a certain firmness but with surprisingly little hostility in my voice.

I asked him what time it was. He answered. That was a good sign. I commented that his watch and the clock on my night table had different times. His said 2:30, mine said 2:45. I had just set mine. I hoped his watch wasn't broken. When had he last set it? He answered. I answered. The time seemed endless. When the atmosphere began to calm a little I asked him how he had gotten into the house. He'd broken through the glass in the back door. I told him that presented me with a problem as I did not have the money to buy new glass. He talked about some financial difficulties of his own. We talked until we were no longer strangers and I felt it was safe to ask him to leave. He didn't want to; said he had no place to go. Knowing I did not have the physical power to force him out I told him firmly but respectfully, as equal to equal, I would give him a clean set of sheets but he would have to make his own bed downstairs. He went downstairs and I sat up in bed, wide awake and shaking for the rest of the night. The next morning we ate breakfast together and he left.

Several things happened that night. I allowed someone who I was afraid of to become human to me and as a result I reacted in a surprisingly human way to him. That caught him off guard. Apparently his scenario had not included a social visit and it took him a few minutes to regain his sense of balance. By that time the vibes were all wrong for violence. Whatever had been motivating him was sidetracked and he changed his mind.

Through the effects of prayer, meditation, training and the experience of lesser kinds of assault, I had been able to allow what I call a context for conversion to emerge. It is what I think Jesus was doing in Gospel examples of self-defense. We can catch a glimpse of what this dynamic looks like by observing how Jesus related to those who threatened him.

Apparently, he did not find it effective to take away a person's ability to choose even when his own welfare was the object of their choice. The scene in the Garden of Gethsemane has interesting implications in the context of dealing with personal assault. Never mind that he was about to be betrayed, that the soldiers were coming, already in sight and armed to the teeth. He knew what to expect from the soldiers. The worse agony was when his closest friends turned and ran. Left him. Abandoned him. His front line of "defense" collapsed. What does Jesus do?

It would have been so easy for him to coerce them to stay; guilt, physical restraint, public censure and embarrassment would have been effective. Instead, he let them go.

There is a terrible respect for the truth here; the truth of the apostles' inability to be faithful. They simply were not ready. Perhaps Jesus let them go because he knew that a coerced choice is no choice at all. To coerce them would have blocked their achieving the insight needed to choose to come back. Neither the Kingdom, nor truth can be taken by force. The nature of insight and truth requires that they be freely accepted. If these men were going to choose to be faithful, they had to be allowed the freedom not to choose it. Jesus' action reflected his willingness to suffer the consequences of their free choice rather than take away their ability to know the truth—even though that choice could involve evil.

But he seems to have required more of people than a moment's choice. Jesus showed himself to be willing to accompany the choice-making person by attempting to create a context for conversion. He fostered situations which caused wonder and could reflect the consequences of people's actions back to them in order to create more inner availability to the truth. He worked to create a context for conversion. His parables are models of this dynamic.

In verses forty and forty-one of Matthew's fifth chapter the author writes, ". . . and if anyone would sue you and take your coat, let him have your cloak as well." If someone takes one garment, the owner is advised to hand over the other. Why? Because, given the climate of the area, without both garments, the person would die from exposure to the elements. So, he is told, give away the other one also. Let your adversary see in your nakedness the truth of what he is doing. Do something wonderful and open his eyes. Later, in verse forty-one we find the admonition to walk the extra mile: ". . .and if any one forces you to go one mile, go with him two miles." This statement refers to walking the extra mile for an enemy understood to be the Roman soldiers who had the right to impress any Jew to carry his gear for one mile. For the first mile, the soldier has the power. But, imagine the Jew refusing to lay down the burden after that first mile and walking on, freely, for the second mile. Who has the power after the second mile? Power relationships change. The Jew has the chance to work on the soldier during the second mile; to help him come to insight about his actions and to help him see this Jewish person as a person and not an object.

Radical respect for the humanity of the person who confronts us as an enemy and creating a context for conversion are ingredients in effective nonviolent defense. But they require a kind of blending or integration that comes from our own struggles to learn to love our enemies.

Our ability to facilitate disarmament in crisis situations, and thus gain real safety, can depend as much on our fundamental desire as it does on the assailant's intention. If I relate to an assailant out of a desire to win, to teach a lesson, or to get revenge, my behavior will reflect those desires. If my own safety is my only concern, I will act against the safety of the assailant, thus becoming threatening. The assailant is then put in a defensive position and I lose any possible control of the interpersonal dynamic.

It is a hard journey from these desires to desiring the assailant's safety as well as my own. Yet this is the base of our ability to disarm someone else's will to hurt us. This is the journey of our own personal disarmament. If we are in the process of disarming ourselves, we will begin to understand what is necessary to disarm another person. In the midst of the fear and vulnerability which we feel in the face of personal assault, something other than the will to destroy can surface and my behavior can reflect that. I will be freer to create a context for conversion because I know my self-preservation does not require the destruction of the other. Along the way, if I cannot yet love the person who threatens me, if I cannot desire their well-being, perhaps I can nurture that ability by remembering that, regardless of how I feel, this is a loved person.

The Gospels tell us that "God's love rains on the just and unjust alike." Whether the person confronting me is an enemy or a friend, they confront me as loved and valued by God, and I need to be careful with what God values. Try as I might, I cannot escape the fact that the God whom Jesus revealed loves unconditionally. With the inbreaking of the Kingdom, the favored nation status ended. We are all loved with the same love originating in the same parent God. Thus the assailant's safety and well-being are as important as my own. Nonviolence means I realize that this is a loved person and I act out of a concern for our mutual safety. My actions are merely the consequence of my belief that as God's love is for me, so it is for everyone. Nonviolence is the manifestation of my commitment to and participation in that love.

When the assailant's safety is as important to me as my own, I can be free enough to disarm the crisis. It is at this level of desire that nonviolence primarily resides and this is one reason why internal personal disarmament work is crucial if I want to interact nonviolently with others in moments of crises.

As a victim I have the power to help facilitate the assailant's ability to change his or her mind, or to encourage, however unconsciously, their desire to hurt me. An assailant is fully prepared for a hostile response, or a response of fear or panic. Sociologists tell us that most assailants work from a definite set of expectations about how the victim will repond and they need the victim to act as a victim in order to feed the polarization in the action/reaction interplay. A violent or hostile response, as well as a response of panic or helplessness, tends to reinforce the assailant's expectations, self-confidence and sense of control. It also tends to increase cruelty within an already hostile person. This is a game the assailant knows how to play. They can handle what they are prepared for. It is important to note here that using violent resistance to resolve the situation is limiting oneself to the rules of the game as laid down by the assailant. To reach a safe resolution within these confines is often impossible.

While fear, panic, helplessness, and counter-violence can heighten hostility and cruelty, psychologists tell us that wonder tends to diffuse them. It seems to be nearly impossible for the human psyche to be in a state of wonder and a state of cruelty at the same time. Thus, introducing an element of wonder into the assault situation tends to be disarming—both to the person initiating the wonder and to the person responding to it. Creating the context for conversion mentioned earlier means doing something wonder-ful; something non-threatening and unexpected. Wonder not only disarms, it tends to focus attention on that which caused the wonder and places the recipient in a very suggestible state of mind. When the human psyche focuses on what causes wonder, a desire to imitate tends to occur. Just as we have to cultivate within ourselves the desire for the assailant's safety, so we must cultivate within the assailant a desire for our safety. "If you want to conquer another," said nonviolent strategist Richard Gregg, "do it not by outside resistance but by creating inside their own personality a strong new impulse that is incompatible with the previous tendency."

With the assailant temporarily thrown off balance by an unexpected, nonthreatening response on the part of the victim, it is possible to move the interaction to a different level. Gregg has termed this dynamic moral jui-jitsu which he explained in *The Power of Nonviolence* as follows:

> The nonviolent (response) of the victim acts in the same way that the lack of physical opposition by the user of physical jui-jitsu does, causing the attacker to lose his moral balance. He suddenly and unexpectedly loses the moral support which the usual violent resistance of most victims would render him ... He feels insecure because of the novelty of the situation and his ignorance of how to handle it. He loses poise and self-confidence ... The user of nonviolent resistance knowing what he is doing and having a more creative purpose, keeps his moral balance, using a different kind of leverage.

The art of jui-jitsu is based on the knowledge of balance and how to disturb it; so too is nonviolence. The resister short-circuits the flow of the assault by disarming responses and moves to take over the direction of the encounter.

This is where the spirituality behind nonviolence is crucial. As important as techniques may be, the consciousness from which they flow is even more so. The power of nonviolence is the power to tap into the orientation of creation toward wholeness. It requires activating the dynamics mentioned earlier such as the refusal to inhibit achievement of the truth by coercion, radical respect for the other as a loved person, an orientation toward reconciliation rather than victory and domination, and a valuing of the well-being of all. Nonviolence reduced to a technique and not authentically rooted in these desires tends to be manipulative. This can be catastrophic in an assault situation. Successful use of nonviolence in the context of assault requires that the victim is acting from an authentic desire for the common well-being. Such a desire can then be translated into building a common universe made up of a variety of small, seemingly insignificant actions.

Violence arms. It is built into the dynamic. Coercion creates within the adversary the need for self-defense. Thus violence increases itself. The art of nonviolence is the art of breaking the escalating cycle of threat and counter-threat and reversing its direction. The same mutual reinforcement of response which can spiral into violent action can also spiral into nonviolent action.

Disarmament is impossible through violence. However, through nonviolence we can firmly face an enemy and still allow love and grace to so permeate the meeting that aggression becomes unnecessary and new choices become possible.

THE IDOLATRY OF DETERRENCE (1986)

The United Methodist Council of Bishops

*T*HE METHODIST BISHOP'S PASTORAL LETTER, In Defense of Creation: The Nuclear Crisis and a Just Peace, is the most far-reaching statement ever issued by Methodist leadership on the subject of war and peace. It was written specifically to state their position, to evoke discussion within the denomination and to urge United Methodists to work for peace. *The Idolatry of Deterrence,* a section from the pastoral letter, is the strongest condemnation of the policy of nuclear deterrence written by any group of bishops within the United States.

Led by their exploration of Methodist biblical and social traditions in regard to war and peace, the bishops' letter offers a "Theology For A Just Peace" which states that, "Every policy of government must be an act of justice and must be measured by its impact on the poor, the weak, and the oppressed—not only in our own nation but in all nations." They urged all Christians to share a strong moral presumption against "violence, killing, and warfare. . . ," and acknowledged that "Peacemaking in the nuclear age, under the sovereignty of God, requires the defense of creation itself against possible assaults that may be rationalized in the name of 'national defense'." The Gospel command to love one's enemies was called "essential to our own well-being and even to our survival" and not merely a benevolent ideal. Finally, the bishops applied these beliefs to the policy of nuclear deterrence. In a courageous stand they condemned the policy and rejected the view held by other religious bodies that nuclear deterrence could be accepted as an "interim ethic" as long as governments were attempting to reach more moral solutions.

*F*OR FORTY YEARS THE moral function of deterrence doctrine has been to justify the threatened use of nuclear weapons and an unending arms race.

We have already indicated in a preliminary way our opposition to any use of nuclear weapons. We have said that the just-war tradition does more to discredit deterrence doctrine than to support it. We have discerned a lack of coherence in deterrence. We have rejected the nuclear idolatry that presumes the power of ultimate judgement and destruction of other nations.

We do not doubt that the threat of nuclear retaliation can be, and has been, a factor inhibiting the resort to nuclear weapons. Fear is a powerful human motive—although its effects are notoriously unpredictable. Deterrence of some sort seems to operate in most institutional and corporate behavior, including the family, education, law enforcement, and church discipline. But we remain profoundly troubled by the military extremities which deterrence doctrines have legitimized if not motivated.

Deterrence has too long been reverenced as the unquestioned idol of national security. It has become an ideology of conformity too frequently invoked to disparage dissent and to dismiss any alternative foreign policy proposals. In its most idolatrous forms, it has blinded its proponents to the many-sided requirements of genuine security. There can be no unilateral security in the nuclear age. Security has become indivisible. Our vulnerability is mutual. Our security must be mutual. Security requires economic strength, environmental and public health, educational quality, social well-being, public confidence, global cooperation. In short, the indispensable moral qualities of security must not be forfeited to an uncontrolled arms race.

Whatever claims may be made for deterrence policies since 1945, the future is shadowed by the perilous trends of recent years: escalation of the arms race, the spread of nuclear-weapons technologies to other states, the specter of terrorist movements with nuclear bombs, and the unresolved political conflicts in nuclear-prone regions like the Middle East, the Persian Gulf, South Asia, East Asia, and South Africa. Even if it could be proved, as it cannot, that deterrence has had some short-term benefits for several decades, the longer-term consequences of nuclear policies since 1945 threaten to make human survival increasingly precarious.

Some Christian leaders have sought to justify deterrence as an interim ethic while nuclear-weapon states pursue arms reduction. As we have seen, Pope John Paul II offered such an interim ethic in his 1982 UN statement: Deterrence "may still be judged morally acceptable" as a step toward "progressive disarmament."

We believe, however, that the moral case for nuclear deterrence, even as an interim ethic, has been undermined by unrelenting arms escalation. Deterrence no longer serves, if it ever did, as a strategy that facilitates disarmament.

Counterforce, or the "countervailing strategy" for the current "modernization" of nuclear weapons, is offered as a kind of "new morality" of deterrence. But the weapons being developed in its name increase first-strike powers and lead to the escalation of mutual suspicion. Their very development, which is projected over long periods of years and even decades, tends to defer any hope of significant disarmament to yet another generation. We believe the churches of nuclear-weapons states must be sensitive to the charge of inequality and invidious discrimination, which nuclear deterrence tends to ignore. If the United States and Soviet Union continue to maintain their rights to nuclear weapons, and even to multiply those weapons, why should other nations not claim those same rights, especially in view of the superpowers' default on their own treaty promises to end nuclear testing and proceed toward nuclear disarmament? If deterrence is good for national security for some nations, why not for other nations? The persistence of such prejudicial conduct bids to become the prime obstacle to effective international cooperation to control nuclear perils.

Nuclear deterrence has become a dogmatic license for perpetual hostility between the superpowers and for their rigid resistance to significant measures of disarmament. Major General Kermit D. Johnson, former Chief of Chaplains of the U.S. Army, in written testimony submitted to our hearing panel, puts it this way:

> Before any nuclear weapons are ever launched, nuclear deterrence locks us into a permanent state of war, albeit a cold war, with the Soviet Union. They are regarded as an "enemy," imminently deserving of being threatened moment by moment with nuclear destruction. The overall political relationship between the U.S. and the Soviet Union is fixed by this military reality.

The primary reliance on unrelenting terror tends to perpetuate the most distorted and inhuman images of our "enemy." It forsakes the more prudent, positive strategies of offers, inducements, and incentives that might draw on the vast human, economic, and technological resources of the U.S. and its allies.

We believe there is a still more fundamental flaw at the very core of deterrence doctrine: a contradiction between inordinate confidence in the rationality of decision makers and the absolute terror of annihilation. Nothing in our understanding of fallible and fallen human nature warrants the expectation that this relentless strain between reason and terror can endure indefinitely. The foundations of an enduring peace must be constructive and cooperative.

The rejection of nuclear deterrence, however, does not necessarily mean immediate, unilateral disarmament. Those who regard themselves as nuclear pacifists do not hold a fully responsible position if they only say No to nuclear weapons; they must also share the difficult political task of working out a strategy of phased arms reduction.

It is the idolatrous connection between the ideology of deterrence and the existence of the weapons themselves that must be broken. Deterrence must no longer receive the churches' blessing, even as a temporary warrant for the maintenance of nuclear weapons. The interim possession of such weapons for a strictly limited time requires a different justification—*an ethic of reciprocity* as nuclear-weapon states act together in agreed upon stages to reduce and ultimately to eliminate their nuclear arms. Such an ethic is shaped by an acceptance of mutual vulnerability, a vision of common security, and the escalation of mutual trust rather than mutual terror. It insists that the positive work of peacemaking must overcome the fearful manipulation of hostility.

We believe that neither the U.S. nor any other nuclear power can extricate itself unilaterally from all nuclear perils. Indeed, immediate and total nuclear disarmament by the U.S. might well tempt other countries to develop or expand their own nuclear arsenals, thereby increasing the risk of nuclear war. Whatever the objective truth about the effects of deterrence, faith in that doctrine will not die quickly. It will take prudent political leadership in partnership with all other nuclear-weapon states, including "enemies," to conceive and implement step-by-step approaches to disarmament. Prudence is always a moral obligation.

JESUS' THIRD WAY (1987)
Walter Wink

W*ALTER WINK (1935–   ) IS PROFESSOR of Biblical Interpretation at* Auburn Theological Seminary in New York City. Having been active in the civil rights movement, the anti-Vietnam War struggle, and campaigns for nuclear disarmament, Dr. Wink travelled to South Africa in March of 1986. In the opinion of those he spoke with there, "nonviolence was the dirtiest word in South Africa." He also learned that a heritage of quietistic missionary training had led Blacks to associate nonviolence with "submission, passivity, acquiescence, and at most, polite negotiation." During that same visit, Beyers Naude, then general secretary of the South African Council of Churches, commented to Wink, "In South Africa we have never yet had a thorough discussion of the issues of violence or nonviolence. It is vitally important to form a legitimate theological position regarding the question." Wink had travelled to South Africa expecting to be persuaded that only violence could bring down the apartheid system. He returned home unexpectedly convinced that nonviolence was their best hope. He presented his case in his book, *Violence and Nonviolence in South Africa,* from which the following selection is excerpted. When the book was published by New Society Publishers in 1987, they mailed 3,400 copies in plain brown paper wrappers to the English-speaking clergy in South Africa. By the end of 1988 a South African edition had been printed and the Roman Catholic Church had sent copies to its eight hundred priests.

The book stirred significant debate. Not only the subject matter was controversial, but Wink himself, a white North American with little personal experience of the sufferings which black South Africans were enduring, was seen by many as an arrogant outsider. For many, the term "nonviolence" itself was beyond redemption. However, the debate stirred by the book created a dialogue on the church's role in the current conflict over apartheid at the 1986 Emergency Convocation of Churches in South Africa, an historic convening in Johannesburg of the top leaders of virtually all the churches of South Africa except the white Dutch Reformed Church. The explicit purpose of the

Convocation was to devise "effective nonviolent direct actions" to be taken by the churches in opposition to the apartheid system. How did nonviolence move from the "dirtiest word" to the top of the church agenda in only two years?

The reasons are many and varied but Wink's book clearly made a significant contribution. Now, according to Rev. Frank Chikane, current secretary of the South African Council of Churches, the debate between violence and nonviolence is over. "If the church stops short at the traditional line where religion is said to end and politics to begin," said Chikane during the Convocation, "if it does not cross this imaginary line in order to test its nonviolent methods in the field, it will forfeit any legitimate right to condemn those who go further into the arena of life and death for the sake of justice." In a single stroke, one of the most respected black leaders in South Africa had given his blessing to that pariah word, nonviolence, and challenged the churches to become involved in actions against the government.

"The risks," says Wink, "are the stuff of everyday life for those who oppose the South African government, which has rendered a high tribute to nonviolent actions by making them punishable by extremely severe penalties. Please undergird them with your prayers. Few of us have ever known the magnitude of consequences they will have to face if they rise to the challenge facing the churches."

MANY OF THOSE WHO have committed their lives to ending apartheid simply dismiss Jesus' teachings about nonviolence out of hand as impractical idealism. And with good reason. "Turn the other cheek" suggests the passive, Christian doormat quality that has made so many Christians cowardly and complicit in the face of injustice. "Resist not evil" seems to break the back of all opposition to evil and to counsel submission. "Going the second mile" has become a platitude meaning nothing more than "extend yourself," and rather than fostering structural change, encourages collaboration with the oppressor.

Jesus obviously never behaved in any of these ways. Whatever the source of the misunderstanding, it is clearly neither in Jesus nor in his teaching, which, when given a fair hearing in its original social context, is arguably one of the most revolutionary political statements ever uttered: *You have heard that it was said, "An eye for an eye and a tooth for a tooth." But I say to you, Do not resist one who is evil. But if anyone strikes you on the right cheek, turn to him the other also; and if anyone would sue you and take your coat, let him have your cloak as well; and if any one forces you to go one mile, go with him two miles (Matthew 5:38-41, Revised Standard Version).*

When the court translators working in the hire of King James chose to translate *antistenai* as "Resist not evil," they were doing something more than rendering Greek into English. They were translating nonviolent resistance into docility. Jesus did not tell his oppressed hearers not to resist evil. That would have been absurd. His entire ministry is utterly at odds with such a preposterous idea. The Greek word is made up of two parts: *anti*, a word still used in English for "against," and *histemi*, a verb which in its noun form (stasis) means violent rebellion, armed revolt, sharp dissention. Thus Barabbas is described as a rebel "who had committed murder in the insurrection" (Mark 15:7; Luke 23:19, 25), and the townspeople in Ephesus "are in danger of being charged with rioting" (Acts 19:40). The term generally refers to a potentially lethal disturbance or armed revolution.

A proper translation of Jesus' teaching would then be, "Do not strike back at evil (or, one who has done you evil) in kind. Do not give blow for blow. Do not retaliate against violence with violence." Jesus was no less committed to opposing evil than the anti-Roman resistance fighters. The only difference was over the means to be used: how one should fight evil.

There are three general responses to evil: 1) passivity, 2) violent opposition, and 3) the third way of militant nonviolence articulated by Jesus. Human evolution has conditioned us for only the first two of these responses: flight or fight. "Fight" had been the cry of Galileans who had abortively rebelled against Rome only two decades before Jesus spoke. Jesus and many of his hearers would have seen some of the two thousand of their countrymen crucified by the Romans along the roadsides. They would have known some of the inhabitants of Sepphoris (a mere three miles north of Nazareth) who had been sold into slavery for aiding the insurrectionists' assault on the arsenal there. Some also would live to experience the horrors of the war against Rome in 66-70 A.D., one of the ghastliest in human history. If the option "fight" had no appeal to them, their only alternative was "flight": passivity, submission, or, at best, a passive-aggressive recalcitrance in obeying commands. For them no third way existed. Submission or revolt spelled out the entire vocabulary of their alternatives to oppression.

Now we are in a better position to see why King James' faithful servants translated *antistenai* as "resist not." The king would not want people concluding that they had any recourse against his or any other sovereign's unjust policies. Therefore the populace must be made to believe that there are two alternatives and only two: flight or fight. Either we resist not or we resist. And Jesus commands us, according to these king's men, to resist not. Jesus appears to authorize monarchical absolutism. Submission is the will of God. Most modern translations have meekly followed in that path.

Neither of these invidious alternatives has anything to do with what Jesus is proposing. It is important that we be utterly clear about this point before going on: Jesus abhors both passivity and violence as responses to evil. His is a third alternative not even touched by those options. *Antistenai* may be translated variously as "Do not take up arms against evil," "Do not react reflexively to evil," "Do not let evil dictate the terms of your opposition." The Good News Bible (TEV) translates it helpfully: "Do not take revenge on someone who wrongs you." The word cannot be construed to mean submission.

Jesus clarifies his meaning by three brief examples. "If any one strikes you on the right cheek, turn to him the other also." Why the right cheek? How does one strike another on the right cheek anyway? Try it. A blow by the right fist in that right-handed world would have landed on the left cheek of the opponent. To strike the right cheek with the fist would require using the left hand, but in that society the left hand was used only for unclean tasks. Even to gesture with the left hand at Qumran carried the penalty of ten days penance (The Dead Sea Scrolls, 1 QS 7). The only way one could strike the right cheek with the right hand would be with the back of the hand. What we are dealing with here is unmistakably an insult, not a fistfight. The intention clearly is not to injure but to humiliate, to put someone in his or her "place." One normally did not strike a peer thus, and if one did the fine was exorbitant (4 zuz was the fine for a blow to a peer with a fist, 400 zuz for backhanding him; but to an underling, no penalty whatever—Mishna, Baba Kamma 8:1-6). A backhand slap was the normal way of admonishing inferiors. Masters backhanded slaves; husbands, wives; parents, children; men, women; Romans, Jews. One black African told me that during his youth white farmers still gave the backhand to disobedient workers.

We have here a set of unequal relations, in each of which retaliation would be suicidal. The only normal response would be cowering submission.

It is important to ask who Jesus' audience is. In every case, Jesus' listeners are not those who strike, initiate lawsuits or impose forced labor, but their victims ("If anyone strikes you . . . would sue you . . . forces you to go one mile . . ."). There are among his hearers people who were subjected to these very indignities, forced to stifle their inner outrage at the dehumanizing treatment meted out to them by the hierarchical system of caste and class, race and gender, age and status, and as a result of imperial occupation.

Why then does he counsel these already humiliated people to turn the other cheek? Because this action robs the oppressor of the power to humiliate. The person who turns the other cheek is saying, in effect, "Try again. Your first blow failed to achieve its intended effect. I deny you the power to humiliate me. I am a human being just like you. Your status (gender, race, age, wealth) does not alter that fact. You cannot demean me."

Such a response would create enormous difficulties for the striker. Purely logistically, how do you now hit the other cheek? You cannot backhand it with your right hand. If you hit with a fist, you make yourself an equal, acknowledging the other as a peer. But the whole point of the back of the hand is to reinforce the caste system and its institutionalized inequality. Even if you order the person flogged, the point has been irrevocably made. You have been forced, against your will, to regard that person as an equal human being. You have been stripped of your power to dehumanize the other.

The second example Jesus gives is set in a court of law. Someone is being sued for his outer garment. Who would do that and under what circumstances? The Old Testament provides the clues.

If you lend money to any of my people with you who is poor, you shall not be to him as a creditor, and you shall not exact interest from him. If ever you take your neighbor's garment in pledge, you shall restore it to him before the sun goes down; for that is his only covering, it is his mantle for his body; in what else shall he sleep? And if he cries to me, I will hear, for I am compassionate (Exodus 22:25-27).

When you make your neighbor a loan of any sort, you shall not go into his house to fetch his pledge. You shall stand outside, and the man to whom you make the loan shall bring the pledge out to you. And if he is a poor man, you shall not sleep in his pledge; when the sun goes down, you shall restore to him the pledge that he may sleep in his cloak and bless you ... You shall not ... take a widow's garment in pledge (Deuteronomy 24:10-13, 17).

They that trample the head of the poor into the dust of the earth ... lay themselves down beside every altar upon garments taken in pledge ... (Amos 2:7-8).

Only the poorest of the poor would have nothing but an outer garment to give as collateral for a loan. Jewish law strictly required its return every evening at sunset, for that was all the poor had in which to sleep. The situation to which Jesus alludes is one with which all his hearers would have been all too familiar: The poor debtor has sunk ever deeper into poverty, the debt cannot be repaid, and his creditor has hauled him into court to try to wring out repayment by legal means.

Indebtedness was the most serious social problem in first century Palestine. Jesus' parables are full of debtors struggling to salvage their lives. The situation was not, however, a natural calamity that had overtaken the incompetent. It was the direct consequence of Roman imperial policy. Emperors had taxed the wealthy so vigorously to fund their wars that the rich began seeking non-liquid investments to secure their wealth. Land was best, but there was a problem: It was not bought and sold on the open market as today but was ancestrally owned and passed down over generations. Little land was ever for sale, in Palestine at least. Exorbitant interest, however, could be used to drive landowners into ever deeper debt until they were forced to sell their land. By the time of Jesus we see this process already far advanced: large estates (*latifundia*) owned by absentee landlords, managed by stewards, and worked by servants, sharecroppers, and day laborers. It is no accident that the first act of the Jewish revolutionaries in 66 A.D. was to burn the Temple treasury, where the record of debts was kept.

It is in this context that Jesus speaks. His hearers are the poor ("if any one would sue you"). They share a rankling hatred for a system that subjects them to humiliation by stripping them of their lands, their goods, finally even their outer garments.

Why then does Jesus counsel them to give over their inner garment as well?

This would mean stripping off all their clothing and marching out of court stark naked! Put yourself in the debtor's place, and imagine the chuckles this saying must have evoked. There stands the creditor, beet-red with embarrassment, your outer garment in the one hand, your underwear in the other. You have suddenly turned the tables on him. You had no hope of winning the trial; the law was entirely in his favor. But you have refused to be humiliated, and at the same time you have registered a stunning protest against a system that spawns such debt. You have said in effect, "You want my robe? Here, take everything! Now you've got all I have except my body. Is that what you'll take next?"

This unmasking is not simply punitive, however; it offers the creditor a chance to see, perhaps for the first time in his life, what his practices cause, and to repent.

Jesus in effect is sponsoring clowning. In so doing he shows himself to be thoroughly Jewish. A later saying of the Talmud runs, "If your neighbor calls you an ass, put a saddle on your back."

The Powers That Be literally stand on their dignity. Nothing "depotentiates" them faster than deft lampooning. By refusing to be awed by their power, the powerless are emboldened to seize the initiative, even where structural change is not possible. This message, far from being a counsel of perfection unattainable in this life, is a practical, strategic measure for empowering the oppressed. It provides a hint of how to take on the entire system in a way that unmasks its essential cruelty and to burlesque its pretensions to justice, law, and order.

Was Johan Stander, the renegade South African nationalist businessman, thinking of this passage, or was he just fed up, when he removed his trousers in front of the Port Elizabeth city hall in April 1986, while demonstrating against apartheid?

Jesus' third example, the one about going the second mile, is drawn from the very enlightened practice of limiting the amount of forced labor that Roman soldiers could levy on subject peoples. Jews would have seldom encountered legionnaires except in time of war or insurrection. It would have been auxilliaries who were headquartered in Judea, paid at half the rate of legionnaires and rather a scruffy bunch. In Galilee, Herod Antipas maintained an army patterned after Rome's; presumably they also had the right to impose labor. Mile markers were placed regularly beside the highways. A soldier could impress a civilian to carry his pack one mile only; to force the civilian to go farther carried with it severe penalties under military law. In this way Rome attempted to limit the anger of the occupied people and still keep its armies on the move. Nevertheless, this levy was a bitter reminder to the Jew that they were a subject people even in the Promised Land.

To this proud but subjugated people Jesus does not counsel revolt. One does not "befriend" the soldier, draw him aside, and drive a knife into his ribs. Jesus was keenly aware of the futility of armed revolt against Roman imperial might and minced no words about it, though it must have cost him support from the revolutionary factions.

But why walk the second mile? Is this not to rebound to the opposite extreme: aiding and abetting the enemy? Not at all. The question here, as in the two previous instances, is how the oppressed can recover the initiative, how they can assert their human dignity in a situation that cannot for the time being be changed. The rules are Caesar's, but not how one responds to the rules— that is God's, and Caesar has no power over that.

Imagine then, the soldier's surprise when, at the next mile marker, he reluctantly reaches to assume his pack (sixty-five to eighty-five pounds of full gear), and you say, "Oh no, let me carry it another mile." Why would you do that? What are you up to? Normally he has to coerce your kinsmen to carry his pack, and now you do it cheerfully, and will not stop! Is this a provocation? Are you insulting his strength? Being kind? Trying to get him disciplined for seeming to make you go farther then you should? Are you planning to file a complaint? Create trouble?

From a situation of servile impressment, you have once more seized the initiative. You have taken back the power of choice. The soldier is thrown off-balance by being deprived of the predictability of your response. He has never dealt with such a problem before. Now you have forced him into making a decision for which nothing in his previous experience has prepared him. If he has enjoyed feeling superior to the vanquished, he will not enjoy it today. Imagine the hilarious situation of a Roman infantryman pleading with a Jew, "Aw, come on, please give me back my pack!" The humor of this scene may escape those who picture it through sanctimonious eyes, but it could scarcely have been lost on Jesus' hearers, who must have been regaled at the prospect of thus discomfitting their oppressors.

Some readers may object to the idea of discomfitting the soldier or embarrassing the creditor. But can people who are engaged in oppressive acts repent unless they are made uncomfortable with their actions? There is, admittedly, the danger of using nonviolence as a tactic of revenge and humiliation. There is also, at the opposite extreme, an equal danger of sentimentality and softness that confuses the uncompromising love of Jesus with being nice. Loving confrontation can free both the oppressed from docility and the oppressor from sin.

Even if nonviolent action does not immediately change the heart of the oppressor, it does change the heart of the oppressed, it does affect those committed to it. As Martin Luther King, Jr. attested, it gives them new self-respect, and calls up resources of strength and courage they did not know they had. To those who have power, Jesus' advice to the powerless may seem paltry. But to those whose lifelong pattern has been to cringe, bow, and scrape before their masters, and who have internalized their role as inferiors, this small step is momentous. It is comparable to the attempt by black charwomen in South Africa to join together in what will be for some of them an almost insuperable step: to begin calling their employers by their first names.

These three examples amplify what Jesus means in his thesis statement: "Do not violently resist evil (or, one who is evil)." Instead of the two options ingrained in us by millions of years of unreflective, brute response to biological threats from the environment—flight or fight—Jesus offers a third way. This new way marks a historic mutation in human development: the revolt against the principle of natural selection. With Jesus a way emerges by which evil can be opposed without being mirrored:

Jesus' Third Way

Seize the moral initiative
Find a creative alternative to violence
Assert your own humanity and dignity as a person
Meet force with ridicule or humor
Break the cycle of humiliation
Refuse to submit or to accept the inferior position
Expose the injustice of the system
Take control of the power dynamic
Shame the oppressor into repentance
Stand your ground
Make the Powers make decisions for which they are not prepared
Recognize your own power
Be willing to suffer rather than retaliate
Force the oppressor to see you in a new light
Deprive the oppressor of a situation where a show of force is effective
Be willing to undergo the penalty of breaking unjust laws
Die to fear of the old order and its rules

Flight	Fight
Submission	Armed revolt
Passivity	Violent rebellion
Withdrawal	Direct retaliation
Surrender	Revenge

Sadly, Jesus' three examples have been turned into laws, with no reference to the utterly changed contexts in which they were being applied. His attempt to nerve the powerless to assert their humanity under inhuman conditions has been turned into a legalistic prohibition on schoolyard fistfights between peers. Pacifists and those who reject pacifism alike have tended to regard Jesus' infinitely malleable insights as iron rules, the one group urging that they be observed inflexibly, the other treating them as impossible demands intended to break us and catapult us into the arms of grace. The creative, ironic, playful quality of Jesus' teaching has thus been buried under an avalanche of humorless commentary. And as always, the law kills.

How many a battered wife has been counseled, on the strength of a legalistic reading of this passage, to "turn the other cheek," when what she needs, according to the spirit of Jesus' words, is to find a way to restore her own dignity and end the vicious circle of humiliation, guilt, and bruising. She needs to assert some sort of control in the situation and force her husband to regard her as an equal, or get out of the relationship altogether. The victim needs to recover her self-worth and seize the initiative from her oppressor. And he needs to be helped to overcome his violence. The most creative and loving thing she could do, at least in the American setting, might be to have him arrested. "Turn the other cheek" is not intended as a legal requirement to be applied woodenly in every situation, but as the impetus for discovering creative alternatives that transcend the only two that we are conditioned to perceive: submission or violence, flight or fight.

Shortly after I was promoted from the "B" team to the varsity basketball squad in high school, I noticed that Ernie, the captain, was missing shot after shot from the corner because he was firing it like a bullet. So, helpfully I thought, I shouted, "Arch it, Ernie, arch it." His best friend, Ham, thought advice from a greenhorn impertinent and from that day on verbally sniped at me without letup. I had been raised a Christian, so I "turned the other cheek." To each sarcastic jibe I answered with a smile or soft words. This confused Ham somewhat; by the end of the season he lost his taste for taunts.

It was not until four years later that I suddenly woke to the realization that I had not loved Ham into changing. The fact was, I *hated his guts*. It might have been far more creative for me to have challenged him to a fistfight. Then he would have had to deal with me as an equal. But I was *afraid* to fight him, though the fight would probably have been a draw. I was scared I might get hurt. I was hiding behind the Christian "injunction" to "turn the other cheek," rather than asking, What is the most creative, transformative response to this situation? Perhaps I had done the right thing for the wrong reason, but I suspect that creative nonviolence can never be a genuinely moral response unless we are capable of first entertaining the possibility of violence and consciously saying No. Otherwise our nonviolence may actually be a mask for cowardice.

The oppressed of the third world are justifiably suspicious that we of the first world are more concerned with avoiding violence than with realizing justice. Nobel Peace Prize laureate Adolfo Perez Esquivel comments, "What has always caught my attention is the attitude of peace movements in Europe and the United States, where nonviolence is envisioned as the final objective. Nonviolence is not the final objective. Nonviolence is a lifestyle. The final objective is humanity. It is life."

Beyers Naude, when asked about the role of nonviolent direct action in South Africa today, responded that the churches long ago defaulted by failing to develop concrete strategies of militant nonviolence. The churches now must act decisively to develop such strategies and pay the full price in suffering and imprisonment. And, he concluded, we in the churches must not raise a single finger in judgment of those who have despaired of nonviolent change and have turned to violence as a last resort.

Ironically, in South Africa at this very moment, the apartheid regime is, by the stupidity of its brutal over-reactions to funeral processions and minor harrassments, helping to re-create a nonviolent movement among an oppressed people that had largely dismissed nonviolence as ineffectual. The issue is still undecided; and undisciplined and sporadic appeal to nonviolent direct action can quickly collapse when it is caught in the middle of violence from both sides. Any long-term nonviolent struggle must be disciplined, persistent, and broadly supported.

Perhaps it would help to juxtapose Jesus' teachings with Saul Alinsky's principles for nonviolent community action (in his *Rules for Radicals*), so that we have a clearer sense of their practicality and pertinence to the struggles of our time. Among the rules Alinsky developed in his attempts to organize American workers and minority communities are these:

1. Power is not only what you have but what your enemy thinks you have.
2. Never go outside the experience of your people.
3. Wherever possible go outside the experience of the enemy.

Jesus recommended using one's experience of being belittled, insulted, or dispossessed (Alinsky's rule 2) in such a way as to seize the initiative from the oppressor, who finds the reaction of the oppressed totally outside his experience (second mile, stripping naked, turning the other cheek—3) and forces him or her to believe in your power (1) and perhaps even to recognize your humanity.

4. Make your enemies live up to their own book of rules.
5. Ridicule is your most potent weapon.
6. A good tactic is one that your people enjoy.
7. A tactic that drags on too long becomes a drag.

The debtor in Jesus' example turned the law against his creditor by obeying it (4)—and throwing in his underwear as well. The ruthlessness of the creditor is thus used as the momentum by which to expose his rapacity (5), and it is done quickly (7) and in a way that could only regale the debtor's sympathizers (6). All other such creditors are now put on notice, all other debtors armed with a new sense of possibilities.

8. Keep the pressure on.
9. The threat is usually more terrifying than the thing itself.

10. The major premise for tactics is the development of operations that will maintain a constant pressure upon the opposition.

Jesus, in the three brief examples he cites, does not lay out the basis of a sustained movement, but his ministry as a whole is a model of long-term social struggle (8, 10). Mark depicts Jesus' movements as a *blitzkrieg*. "Immediately" appears eleven times in chapter one alone. Jesus' teaching poses an immediate threat to the authorities. The good he brings is misperceived as evil, his following is overestimated, his militancy is misread as sedition, and his proclamation of the coming Reign of God is mistaken as a manifesto for military revolution (9). Disavowing violence, he wades into the hostility of Jerusalem openhanded, setting simple truth against force. Terrified by the threat of this man and his following, the authorities resort to their ultimate deterrent, death, only to discover it impotent and themselves unmasked. The cross, hideous and macabre, becomes the symbol of liberation. The movement that should have died becomes a world religion.

11. If you push a negative hard and deep enough it will break through to its counterside.
12. The price of a successful attack is a constructive alternative.
13. Pick the target, freeze it, personalize it, polarize it.

Alinsky delighted in using the most vicious behavior of his opponents—burglaries of movement headquarters, attempted blackmail, and failed assassinations—to destroy their public credibility. Here were elected officials, respected corporations, and trusted police, engaging in patent illegalities in order to maintain privilege. In the same way, Jesus suggests amplifying an injustice (the other cheek, undergarment, second mile) in order to expose the fundamental wrongness of legalized oppression (11). The law is "compassionate" in requiring that the debtor's cloak be returned at sunset, yes; but Judaism in its most lucid moments knew that the whole system of usury and indebtedness was itself the root of injustice and should never have been condoned (Exod. 22:25). The restriction of enforced labor to carrying the soldier's pack a single mile was a great advance over unlimited impressment, but occupation troops had no right to be on Jewish soil in the first place. Jesus' teaching is a kind of moral jui-jitsu, a martial art for using the momentum of evil to throw it, but it requires penetrating beneath the conventions of legality to issues of fundamental justice and hanging onto them with dogged persistence. As Gandhi put it, "We are sunk so low that we fancy that it is our duty and religion to do what the law lays down." If people will only realize that it is cowardly to obey laws that are unjust, he continued, no one's tyranny will enslave them.

Picking the target, freezing it, personalizing it, and polarizing it are the means, then, by which intensity is focused and brought to bear (13). For example, infant formula merchants were discouraging breast feeding and promoting their product in countries where women could not afford the powder. Often the parents overdiluted the formula causing malnutrition, or mixed it with unsanitary water resulting in diarrhea and death. But you cannot fight all the merchants of infant formula in the third world at once; so you pick the biggest and most visible, Nestle, even though doing so is technically unfair, since their competition gets off scot free. The focus pays off, however. Nestle's recalcitrance leads to world-wide outrage and an international boycott. To avoid similar treatment most of the infant formula manufacturers make some changes. Eventually the boycott leader, the Infant Formula Action Coalition (INFACT), in conjunction the the World Health Organization and the United Nations International Children's Fund, draws up a code regulating the marketing of infant formula. In 1984, after eight years of struggle, Nestle finally signs an agreement promising to comply with the new standards. And the whole campaign has been instigated out of an office the size of a closet.

Jesus' constructive alternative (12) was, of course, the Reign of God. Turning the tables on one's oppressor may be fun now and then, but long-term structural and spiritual change requires an alternative vision. As the means of purveying that vision and living it in the midst of the old order, Jesus established a new counter-community that developed universalistic tendencies, erupting out of his own Jewish context and finally beyond the Roman Empire.

Jesus was not content merely to empower the powerless, however, and here his teachings fundamentally transcend Alinsky's. Jesus' sayings about non-retaliation are of one piece with his challenge to love our enemies. Here it is enough to remark that Jesus did not advocate nonviolence merely as a technique for outwitting the enemy, but as a just means of opposing the enemy in such a way as to hold open the possibility of the enemy's becoming just as well. Both sides must win. We are summoned to pray for our enemies' transformation, and to respond to ill-treatment with a love which is not only godly but also, I am convinced, can only be found in God.

To Alinsky's list I would like to add another "rule" of my own: Never adopt a strategy that you would not want your opponents to use against you. I would not object to my opponents using nonviolent direct actions against me, since such a move would require them to be committed to suffer and even die rather than resort to violence against me. It would mean that they would have to honor my humanity, believe that God can transform me, and treat me with dignity and respect. One of the ironies of nonviolence, in fact, is that those who depend on violent repression to defend their privileges cannot resort to nonviolence. There is something essentially contradictory between crushing the dissent of a society's victims and being willing to give one's life for justice and the truth.

Today we can draw on the cumulative historical experience of nonviolent social struggle over the centuries and employ newer tools for political and social analysis. But the spirit, the thrust, the surge for creative transformation which is the ultimate principle of the universe, is the same we see incarnated in Jesus. Freed from literalistic legalism, his teaching reads like a practical manual for empowering the powerless to seize the initiative even in situations impervious to change. It seems almost as if his teaching has only now, in this generation, become an inescapable task and practical necessity.

To people dispirited by the enormity of the injustices which crush us and the intractability of those in positions of power, Jesus' words beam hope across the centuries. We need not be afraid. We can reassert our human dignity. We can lay claim to the creative possibilities that are still ours, burlesque the injustice of unfair laws, and force evil out of hiding from behind the facade of legitimacy.

To risk confronting the Powers with such harlequinesque vulnerability, simultaneously affirming our own humanity and that of those whom we oppose, and daring to draw the sting of evil by absorbing it in our own bodies— such behavior is not likely to attract the faint of heart. But I am convinced that there is a whole host of people simply waiting for the Christian message to challenge them, for once, to a heroism worthy of their lives. Has Jesus not provided us with that word?

INDEX

A

Abolitionist movement
  Angelina Grimke's introduction to, 51
  Grimke sisters and, 49-53
  nonresistance as strategy of, 4
  Sojourner Truth and, 96
  statement of principles of, 65-69
Action, nonviolent liberating, axioms for, 227-229
Action-contemplation synthesis, 226
Acts 19:40, 255
Adversaries. *See also* Enemies
  learning from, 200-201
Aggression, provocation of, 129
Ahimsa, 228
Alabama Christian Movement for Human Rights, 172, 173
Aldridge, Bob, 235
Alinsky, Saul
  Cesar Chavez and, 228
  principles for nonviolent community action, 262-263
Amalgamated Textile Workers of America, A.J. Muste and, 106
American Antislavery Society, men-only policy of, 85
American Peace Society, 59, 65
American Revolution
  nonviolent approach to, 59
  and use of violence, 207
American Workers Party, A.J. Muste and, 107
Amos, as extremist for justice, 180
An Appeal to the Christian Women of the South, 52
Antistenai, translations of, 254-255
Appeal to the Christian Women of the South, 5
Aquinas, Saint Thomas
  and social justice, 119
  on unjust laws, 176
Assault, personal, nonviolence and, 241-247
Association of Catholic Trade Unionists, 120
Atman, Vedantist doctrine of, 196
Atomic weapons, 133-134. *See also* Nuclear war; Nuclear weapons
  Christianity and, 134
Austin, Ann, 10

B

Bacon, Margaret Hope, biographical note, 13
Ballou, Adin
  biographical note, 75
  and New England Non-Resistance Society, 65
Baltimore Four, 205
Barclay, Robert, 4
  An Apology for the True Christian Divinity, 15-17
  biographical note, 15
Baumfree, Isabella. *See* Truth, Sojourner
Beatitudes, 197, 202
  as basis for Christian nonviolence, 197
Berrigan, Daniel
  and Catonsville raid, 203
  and destruction of draft records, 204
  Weathermen and, 213-219
Berrigan, Philip
  and Catonsville raid, 203
  and destruction of draft records, 204
Bett, Mau Mau, 95
Bevel, James, 154
  Fannie Lou Hamer and, 157

Bhagavad-Gita, Gandhi's study of, 229
Bhave, Vinoba
  on international conflict, 192-193
  and land-trust movement, 194
Black Muslims, 179
Blessed Are the Meek: the Christian Roots of Nonviolence, 162
Boston Defense Committee, A.J. Muste and, 106
Bowdoin Street Young Men's Peace Society, 59
Boycotts
  Montgomery, 6, 181
  Nestle, 264
  as nonviolent strategy, 75
Bradford, Sarah H., Harriet Tubman and, 83
Brethren, conscientious objectors and, 107
Brookwood Labor College, A.J. Muste and, 106
Brown, John
  advocacy of violence by, 88
  Harriet Tubman and, 81, 82
Buber, Martin, on segregation, 176
Bunyan, John, as extremist, 180
Bus boycott, Montgomery, 6, 181

C

Camara, Dom Helder, 109, 223
Cannon, James P., comments on A.J. Muste, 107
Capital punishment
  Garrison's opposition to, 65
  Whipple's views on, 98-100
Capitalism, Catholic Worker position on, 123-124
Catholic Church, position on social order, 119
Catholic Worker, 118
  position on World War II, 119
Catholic Worker Movement, 118
  draft card burning and, 109
  pacifism of, 118, 119
  purpose of, 123
Catholic Worker Positions, 123-125
Catonsville Nine, 203-208
Central American refugees, 5
  sanctuary movement and, 231-234
Change
  consciousness as basis of, 223-224, 227
  first-order, 224-225, 228-229
  second-order, 224-227, 229
Change: Principles of Problem Formation and Problem Resolution, 224
Change theory, 222
Channing, William Ellery, biographical note, 71
Chant to be Used in Processions Around a Site with Furnaces, 161
Charles II, 12
Chavez, Cesar
  and appropriation of suffering, 228
  Dorothy Day and, 120
  and United Farm Workers Union, 209-212
Chesterton, G.K., on St. Francis of Assisi, 225
Chevrier, David, 234
Chicago Eight, 189
Chikane, Frank, 254
Children of the Light. *See* Quakers
Christian realism, Reinhold Niebuhr and, 107
Christianity
  atomic weapons and, 134
  organized, failure of, to address Christian teachings, 7
  roots of nonviolence in, 195-202
  Whipple's definition of, 100
Christianity and the Social Crisis, 101

Christians
  nonresistance obligations of, 76
  and obligation to oppose war, 48, 74
  social commitment of, 101
  Whipple's definition of, 100
  World War II and, 127-131
Church, white, role in maintaining segregation,
  181
Civil disobedience, and "Letter from a
  Birmingham Jail", 171-184
Civil rights movement
  Fannie Hamer and, 153-158
  Fellowship of Reconciliation and, 185
  and "Letter from a Birmingham Jail", 171-184
Class war, pacifism and, 111-116
Committee for Nonviolent Action (CNVA),
  A.J. Muste and, 108
Communal living, Koinonia Farm experiment
  in, 135-136
Communism
  attitudes toward violence, 114
  Mennonite statement on, 167-169
Communism and Anti-Communism, 167-169
Communist Party USA, and Mobilization
  against the War in Vietnam, 109
Community, purpose of, 99
Congress on Racial Equality (CORE), Freedom
  Rides and, 108, 185
Connor, Bull, 171, 173, 174, 182-184, 192, 229
Conscientious objection
  A.J. Muste and, 107
  Catholic Worker position on, 125
  Mennonites and, 167
  Selective Service and, 107
Consciousness
  as basis for change, 223-224
  impasse situations and, 222-224
Conscription, resistance to. See Draft resistance
Corbett, Jim, 232
I Corinthians 1:27, 226
I Corinthians 13:7, 202
I Corinthians 3:10-15, 197
Cornell, Tom, 5
  on property destruction as nonviolent action,
  203-208
Cotton Patch versions of New Testament, 136
Creative tension, 228-229
  role in nonviolent direct action, 174-175
Cuker, Mr. and Mrs. Robert, 155

D
Dabbs, James, 180
Darst, David, and destruction of draft records,
  204
Day, Dorothy, 109, 161
  conversion to Catholicism, 118
  draft card burning and, 109
  labor movement and, 118
  nonviolence of, 117-122
"Days of Rage", 213
Death penalty, Quakers and, 11, 12
Declaration of Independence, 61
Dellinger, David, 108
  biographical note, 189
  on theory and practice of nonviolence,
  189-194
Democratic National Convention of 1964,
  Fannie Lou Hamer and, 153
Democratic National Convention of 1968,
  Chicago Eight and, 189
Demonstrations, 187
Deterrence, nuclear. See Nuclear deterrence

Direct action, nonviolent. See Nonviolent direct
  action
Disarmament, personal, 241-247
Dodge, David Low, biographical note, 39
Dolci, Danilo, 227
Douglass, Frederick
  Harriet Tubman and, 80
  Sojourner Truth and, 95
Douglass, Shelley
  biographical note, 235-236
Draft cards, burning of, as nonviolent strategy,
  203
Draft records, destruction of, 204
Draft resistance
  A.J. Muste and, 109, 149-152
  Catholic Worker position on, 125
  David Dellinger and, 189
Dumont, John J., 95
"Duty of A Christian in A Trying Situation", 39
Dyer, Mary, 4, 9-12
  conversion to Quakerism, 10
Dyer, Will, 11, 12

E
Eberhardt, David, and destruction of draft
  records, 204
Economics, Catholic Worker position on, 123
Education, peace. See Peace education
"Eighteen Articles", 167
El Salvador, martyrs of, 233
Eliot, T.S., 183, 198
Emergency Convocation of Churches in South
  Africa, 253
Enemies
  learning from, 200-201
  love of, Jesus' teaching of, 2
Esquivel, Adolfo Perez, 261
Evers, Medger, murder of, 157
Evil
  disarming of, 242
  Jesus' attitude toward, 3
  noncooperation with, 235-240
  nonresistance to, misinterpretation of, 4,
  254-255
  overcoming with good, 97-100
  responses to, 255
  social structure and, 101
Exodus, implications for sanctuary movement,
  232-233
Exodus 20:2, 232
Exodus 22:25, 263

F
Fellowship of Reconciliation, 161
  A.J. Muste and, 105, 107
  Freedom Rides and, 185
  "how to's" in nonviolence, 185-188
  Kirby Page and, 133
Felmet, Joe, 185
Feminism. See also Women; Women's rights
  Grimke sisters and, 52
Fisch, Richard, 224
Fisher, Mary, 10
Flynn, Elizabeth Gurley, Lawrence textile strike
  and, 106
Forest, Jim, 161
Forman, James, 154
Freedom Rides, 108
  Congress on Racial Equality and, 185
  Fellowship of Reconciliation and, 185
Freire, Paulo, 223
  and struggle for consciousness, 227

French Revolution, 115
Friends, Religious Society of. *See* Quakers
Fugitive Slave Law, 65
Fund for Humanity, 137

G
Galilea, Segundo, 222
Gandhi, Mahatma
 influence on Thomas Merton, 161-162
 and Jan Christiaan Smuts, 228
 nonviolence of, 191
 nonviolence theory and, 207
 and religious basis of nonviolence, 196
 and satyagraha concept, 227
 and work of Adin Ballou, 75
Garrison, William Lloyd
 A. Grimke's support of, 51
 and American Antislavery Society, 85
 biographical note, 65
 and New England Non-Resistance Society, 65
 Sojourner Truth and, 95
 at Woman's Rights Convention of 1853, 87
Genesis 37:19-20, 230
Germany, Nazi, legality of, 177
Gilmore
 Joyce, 109
 Robert, 109
*Giving up the Gun: Japan's Reversion to the
 Sword, 1543-1879*, 221
Godse, N.V., 230
Golden, Harry, 180
Golden, Renny
 biographical note, 231
Goodyear strike, sit-in tactics of, 111
Gospel(s). *See also* specific gospels
 nonviolence theme in, 1
 social. *see* Social Gospel
Government
 oppression by, 112
 resistance to, 71-74
Greene, "Old Rit" (Harriet), 80
Gregg, Richard, 246
Grimke, Angelina, 5, 49-54
 "Appeal to the Christian Women of the
 South", 55-58
 feminist views of, 52
Grimke, John Faucheraud, 49
Grimke, Sarah, 49-54
 conversion to Quakerism, 50
 feminist views of, 52
Ground Zero Center for Nonviolent Action, 235,
 236
Guatemala, martyrs of, 233
Gutierrez, Gustavo, and liberation of oppressors
 and oppressed, 227-228

H
Hamer, Fannie Lou, 153-158
 police abuse of, 156-158
 as SNCC Field Secretary, 156
 voter registration work of, 154-156
Harlem, institutional violence and, 191
Hebrew Testament. *See also* Old Testament;
 specific books of the Old Testament
 roots of Jesus' teaching in, 2
Heraclitus, 225
Hinduism, and basis for nonviolence, 196
Hitler, Adolph, legality of actions, 177
Hitlerism, 127, 128
Hogan, John, and destruction of draft records,
 204
Hoover, J. Edgar, 153

Houser, George, 108
Humphrey, Hubert, 153
Hutchinson, Anne, 10
 death of, 10

I
Impasse situations, consciousness and, 222-224
Imprisonment, evils of, 98
Infant Formula Action Coalition (INFACT), 264
Injustice, as violence, 223
Intervention, nonviolent direct, 5

J
James 1:2, 223
Japan, Samurai tradition in, 221-222
Japanese-Americans, during World War II, 206
Jefferson, Thomas, as extemist, 180
Jesus
 attitudes toward Messiahship, 103
 attitudes toward nonviolence, 103
 as extremist for love, 180
 interpretation of King of God, 101-104
 seen as radical, 112
 teachings about love toward enemies, 2-3
 teachings about nonviolence, 254-265
 third way of, 255
John 13:35, 196
John 17:21, 196
John Paul II, on nuclear deterrence, 250
John the Baptist, 103
Johnson, Kermit D., 251
Johnson, Lyndon B.
 draft card burning legislation and, 109
 and Mississippi Freedom Democratic Party,
 153
 on use of violence, 207
Jordan, Clarence
 biographical sketch, 135-137
 and *Cotton Patch* Sermon on the Mount, 139,
 141-143
 and *Cotton Patch* version of Luke 12:13-21,
 139, 145-148
 founding of Koinonia Farm, 135-136
Judaism, Hellenistic, key values in, 2
Judson, Sylvia Shaw, 9
Just war theory, 242
 deterrence and, 250

K
King, Martin Luther, Jr., 6, 229
 epitaph of, 230
 Fannie Lou Hamer and, 157
 "Letter from a Birmingham Jail", 171-184
 nonviolence theory and, 207
 on United Farm Workers' grape boycott, 210
Kingdom of God
 Christian nonviolence and, 197
 Jesus' reinterpretation of, 101-104
Koan, change theory and, 222
Koinonia Farm, founding of, 135-136
Koinonia Partners, 137

L
Labor movement
 A.J. Muste and, 106
 Catholic Worker and, 119-120
 Dorothy Day and, 118
 Goodyear strike, 111
 in New York City, 115
 nonviolence and, 113-116
Ladies' Anti-Slavery Society of Boston, 58
Laing, R.D., 222
Landscapes of the Sacred, 221

Land-trust movement, 194
Lane, Beldon, biographical note, 221
Latin America, U.S. role in, 193, 194
Lawrence textile strike, 106
Laws
  just and unjust, 176-177
  obedience to, as idolatry, 234
  resistance to, 71
Lazarus, Clarence Jordan's commentary on,
  145-148
Letter from a Birmingham Jail, 210
Letter to a Young Activist, 161
Leviticus 19:18,34, 2
Lewis, Thomas, and destruction of draft records,
  204
Liberation, axioms for nonviolent achievement
  of, 227-229
Liberation magazine, 189
Liberation Press, 189
Liberation theology, of nonviolence, 221-230
Lincoln, Abraham, as extremist, 180
Love, of enemies, Jesus' teaching of, 2
Love of Enemies Tradition, 2
Luke 23:19, 255
Luke 6:27-36, 2
Luke 12:13-21, Clarence Jordan's commentary
  on, 139, 145-148
Luke 17:20-21, 103
Luther, Martin, as extremist, 180
Lynn, Conrad, 108

M
Maglon, Joe, 155
Mark 15:7, 255
Marriage, equality in, 93
Marxism-Leninism, A.J. Muste and, 106
Massachusetts Bay Colony, persecution of
  Quakers in, 9
Massachusetts Peace Society, 43, 65
  William Ellery Channing and, 71
Matthew 3:10-12, 103
Matthew 4:8-10, 103
Matthew 5:38, 16
Matthew 5:39, 3
Matthew 5:3-4, 197
Matthew 5:38-41, 254
Matthew 5:38-48, 2
Matthew 5:40-41, 244
Matthew 14:22-23, 103
Matthew 23:23, 234
Maurin, Peter
  three-point program of, 118
  and Works of Mercy, 119
McConnell, Michael, biographical note, 231
McGill, Ralph, 180
Meade Missile Base, direct action at, 108
Meditation, role in liberating change, 229
Meekness, Christian, interpretation of, 197
Melville, Mr. and Mrs. Thomas, and destruction
  of draft records, 204
Mengel, James, and destruction of draft records,
  204
Mennonites
  on conflict over ideology, 167-169
  conscientious objectors and, 107
  early struggles of, 4
  "Eighteen Articles" of, 167
  first settlement of, 21
  nonresistance form of nonviolence and, 167
Meredith, George, 191
Meredith, James, 183

Merton, Thomas
  on cold war, 160
  influence of Gandhi, 161-162
  on peace in the nuclear age, 159-160
  personalist nonviolence of, 159-162
  on racism, 160
  on roots of Christian nonviolence, 195-202
  on self-knowledge as basis for nonviolence,
    160-161
Messiahship, Jesus' attitude toward, 103
Methodist Bishops, on war and peace, 249-252
Military, power of, 112
Mische, George, and destruction of draft
  records, 204
Mississippi Freedom Democratic Party, and
  Democratic National Convention of 1964, 153
Mobilization against the War in Vietnam,
  A.J. Muste and, 109
Mondale, Walter, 153
Montgomery bus boycott, 6, 181
Moral Man, Immoral Society, 107
Morality, Catholic Worker position on, 124
Morris, Israel, 50
Moses
  Robert, support for Fannie Lou Hamer, 156
  sanctuary established by, 233
Mott, James, 85
Mott, Lucretia, 85-88
  anti-slavery position of, 85
  attitudes toward marriage, 86
  nonviolence of, 86, 87-88, 89
  and organizing of Philadelphia Female
    Antislavery Society, 85-86
  Sojourner Truth and, 96
Moylan, Mary, and destruction of draft records,
  204
Muhammad, Elijah, 179
Murder in the Cathedral, 198
Murray, Gilbert, on Gandhi, 229
Muslims, Black, 179
Muste, A.J., 105-110
  and Boston Defense Committee, 106
  Brookwood Labor College and, 106
  and Committee for Nonviolent Action, 108
  draft resistance and, 109
  education of, 105
  and Fellowship of Reconciliation, 105
  labor movement and, 106
  Marxism-Leninism of, 106
  nonviolence theory and, 207
  and war in Southeast Asia, 109
  work against racism, 108
  work with David Dellinger, 189
  World War II and, 107-108
Musteites, 107
Mysticism for the Nuclear Age, 161

N
National Anti-Slavery Society, 52-53
Native Americans
  John Woolman and, 25
  Penn's letter to, 19-20
  Quaker relations with, 19
Naude, Beyers, 253, 261
Nazi Germany, legality of, 177
Negotiation, 186-187
Nelson, Wally, 108
Nestle boycott, 264
New England Antislavery Society, 86
New England Non-Resistance Society, 65
  women's rights and, 65

New Testament
concept of sanctuary in, 233-234
Cotton Patch versions of, 136
New York Peace Society, 65
Newark Commune, 189
Niebuhr, Reinhold, 174
"Christian realism" of, 107
Noncooperation, 235-240
Nonresistance. *See also* Nonviolence
Christian obligations in, 76
early concept of, 4
origin of term, 3
as social change strategy, 4
Non-Resistance Applied to the Internal Defense of A Community, 4
Nonviolence. *See also* Nonresistance
as alternative to American Revolution, 59
advantages and disadvantages of, 62-64
and attitudes of society defended, 193-194
Christian
in face of personal assault, 241-247
and love of enemies tradition, 3
Christian roots of, 195-202
conditions for honest practice of, 199-202
criticisms of, 190
David Dellinger on theory and practice of, 189-194
detachment in, 161
Dorothy Day and, 117-122
Gandhian, 117
as basis for Committee for Nonviolent Action, 108-109
Garrison's views on, 65
Gospel-based, 1, 2-3
antithetical interpretations of, 75
forms of, 3-5
root dynamic of, 5-7
Harriet Tubman and, 82
Hindu basis for, 196
"how to's" in, 185-188
Jesus' attitudes toward, 103
and knowledge of balance, 246
labor movement and, 113-116
liberation theology of, 221-230
as lifestyle, 189
Lucretia Mott and, 86, 88, 89
modern, characteristics of, 5
and nuclear war, 199
police force adopting methods of, 97
potential uses of, 193
as practical strategy vs. end in itself, 190-191
principles of, 185-186
property destruction and, 203-208
psychological basis for, 112-113
requirements of, 6-7
revolution through, Catholic Worker position on, 124
and risk of pharisaism, 196
in South Africa, 253-254
strategic steps in, 186-188
theory of, Ballou's contribution to, 75
Thomas Merton on, 160-161
and unity of human beings, 191
Vedantist doctrine and, 196
Whipple's strategies for, 59
William Lloyd Garrison's advocacy of, 51
Nonviolent action, Alinsky's principles for, 262-263
Nonviolent direct action, 5
Catholic Worker and, 124
Freedom Riders and, 108
steps in, 173

Nonviolent Napalm in Catonsville, 5
Nonviolent resistance
draft resistance as, 149-152
as final step in nonviolence, 187
as strategy for peace and justice, 130-131
Northamptom Association, Sojourner Truth and, 95
Northrop, Edward, 204, 205
Now is the Time to Prevent a Third World War, 133
Nuclear deterrence, fundamental flaw of, 251
Nuclear war, nonviolence and, 199
Nuclear weapons, personal involvement with, 238-239
Numbers 35:15, 233

O
Objectives, definition of, 185-186
Old Testament. *See also* specific books of Old Testament
concept of sanctuary in, 233
Oppression, by governments, 112
Oppressor, respect for, 227-228
Oriental Exclusion Act, 130

P
Pacem in Terris, 201
Pacific Life Community, 235
Pacifism
of *Catholic Worker*, 118
of Catholic Worker movement, 119
class war and, 111-116
as national policy, 130-131
Pack, Jim, 108
Page, Kirby, biographical note, 133
Paul, as extremist for Gospel of Jesus, 180
Peace education
advocacy of, 48
Worcester's advocacy of, 43
Peace societies, advocacy of, 47-48
Penal system, Whipple's views on, 98-100
Penn, William, biographical note, 19
Pennsylvania Antislavery Society, 86
Perrin, Noel, 221
Peter 3:9, 2
Pharisaism, 196
Pharisees, 112
Philadelphia Female Antislavery Society, 51
founding of, 85-86
Phillips, Wendell, 53
Sojourner Truth and, 95
Pirsig, Robert, 223-224
Plea to the Poor, 5
Polaris Actions, 108
Police force, nonviolent, 97
Ponder, Ann, 156, 157
Power of Nonviolence, 246
Property, destruction of, nonviolence and, 203-208
Provocation, response to, 187
Psalm 42, 233
Psalm 46, 233
Psychoanalysis, Laingian, 222
Psychology, Catholic Worker position on, 123-124
Puritans, in Massachusetts Bay Colony, religious persecution by, 9

Q

Quakers
  during American Revolution, 35
  attitudes toward women, 9, 10, 50
  beliefs of, 9
  conscientious objectors and, 107
  early struggles of, 4
  laws regarding, 11
  participation in slavery, 22
  persecution of, 10-11
  position of women and, Lucretia Mott's
    struggle with, 87
  protest against slavery, 21-23
  relations with Native Americans, 19
  religious persecution of, 9
  struggles for religious freedom, 2

R

Racism
  A.J. Muste and, 108
  Catholic Worker position on, 124-125
  Thomas Merton on, 160
  in United States, 130
Rauschenbusch, Walter, biographical note, 101
Refugees, Central American, 5
  sanctuary movement and, 231-234
Religious Society of Friends. *See* Quakers
Resistance, passive, 4-5
Reuther, Walter, 153
Revolution
  American. *See* American Revolution
  internal, 161
  nonviolent, Catholic Worker position on, 124
*Reweaving the Web of Life: Feminism and
    Nonviolence*, 154
Rhode Island, religious freedom in, 10
Robinson, William, 11
Romans 12:14, 17-20, 2
Roodenko, Igal, 108, 185
Ross, Araminta. *See* Tubman, Harriet
Ross, "Old Ben", 80
Ruggles, David, Sojourner Truth and, 95
Russian Revolution, 115
Rustin, Bayard, 108, 185
Rynder gang, 87

S

Sadducees, 113
St. Augustine
  just war theory of, 242
  on unjust laws, 176
St. Francis, 114
St. Francis of Assisi, 225
St. Gertrude, 124
Salt March, 237
Samurai warrior, spirituality of, 221-222
Sanctuary
  biblical and historical tradition of, 233-234
  theology of, 231-234
Sanctuary: the Underground Railroad, 231
Sanctuary Movement, 5
  Exodus event and, 232-233
Sanctuary Nuts and Bolts, 231
Satyagraha
  defined, 117
  and respect for oppressor, 227
Scott, Job
  biographical note, 35
Scott, Patience, 11
Security, moral qualities of, 250
Segregation
  Martin Buber on, 176
  role of white moderates in, 177-180

Select Panel on Mississippi and Civil Rights, 154
Selective Service System, conscientious
  objectors and, 107
Self-defense, justification of, repudiation of,
  77-78
Self-purification, as stage in nonviolent direct
  action, 173
Self-rule, Gandhi's concept of, 236-237
Seneca Falls Convention
  A. Grimke and, 53
  Lucretia Mott and, 87
Sermon on the Mount, 39-40
  as basis for Christian nonviolence, 197
  Cotton Patch version of, 141-143
  Gandhi and, 229
  as theology of the unexpected, 222
Seven Storey Mountain, 160
Seward, William, as supporter of Harriet
  Tubman, 83
Sexual abuse, A. Grimke's denounciation of, 52
Sissel, Herman, 155
Sit-in strategy, in Goodyear strike, 111
Slavery
  contrasted with Jewish servitude, 56
  Garrison's opposition to, 65
  Grimke sisters' opposition to, 49-53
  John Woolman and, 25
  in New World, 3
  opposition to, 44
  Quaker participation in, 22
  Quaker protest against, 21-23
  southern laws concerning, 55-58
Slaves, Underground Railroad and, d5
Smith, Lillian, 180
Smuts, Jan Christiaan, Gandhi and, 228
SNCC. *See* Student Nonviolent Coordinating
  Committee
Social change. *See also* Change
  nonviolent, 4
Social Gospel, Walter Rauschenbusch and, 101
Socialist Workers Party, and Mobilization
  against the War in Vietnam, 109
Sophia 2:3, 197
South Africa, attitudes toward nonviolence in,
  253-254
South African Council of Churches, 253
Southern Christian Leadership Conference, 154,
  172
Southside Presbyterian Church, sanctuary
  declared by, 232
Spanish Civil War, Catholic Worker position on,
  118-119
Spiritual discipline, role in liberating change, 229
Spirituality, political commitment and, 221-230
Stander, Johan, 258
Stanton, Elizabeth Cady
  meeting with Lucretia Mott, 87
  Sojourner Truth and, 96
State, violence of, 112
Stephenson, Marmaduke, 11
Stone, Lucy, 53
Strikes
  nonviolent, Catholic Worker position on, 125
  United Farm Workers and, 209
Student Moratorium Group, in anti-Vietnam
  War movement, 109
Student Nonviolent Coordinating Committee
  (SNCC), 154
  Fannie Lou Hamer and, 155-156
Students for a Democratic Society (SDS), 213
Suffering, appropriation of, 228

T

Tax resistance
  Catholic Worker position on, 125
  as means of noncooperation, 238
Taxes, war. *See* War taxes
Tension, creative, 228-229
  role in nonviolent direct action, 174-175
Therese of Lisieux, 120
Thessalonians 5:15, 1, 2
Third House, 121
Third way, 4
Third way, 253-265
Thomas a Becket, 198
Thompson, George, 51
Tillich, Paul, on sin, 176
Tittle, Ernest Fremont, biographical note, 127
Tolstoy, Leo, and work of Adin Ballou, 75
Tresca, Carlo, Lawrence textile strike and, 106
Trident Campaign, 235
Trident missile system, 235
Trotsky, L., A.J. Muste and, 106, 107
Truth, Sojourner
  biography of, 95-96
  at Woman's Rights Convention of 1853, 87
Tubman, Harriet, 5, 79-83
  educational work with women, 82
  nonviolence and, 82
  role with Union Army, 82
  Underground Railroad and, 80

U

Underground Railroad, 5, 231
  Harriet Tubman and, 80
  as nonviolent strategy, 75
United Farm Workers Union, 209-212, 228
  Dorothy Day and, 120
United Methodist Council of Bishops, on war and peace, 249-252

V

Vedantist doctrine of Atman, nonviolence and, 196
Vietnam War
  and advocates of nonviolent resistance, 203
  A.J. Muste and, 109
  nonviolent direct intervention during, 5
Violence
  in American Revolution, 207
  Communism and, 114
  injustice as, 223
  institutionalized, 191, 223
  responses to, 6
  spiral of, 223
Violence and Nonviolence in South Africa, 253

W

Wagner, Robert, 191
War
  aggressive, justification of, 46
  alternatives to, 43-48, 59-64
  in atomic age, 133-134
  Christian obligation to resist, 48, 74
  defenses of, 44-45, 47
  defensive, justification of, 39
  evils of, 98
  inadequacy in serving peace and justice, 128-130
  Job Scott's denunciation of, 35-37
  just
    Channing's questioning of, 71-74
    St. Augustine's theory of, 242
  lawfulness of, 39-42
  nuclear. *See* Nuclear war
  resistance to, 149-152. *See also* Draft resistance
  roots of, Thomas Merton on, 160
  scriptural advocacy of, 44-45
War taxes
  Catholic Worker position on, 125
  John Woolman and, 25-29
  non-payment of, 4
  opposition to, 35
  resistance to, 60
Washington, Booker T.
  tribute to Harriet Tubman, 83
Washington, George
  and use of violence, 207
Watzalawick, Paul, 224
Weakland, John, 224
Wealth, *Cotton Patch* lecture on, 145-148
Weathermen, Daniel Berrigan and, 213-219
Weil, Simone, 227
  Dorothy Day and, 120
Weisgal, Fred, 204
Weld, Theodore D., 53
Wellington Ave. United Church of Christ, sanctuary declared by, 234
Whipple, Charles K., 4
  biographical note, 59
  views on nonresistance, 97-100
White church, role in maintaining segregation, 181
White moderates, role in segregation, 177-180
White Train, 235
White Train Campaign, 236
Williams, Roger, 10
Wink, Walter, 4
  biographical note, 253
Woman Question, 86, 87. *see also* Feminism; Women; Women's rights
Woman's Rights Convention of 1853, 87
Women
  anti-slavery work of, 58
  Biblical, role in achieving freedom, 57-58
  Biblical references to role of, 89-90
  Quaker attitudes toward, 9, 10, 50
  rights of, 3
Women's rights
  Lucretia Mott and, 87, 89-94
  and New England Non-Resistance Society, 65
Women's rights movement, Sojourner Truth and, 96
Woolman, John, 5
  biographical note, 25-26
  and Quaker anti-slavery movement, 21
  war taxes and, 25-29
Worcester, Noah
  biographical note, 43
  and constitution of American Peace Society, 65
Work slowdowns, 5
Works of Mercy, 119
World court, Worcester's advocacy of, 43, 45-46
World War II
  A.J. Muste and, 107
  Catholic Worker position on, 119
  Christian pacifism and, 127-131
  Japanese-Americans during, 206
Worrell, Richard, 21
Wright, Elizur, 53

Y

Young, Andrew, Fannie Lou Hamer and, 157

Z

Zen, koan concept of, 222
Zen and the Art of Motorcycle Maintenance, 223-224